VOLU
OLD TES

THE NEW COLLEGEVILLE BIBLE COMMENTARY

JEREMIAH
BARUCH

Pauline A. Viviano

SERIES EDITOR

Daniel Durken, O.S.B.

LITURGICAL PRESS
Collegeville, Minnesota

www.litpress.org

Nihil Obstat: Reverend Robert Harren, *Censor deputatus*.
Imprimatur: ✠ Most Reverend John F. Kinney, J.C.D., D.D., Bishop of St. Cloud, Minnesota, May 28, 2013.

Design by Ann Blattner.

Photos: pages 8 and 144, Wikimedia Commons; pages 54, 58, 69, and 156, Thinkstock Photos.

Maps created by Robert Cronan of Lucidity Information Design, LLC.

1   2   3   4   5   6   7   8   9

Library of Congress Cataloging-in-Publication Data

Viviano, Pauline A., 1946–
    Jeremiah, Baruch / Pauline A. Viviano.
        pages   cm. — (New Collegeville Bible commentary. Old Testament ; Volume 14)
    Includes index.
    ISBN 978-0-8146-2848-5 (alk. paper)
    1. Bible. O.T. Jeremiah—Commentaries.   2. Bible. O.T. Apocrypha. Baruch—Commentaries.   I. Title.
    BS1525.53.V58   2013
    224'.207—dc23   2013008343

CONTENTS

ABBREVIATIONS

Books of the Bible

Acts—Acts of the Apostles
Amos—Amos
Bar—Baruch
1 Chr—1 Chronicles
2 Chr—2 Chronicles
Col—Colossians
1 Cor—1 Corinthians
2 Cor—2 Corinthians
Dan—Daniel
Deut—Deuteronomy
Eccl (or Qoh)—Ecclesiastes
Eph—Ephesians
Esth—Esther
Exod—Exodus
Ezek—Ezekiel
Ezra—Ezra
Gal—Galatians
Gen—Genesis
Hab—Habakkuk
Hag—Haggai
Heb—Hebrews
Hos—Hosea
Isa—Isaiah
Jas—James
Jdt—Judith
Jer—Jeremiah
Job—Job
Joel—Joel
John—John
1 John—1 John
2 John—2 John
3 John—3 John
Jonah—Jonah
Josh—Joshua
Jude—Jude
Judg—Judges
1 Kgs—1 Kings

2 Kgs—2 Kings
Lam—Lamentations
Lev—Leviticus
Luke—Luke
1 Macc—1 Maccabees
2 Macc—2 Maccabees
Mal—Malachi
Mark—Mark
Matt—Matthew
Mic—Micah
Nah—Nahum
Neh—Nehemiah
Num—Numbers
Obad—Obadiah
1 Pet—1 Peter
2 Pet—2 Peter
Phil—Philippians
Phlm—Philemon
Prov—Proverbs
Ps(s)—Psalms
Rev—Revelation
Rom—Romans
Ruth—Ruth
1 Sam—1 Samuel
2 Sam—2 Samuel
Sir—Sirach
Song—Song of Songs
1 Thess—1 Thessalonians
2 Thess—2 Thessalonians
1 Tim—1 Timothy
2 Tim—2 Timothy
Titus—Titus
Tob—Tobit
Wis—Wisdom
Zech—Zechariah
Zeph—Zephaniah

The Book of Jeremiah

The historical context

The Assyrian Empire, which dominated the Syro-Palestinian region in the eighth to seventh centuries B.C., gave way to the Babylonian Empire in the late seventh century B.C. shortly after the reign of Josiah, king of Judah (640–609 B.C.). The prophetic call of Jeremiah is dated to the thirteenth year of Josiah's reign, that is, 626 B.C. There are few oracles in the book of Jeremiah that can be dated to Josiah's reign with certainty, but it is possible that the oracles of chapters 2–6 belong to the period when Josiah was king of Judah.

According to 2 Kings 22:3–23:3 a law code was discovered in the temple in 621 B.C.; this law code was authenticated as the word of the Lord by Hulda the prophetess, and King Josiah aligned the reform he had begun with the terms of this law. It is not certain whether the story of the discovery of the law code reflects an actual event or was a story created to support Josiah's reform, but whichever is the case, Deuteronomic law and the theology expressed in that law came to the fore in the late seventh century B.C. and played a major role in the shaping of Israel and its Scriptures in the exilic and postexilic periods. It is thought that the Deuteronomic law code of Deuteronomy 12–26, though in an earlier form, was the law code discovered at the time of King Josiah. The Deuteronomic law code has similarities to Josiah's reform, especially with respect to the centralization of worship. Jeremiah may have supported Josiah's reform, but his prophetic message suggests that the reform of Josiah did not significantly impact the behavior of the people, for they continued to worship other gods at various shrines. The book of Jeremiah shows the influence of Deuteronomic theology and it is generally agreed that the book reached its final form through the hands of Deuteronomic editors.

Most of the book of Jeremiah reflects the period of Babylonian dominance over Judah, especially during the reigns of Jehoiakim and Zedekiah. This was a period of turmoil that resulted from conflicting political policies in the royal court of Judah. Jehoiakim had been placed on the throne by the

Egyptian pharaoh Necho II who deposed Jehoahaz. Jehoahaz assumed the throne of Judah upon the death of Josiah in 609 B.C. Josiah had attempted to prevent the Egyptians from assisting the Assyrians against the Babylonians, but he was slain in battle at Megiddo (2 Kgs 23:29). Jehoiakim began his reign as a vassal to Egypt, but when Nebuchadnezzar of Babylon defeated the Egyptians at the Battle of Carchemish (605 B.C.), he became a vassal of Babylon. Jehoiakim was caught between two factions: those who sought to throw off Babylonian rule and those who sought to remain loyal vassals of Babylon. Jeremiah's position is consistent with this latter group. Jehoiakim's policy of vacillation between these factions brought the Babylonian army to Jerusalem in 597 B.C. Jehoiakim died before feeling the full wrath of the Babylonians. Though the Babylonians did not destroy the city at this time, they did take the new king, Jehoiachin, into exile with several thousand leading citizens and they put Zedekiah on the throne of Judah. Zedekiah's reign was marked by the same divided policies of Jehoiakim and, as a result, the Babylonians laid siege against Jerusalem in 588 B.C.; the city and its temple were destroyed in August of 587 B.C. Zedekiah attempted to escape but was captured by the Babylonians. They killed his family in his presence; then he was blinded and taken to Babylon. Jeremiah was most active as prophet during the reigns of Jehoiakim and Zedekiah.

The book of Jeremiah

The book of Jeremiah contains poetic oracles, prose biographical stories about the prophet, and additions from the Deuteronomic compilers of the book. The poetic oracles, particularly those found in chapters 1–25, are thought to contain the heart of Jeremiah's message. The oracles against the nations (chs. 46–51) are also in poetic form, but it is doubtful that Jeremiah authored these oracles. The biographical stories about Jeremiah have been traditionally attributed to Baruch, but they may have developed as the traditions about the prophet grew over time. They are located primarily in chapters 26–45. Most of these stories show the prophet coming into conflict with various groups, performing symbolic acts, or presenting a prophetic message at a particular time and place or addressed to a specific person. The additions attributed to the Deuteronomic compilers appear throughout the book.

That the book of Jeremiah grew over time is clearly evidenced in the differences between the Greek (Septuagint, or LXX) and the Hebrew (Masoretic text) versions of the book. The Greek version is one-eighth shorter than the Hebrew version and the oracles against the nations are found in chapters 26–32 of the LXX, but these oracles are the end of the Masoretic text (chs. 46–51).

As with other prophetic books, the words of the prophet Jeremiah were collected and passed on from one generation to the next. Though the prophet spoke at a particular time and to a particular audience, it was thought that the prophetic word continued to have meaning for subsequent generations. Indeed the book of Jeremiah seemed to have been shaped primarily to address the concerns of the exiles, even though Jeremiah's primary audience lived in the preexilic period. The book of Jeremiah explains the cause of the exile, but at the same time it gives the exiles hope for the future.

The prophet Jeremiah and his poetry

Nowhere in the book of Jeremiah is the prophet described, but we come away from the book with an image of a person who is strong and passionate. This image of Jeremiah is conveyed in his commitment to his message in spite of the suffering that he endured as a result. It is conveyed in his reaction to the painful message he was called upon to proclaim and his complaints to the Lord. It is even conveyed in the style of his poetry, with its often harsh and vehement language. Though poetic devices that play on the repetition of sound are lost in translation, we can still appreciate the vividness of Jeremiah's imagery and become engaged by Jeremiah's frequent use of rhetorical questions. We can be stunned and even outraged by his hyperbole and crude language, but we are drawn to the figure of Jeremiah who came to embody the sorrow and pain of the community that cherished his memory.

HIEREMIAS

The Book of Jeremiah

I. Oracles in the Days of Josiah

1 ¹The words of Jeremiah, son of Hilkiah, one of the priests from Anathoth, in the land of Benjamin. ²The word of the LORD came to him in the days of Josiah, son of Amon, king of Judah, in the thirteenth year of his reign, ³and again in the days of Jehoiakim, son of Josiah, king of Judah, until the end of the eleventh year of Zedekiah, son of Josiah, king of Judah—down to the exile of Jerusalem, in the fifth month.

ORACLES IN THE DAYS OF JOSIAH

Jeremiah 1:1–6:30

The first chapter grounds the entire book of Jeremiah. The central theme of the book is set forth: the Lord will punish the people of Judah for their stubborn persistence in the worship of other gods. Jeremiah is commissioned as the Lord's prophet and, as such, he will come into conflict, especially with the leaders of the community. He will be treated brutally and imprisoned for proclaiming the unwelcome message that the end of the nation is inevitable, but the Lord will stand by the word of Jeremiah and will deliver the prophet from the hands of his enemies.

1:1-3 Introductory verses

The opening verses of the book of Jeremiah situate the activity of the prophet during the reigns of three of the last five kings of Judah: Josiah, Jehoiakim, and Zedekiah. Jehoahaz II (2 Kgs 25:31), who reigned after Josiah, and Jehoiachin (2 Kgs 24:8), who reigned after Jehoiakim, are passed over, probably because both of these kings reigned for only three months. Jeremiah prophesies from 626 B.C. to the fifth month of exile of 587 B.C., roughly the last forty years of the southern kingdom, Judah. These verses identify Jeremiah as a priest, but he functions only as prophet in the book itself. He is from Anathoth, a small village not too far from Jerusalem. It was the village to which Solomon had banished the priest Abiathar. Presumably the descendants of Abiathar's branch of the priestly family continued to live in Anathoth.

9

The prophet Jeremiah by Michelangelo in the ceiling of the Sistine Chapel.

Call of Jeremiah

⁴The word of the LORD came to me:

⁵Before I formed you in the womb I
 knew you,
 before you were born I dedicated you,
 a prophet to the nations I
 appointed you.
⁶"Ah, Lord GOD!" I said,
 "I do not know how to speak. I
 am too young!"
⁷But the LORD answered me,
Do not say, "I am too young."
 To whomever I send you, you
 shall go;
 whatever I command you, you
 shall speak.

⁸Do not be afraid of them,
 for I am with you to deliver
 you—oracle of the LORD.

⁹Then the LORD extended his hand and
touched my mouth, saying to me,

See, I place my words in your
 mouth!
¹⁰Today I appoint you
 over nations and over kingdoms,
To uproot and to tear down,
 to destroy and to demolish,
 to build and to plant.

¹¹The word of the LORD came to me:
What do you see, Jeremiah? "I see a
branch of the almond tree," I replied.

1:4-19 Call of Jeremiah

The prophetic call form is an ancient form whose purpose was to underscore that the commissioning of the prophet was done by God and therefore the words of the prophet are to be understood as the words of God. This form consists of several elements, each of which can be found in these opening verses: divine confrontation (1:4), preparatory word (1:5ab), commission (1:5c, 7, 10), objection from the prophet (1:6), divine assurance (1:8), and sign (1:9 or 1:11-14). The divine confrontation in the book of Jeremiah is very brief. There are no elaborate visions as in the call of Isaiah (Isa 6) or Ezekiel (Ezek 1–3). Visions will play only a minor role in the book of Jeremiah (1:11-12; 13–14; 24:1-10). There is no description of the circumstances surrounding Jeremiah's call as we find with Moses (Exod 3:1-3) and Gideon (Judg 6:1-10). Verse 4 simply announces that the word of the Lord came to Jeremiah.

The preparatory word (1:5ab) is considerably expanded. A call from the womb is unprecedented in the Old Testament, but the birth accounts of Moses, Samuel, and Samson imply a destiny from birth. It is notable that verse 5ab bears a similarity to statements found in ancient Near Eastern texts regarding their rulers. Of Shulgi of Ur (2050 B.C.) it is said, "I, the king, a warrior from the (mother's) womb am I" ("Hymn of Shulgi," in *History*

► This symbol indicates a cross reference number in the *Catechism of the Catholic Church*. See page 166 for number citations.

¹²Then the LORD said to me: You have seen well, for I am watching over my word to carry it out. ¹³A second time the word of the LORD came to me: What do you see? I replied, "I see a boiling kettle whose mouth is tipped away from the north."

¹⁴The LORD said to me, And from the north evil will pour out over all who dwell in the land.

¹⁵Look, I am summoning
    all the kingdoms of the north—
        oracle of the LORD—
Each king shall come and set up his throne
    in the gateways of Jerusalem,
Against all its surrounding walls
    and against all the cities of Judah.
¹⁶I will pronounce my sentence
    against them

Begins at Sumer, 3rd rev. ed., Samuel Noah Kramer, 285 [Philadelphia: University of Pennsylvania, 1981]); and of Ashurbanipal of Assyria (668–627 B.C.), "Assurbanipal whom . . . the great gods, truly desired (while still) in the womb of his mother, and decreed his rule" (Shalom M. Paul, "Deutero-Isaiah and Cuneiform Royal Inscriptions," *JAOS* 88 [1968]: 184). A close parallel from Egypt regarding Pharaoh Pianchi (751–730 B.C.) reads, "It was in the belly of your mother that I said concerning you that you were to be ruler of Egypt; it was as seed and while you were in the egg that I knew you were to be Lord" (M. Gilula, "An Egyptian Parallel to Jeremiah I 4-5," *VT* 17 [1967]: 114). The "borrowing" of these kinds of statements underscores the importance of Jeremiah and suggests that the prophet has been destined from birth and, in speaking on behalf of the Lord, carries the authority of a king. The use of "know" and "dedicate" in this preparatory word is significant. "Know" in the Old Testament is a relational term that indicates an intimacy between the knower and the known; it is used in covenants and thus carries the notion of a bond between the parties of the covenant. To be "dedicated" is to be consecrated for the Lord's service; the one dedicated belongs to the Lord in a special way.

Jeremiah is "appointed," that is, he is assigned a particular task. Jeremiah is commissioned as "a prophet to the nations" (1:5c), but in the book itself Jeremiah functions as prophet only to Judah. His appointment as prophet "to the nations" may indicate his sphere of activity. As the Lord is active in the affairs of the nations, so Jeremiah as the Lord's prophet will likewise have an impact on the affairs of the nations. Though Jeremian authorship of the "oracles against the nations" (chs. 46–51) is doubtful, these oracles give substance to Jeremiah's role as a "prophet to the nations."

Jeremiah's objection to his commissioning (1:6) echoes statements predicated of Moses, who claims that he has difficulty speaking (Exod 4:10; 6:12, 30), and of Samuel, who is described as a "youth" (1 Sam 3:1, 8) when he

for all their wickedness in
forsaking me,
In burning incense to other gods,
in bowing down to the works of
their hands.
¹⁷But you, prepare yourself;
stand up and tell them
all that I command you.
Do not be terrified on account of
them,
or I will terrify you before them;

¹⁸For I am the one who today
makes you a fortified city,
A pillar of iron, a wall of bronze,
against the whole land:
Against Judah's kings and princes,
its priests and the people of the
land.
¹⁹They will fight against you, but
not prevail over you,
for I am with you to deliver
you—oracle of the LORD.

---

received his prophetic call. It may be that Jeremiah was called as a young man, but it may be that the terms of this objection are meant to put Jeremiah in the tradition of Moses and Samuel. It is noteworthy that these two prophets are mentioned by name in the book of Jeremiah (15:1).

The Lord counters Jeremiah's objection using the technical vocabulary found in prophetic call forms for a commissioning: "send"/"go," "command"/"speak" (1:7). The use of this vocabulary underscores that the prophet acts and speaks under divine compulsion. As in verse 6 we find echoes from the traditions surrounding the figure of Moses (cf. Exod 7:2; Deut 18:18). Using a formula drawn from oracles of salvation, "Do not be afraid" (1:8), the Lord assures Jeremiah that God will be with him and will "deliver" him. A similar assurance, "I will be with you," was given to Moses (Exod 3:12) and Gideon (Judg 6:16). The sign, which is a characteristic element of the prophetic call form, may be seen in verse 9, with the transference of the Lord's word to Jeremiah's mouth, or in the two visions that follow (1:11-12 and 1:13-14). Prophecy as the mediation of the divine word represents the Deuteronomic view of prophecy. Indeed the term "to place," found in 1:9 and 5:14, is also found in Deuteronomy 18:18, which speaks of a future prophet who will be like Moses.

In a restatement of the commissioning, the Lord reiterates the appointment of Jeremiah, but now specifies that his task will be "[t]o uproot and to tear down, to destroy and to demolish, to build and to plant" (1:10). Throughout the book of Jeremiah these six verbs will be repeated (12:14-17; 18:7-9; 24:6; 31:4-5, 28, 38, 40; 42:10; 45:4), but it is the Lord who is their subject, not Jeremiah. This underscores the identification of the prophet's words/actions with the Lord's words/actions. The final verse in this call of Jeremiah anticipates the message of the book of Jeremiah. It is a message announcing a harsh judgment of destruction and exile, but that judgment contains seeds of hope for the future.

◄ **2** **Infidelity of Israel.** ¹The word of the LORD came to me: ²Go, cry out this message for Jerusalem to hear!

> I remember the devotion of your youth,
>> how you loved me as a bride,
> Following me in the wilderness,
>> in a land unsown.
> ³Israel was dedicated to the LORD,
>> the first fruits of his harvest;
> All who ate of it were held guilty,
>> evil befell them—oracle of the LORD.
> ⁴Listen to the word of the LORD, house of Jacob!
>> All you clans of the house of Israel,

> ⁵thus says the LORD:
> What fault did your ancestors find in me
>> that they withdrew from me,
> Went after emptiness,
>> and became empty themselves?
> ⁶They did not ask, "Where is the LORD
>> who brought us up from the land of Egypt,
> Who led us through the wilderness,
>> through a land of wastes and ravines,
> A land of drought and darkness,
>> a land which no one crosses,
>> where no one dwells?"
> ⁷I brought you into the garden land
>> to eat its fine fruits,

The two visions (1:11-12 and 1:13-14) attached to Jeremiah's call address aspects of Jeremiah's prophetic message. In a play on words in the first vision, the "almond tree" (*šāqēd*) becomes a "watching-tree" (*šōqēd*) as the Lord "watches" over the fulfillment of the Lord's word. In the book of Jeremiah this "watching" is to secure destruction, but beyond the time of destruction, Israel "watches" for the fulfillment of the hope announced by Jeremiah. The vision of the boiling pot introduces a concept that will recur in the book of Jeremiah, that is, there is a foe coming from the north against the people of Judah (4:6; 6:1, 22; 10:22; 13:20).

The chapter ends with an oracle that summarizes the contents of the book of Jeremiah: Judah will face destruction (1:15-16a) because the people of Judah are worshiping other gods (1:16). As the book of Jeremiah unfolds, it is clear his message was not well received by leaders and the people; Jeremiah suffered greatly as a result. Verses 17-19 encourage the prophet to stand firm in the face of rejection, for the Lord promises to deliver the prophet. Jeremiah will come into conflict with "kings and princes . . . priests and the people of the land" (1:18); he will also come into conflict with prophets and even the Lord. Nevertheless, he is assured that the Lord is with him to deliver him (1:19).

2:1–3:5 Infidelity of Israel

The opening oracles of Jeremiah read as a divine lament. Reflections on the past are interwoven with complaints about the present; there is an

But you entered and defiled my
   land,
   you turned my heritage into an
      abomination.
8The priests did not ask,
   "Where is the LORD?"
The experts in the law did not
      know me:
   the shepherds rebelled against
      me.
The prophets prophesied by Baal,
   and went after useless idols.
9Therefore I will again accuse you—
   oracle of the LORD—
   even your children's children I
      will accuse.
10Cross to the coast of Cyprus and
      see,
   send to Kedar and carefully
      inquire:
   Where has anything like this
      been done?
11Does any other nation change its
      gods?—
   even though they are not gods
      at all!
But my people have changed their
      glory
   for useless things.
12Be horrified at this, heavens;
   shudder, be appalled—oracle of
      the LORD.
13Two evils my people have done:

they have forsaken me, the
      source of living waters;
They have dug themselves cisterns,
   broken cisterns that cannot hold
      water.
14Is Israel a slave, a house-born
      servant?
Why then has he become
      plunder?
15Against him lions roar,
   they raise their voices.
They have turned his land into a
      waste;
   his cities are charred ruins,
      without an inhabitant.
16Yes, the people of Memphis and
      Tahpanhes
   shave the crown of your head.
17Has not forsaking the LORD, your
      God,
   done this to you?*k*
18And now, why go to Egypt,
   to drink the waters of the Nile?
Why go to Assyria,
   to drink the waters of the River?
19Your own wickedness chastises
      you,
   your own infidelities punish
      you.
Know then, and see, how evil and
      bitter
   is your forsaking the LORD, your
      God,

---

interplay of rhetorical questions and accusations. Relational imagery abounds, but especially that of a marriage that has moved from fidelity to eventual breakdown because of persistent infidelity. The overtly sexual language of Jeremiah is often crude and offensive, but it is used to shock the people into repentance. *Šûb*, the Hebrew word meaning "turn"/"return," is often found in these oracles and throughout the book of Jeremiah. The people "turn" away from the Lord in apostasy (a "turning away"); the prophet calls the people to "return" to the Lord in faithful obedience and exclusive worship of the Lord.

The special relationship between the Lord and Israel is set forth using first a marital image (2:1-2) and then an agricultural image (2:3). As in the

And your showing no fear of me,
oracle of the Lord, the GOD of
hosts.
²⁰Long ago you broke your yoke,
you tore off your bonds.
You said, "I will not serve."
On every high hill, under every
green tree,
you sprawled and served as a
prostitute.
²¹But I had planted you as a choice
vine,
all pedigreed stock;
How could you turn out so
obnoxious to me,
a spurious vine?^{*n*}
²²Even if you scour it with lye,
and use much soap,
The stain of your guilt is still before
me,
oracle of the Lord GOD.
²³How can you say, "I am not defiled,
I have not pursued the Baals"?
Consider your conduct in the Valley,
recall what you have done:
A skittish young camel,
running back and forth,
²⁴a wild donkey bred in the
wilderness,
Sniffing the wind in her desire—
who can restrain her lust?
None seeking her need tire
themselves;
in her time they will find her.
²⁵Stop wearing out your feet
and parching your throat!
But you say, "No use! No!
How I love these strangers,
after them I must go."

²⁶As the thief is shamed when
caught,
so shall the house of Israel be
shamed:
They, their kings, their princes,
their priests and their prophets;
²⁷They say to a piece of wood, "You
are my father,"
and to a stone, "You gave me
birth."
They turn their backs to me, not
their faces;
yet in their time of trouble they
cry out,
"Rise up and save us!"
²⁸Where are the gods you made for
yourselves?
Let them rise up!
Will they save you in your time
of trouble?
For as numerous as your cities
are your gods, O Judah!
And as many as the streets of
Jerusalem
are the altars you have set up
for Baal.
²⁹Why are you arguing with me?
You have all rebelled against
me—oracle of the LORD.
³⁰In vain I struck your children;
correction they did not take.
Your sword devoured your
prophets
like a ravening lion.
³¹You people of this generation,
consider the word of the Lord:
Have I become a wilderness to
Israel,
a land of gloom?

---

book of Hosea (Hos 2:15), the time of wilderness is seen as a time when Israel was the faithful "bride" of the Lord. "Devotion" (*hesed*) refers to a love that is characterized by steadfastness or loyalty. It is the love the Lord has for Israel as its covenant lord and it is the faithful love the Lord expects from Israel in return. Israel is said to be the "first fruits" that are dedicated

15

Why then do my people say, "We
have moved on,
we will not come to you any
more"?
³²Does a young woman forget her
jewelry,
a bride her sash?
Yet my people have forgotten me
days without number.
³³How well you pick your way
when seeking love!
In your wickedness,
you have gone by ways
unclean!
³⁴On your clothing is
the life-blood of the innocent,
you did not find them committing burglary;

³⁵Nonetheless you say, "I am
innocent;
at least, his anger is turned
away from me."
Listen! I will judge you
on that word of yours, "I have
not sinned."
³⁶How frivolous you have become
in changing your course!
By Egypt you will be shamed,
just as you were shamed by
Assyria.
³⁷From there too you will go out,
your hands upon your head;
For the LORD has rejected those in
whom you trust,
with them you will have no
success.

---

to the Lord. The guilt of those who "ate of it" is probably in reference to the guilt incurred by those who attacked Israel in the wilderness (e.g., the Amalekites).

In contrast to the memory of Israel's initial fidelity, the oracle shifts to the present broken relationship between the Lord and Israel. Israel's unfaithfulness has a long history; it goes back to Israel's ancestors who rather quickly turned away from the Lord to pursue idols. Idols are here spoken of as "emptiness" and the pursuit of idols makes the pursuers themselves "empty." The exodus, the trek through the wilderness, coming into the Promised Land—all reveal that the Lord has acted on behalf of the people, and so the infidelity of the people is all the more inexplicable. The betrayal of their relationship to the Lord stems from their neglect of the Lord and their enthusiasm for false gods. Israel's turning away from the Lord may have resulted from political alliances with other nations, which are represented by reference to Egypt and Assyria (2:16-18), but it is not just the leaders who stand guilty; the people as well as their leaders are complicit.

As the passage develops, there is an interplay between the Lord's complaint against the people and quotes from the people representing their refusal to serve the Lord, their persistence in the worship of other gods, and their insistence that they are guiltless. The repeated reference to the sinful actions of the people and the vivid use of sexual imagery comparing the people to camels in heat or lustful wild donkeys are certainly meant to shock the people into recognizing the depth of their sin and bringing them

3 ¹If a man divorces his wife
and she leaves him
and then becomes the wife of
another,
Can she return to the first?
Would not this land be wholly
defiled?
But you have played the prostitute
with many lovers,
and yet you would return to
me!—oracle of the LORD.
²Raise your eyes to the heights, and
look,
where have men not lain with
you?
Along the roadways you waited for
them
like an Arabian in the wilderness.
You defiled the land
by your wicked prostitution.
³Therefore the showers were
withheld,
the spring rain did not fall.
But because you have a prostitute's
brow,
you refused to be ashamed.

⁴Even now do you not call me, "My
father,
you are the bridegroom of my
youth?
⁵Will he keep his wrath forever,
will he hold his grudge to the
end?"
This is what you say; yet you do
all the evil you can.

Judah and Israel. ⁶The LORD said to me in the days of King Josiah: Do you see what rebellious Israel has done? She has gone up every high mountain, and under every green tree she has played the prostitute. ⁷And I thought: After she has done all this, she will return to me. But she did not return. Then, even though that traitor her sister Judah, saw ⁸that, in response to all the adulteries rebel Israel had committed, I sent her away and gave her a bill of divorce, nevertheless Judah, the traitor, her sister, was not frightened; she too went off and played the prostitute. ⁹With her casual prostitution, she polluted the

to repentance. Sexual imagery dominates much of this section, but the passage draws on other imagery as well to speak of the unfaithfulness of the people: they broke the yoke of the law; they have become a wild vine; they are permanently stained; they are thieves.

Chapter 3:1 raises the possibility of the Lord's forgiveness, but it is ruled out based on the divorce laws of Deuteronomy 24:1-4: a man was forbidden to remarry a wife whom he had previously divorced. However, as the passage continues in 3:12–4:18, the Lord extends forgiveness to the people, if only they would repent. The accusations against the people draw again on sexual imagery to indict the people: they act as shameless prostitutes. Though they may pray that the Lord's wrath will pass, their persistence in their evil actions shows the hollowness of their prayer.

3:6-10 Judah and Israel

Israel, the northern kingdom, had been destroyed by the Assyrians and its leading citizens were taken into exile in 721 B.C. Thus the northern

land, committing adultery with stone and wood. ¹⁰In spite of all this, Judah, the traitor, her sister, did not return to me wholeheartedly, but insincerely—oracle of the Lord.

Restoration of Israel. ¹¹Then the Lord said to me: Rebel Israel is more just than traitor Judah. ¹²Go, proclaim these words toward the north, and say:

Return, rebel Israel—oracle of the
Lord—
I will not remain angry with
you;
For I am merciful, oracle of the
Lord,
I will not keep my anger forever.
¹³Only admit your guilt:
how you have rebelled against
the Lord, your God,
How you ran here and there to
strangers
under every green tree
and would not listen to my
voice—oracle of the
Lord.

¹⁴Return, rebellious children—oracle
of the Lord—
for I am your master;
I will take you, one from a city, two
from a clan,
and bring you to Zion.
¹⁵I will appoint for you shepherds
after my own heart,
who will shepherd you wisely
and prudently.
¹⁶When you increase in number and
are fruitful in the land—
oracle of the Lord—
They will in those days no longer
say,
"The ark of the covenant of the
Lord!"
They will no longer think of it, or
remember it,
or miss it, or make another one.

¹⁷At that time they will call Jerusalem "the Lord's throne." All nations will gather together there to honor the name of the Lord at Jerusalem, and they will no longer stubbornly follow their

kingdom was punished for its idolatrous practices. This should have been a warning to Judah, but Judah did not learn. Inexplicably Judah followed Israel in its infidelity to its God and made only a halfhearted move toward repentance. Surprisingly the Lord announces that of the two nations, Israel was more just and the next words are addressed to the northern kingdom.

3:11-18 Restoration of Israel

The harsh tone of the previous passages gives way to the Lord's plaintive longing that Israel return and confess its sin of idolatry so that the Lord can heal them. The language of promise regarding Israel's return and restoration (3:14-18) is grounded in the mercy of the Lord and the Lord's anger will pass (3:12). The ark of the covenant was thought to be the throne of the Lord and, as such, it symbolized the Lord's presence in the midst of the people. The fate of the ark of the covenant is unknown; it was probably taken away or destroyed by the Babylonians. The loss of the ark is assumed in this passage with its assurance that the ark is no longer needed; Jerusalem itself will

wicked heart. [18]In those days the house of Judah will walk alongside the house of Israel; together they will come from the land of the north to the land which I gave your ancestors as a heritage.

Conditions for Forgiveness

[19]I thought:
How I would like to make you
my children!
So I gave you a pleasant land,
the most beautiful heritage
among the nations!
You would call me, "My Father," I
thought,
and you would never turn away
from me.
[20]But like a woman faithless to her
lover,
thus have you been faithless to
me,
house of Israel—oracle of the
LORD.
[21]A cry is heard on the heights!
the plaintive weeping of Israel's
children,
Because they have perverted their
way,
they have forgotten the LORD,
their God.
[22]Return, rebellious children!
I will heal your rebellions.
"Here we are! We belong to you,
for you are the LORD, our God.
[23]Deceptive indeed are the hills,
the mountains, clamorous;

Only in the LORD our God
is Israel's salvation.
[24]The shameful thing has devoured
our ancestors' worth from our
youth,
Their sheep and cattle,
their sons and daughters.
[25]Let us lie down in our shame,
let our disgrace cover us,
for we have sinned against the
LORD, our God,
We and our ancestors, from our
youth to this day;
we did not listen to the voice of the
LORD, our God."

[1]If you return, Israel—oracle
of the LORD—return to me.
If you put your detestable
things out of my sight,
and do not stray,
[2]And swear, "As the LORD
lives,"
in truth, in judgment, and in
justice,
Then the nations shall bless
themselves in him
and in him glory.

[3]For to the people of Judah and Jerusalem, thus says the LORD:

Till your untilled ground,
and do not sow among thorns.
[4]Be circumcised for the LORD,
remove the foreskins of your
hearts,

---

be the Lord's throne. Even though the northern kingdom had been destroyed about one hundred years earlier, the hope for the reunification of the north and south finds expression here. That all nations will come to honor the Lord in Jerusalem is a theme that recurs throughout the book of Jeremiah.

3:19–4:4 Conditions for forgiveness

The disappointment of the Lord's expectations in making Israel the Lord's people draws on the language of lament and gives a poignant tone

people of Judah and inhabitants
of Jerusalem;
Or else my anger will break out like
fire,
and burn so that no one can
quench it,
because of your evil deeds.

The Invasion from the North

⁵Proclaim it in Judah,
in Jerusalem announce it;
Blow the trumpet throughout the
land,
call out, "Fill the ranks!"
Say, "Assemble, let us march
to the fortified cities."
⁶Raise the signal—to Zion!
Seek refuge! Don't stand there!
Disaster I bring from the north,
and great destruction.
⁷Up comes the lion from its lair,
the destroyer of nations has set
out,
has left its place,
To turn your land into a desolation,

your cities into an uninhabited
waste.
⁸So put on sackcloth,
mourn and wail:
"The blazing anger of the Lord
has not turned away from us."
⁹In that day—oracle of the
Lord—
The king will lose heart, and the
princes;
the priests will be horrified,
and the prophets stunned.
¹⁰"Ah! Lord God," they will say,
"You really did deceive us
When you said: You shall have
peace,
while the sword was at our very
throats."
¹¹At that time it will be said
to this people and to Jerusalem,
A scorching wind from the bare
heights comes
through the wilderness toward
my daughter, the people.
Not to winnow, not to cleanse,

---

to this call for repentance. The pathos of the Lord is revealed as the Lord speaks of inner hopes. Perhaps this will lead the people away from the worship of other gods. It is not clear whether the response of the people indicates a genuine or superficial repentance, but in their confession, the people acknowledge that the Lord alone is their God and that the Lord alone brings salvation. They admit that they have sinned and are deserving of punishment. Their failure to "listen" to the Lord is a frequent complaint that the Lord raises against the people throughout the book of Jeremiah. The final call to repentance in this passage (4:1a) includes what that repentance entails (4:1b-4a), the positive consequence of repentance on the other nations (4:2b), and the negative consequence for the Lord's people if they do not repent (4:4b).

4:5-31 The invasion from the North

A dramatic call to war dominates the opening verses of this passage. War is used here as a means of punishment against the people of Judah and Jerusalem. The people are to prepare for war, but at the same time, the horror of the coming destruction should lead them to acts of penance and

¹²a strong wind from there
  comes at my bidding.
Now I too pronounce
  sentence upon them.
¹³See! like storm clouds he advances,
  like a whirlwind, his chariots;
Swifter than eagles, his horses:
  "Woe to us! we are ruined."
¹⁴Cleanse your heart of evil,
  Jerusalem,
  that you may be saved.
How long will you entertain
  wicked schemes?
¹⁵A voice proclaims it from Dan,
  announces wickedness from
  Mount Ephraim:
¹⁶"Make this known to the nations,
  announce it against Jerusalem:
Besiegers are coming from the
  distant land,

shouting their war cry against
  the cities of Judah."
¹⁷Like watchers in the fields they
  surround her,
for she has rebelled against
  me—oracle of the Lord.
¹⁸Your conduct, your deeds, have
  done this to you;
how bitter is this evil of yours,
  how it reaches to your very heart!
¹⁹My body! my body! how I writhe!
  The walls of my heart!
My heart beats wildly,
  I cannot be still;
For I myself have heard the blast of
  the horn,
  the battle cry.
²⁰Ruin upon ruin is reported;
  the whole land is laid waste.
In an instant my tents are ravaged;

---

mourning. It is the anger of the Lord that has been unleashed and before that anger the leaders of the people will lose courage. It is difficult to determine whether the speaker in several of Jeremiah's oracles is the Lord, Jeremiah, or the people. Jeremiah is probably the speaker in verse 10, but he is giving voice to the people's response to the Lord's announcement of war. The people feel deceived by the Lord because they listened to prophets who proclaimed "peace." The issue of true and false prophecy comes to the fore in the book of Jeremiah, for Jeremiah sees himself as the true prophet announcing that judgment is at hand; he stands against those prophets who speak in the Lord's name a prophecy of peace. It is difficult to know how the people of the day would have viewed this disagreement between prophets, but the test of time supports Jeremiah's claim to be a true prophet.

Though war as punishment dominates this passage, there is a shift in verses 11-12 to the hot desert wind known as sirocco as the means of the punishment to come. Whether through an army or a desert wind, God's judgment against the people is coming. The wickedness of the people arises from the core, their heart (4:14), and is reflected in their rebellion (4:17). Nevertheless, the people are still addressed in a personal way: *my* daughter (4:11). In the midst of this announcement of judgment there is a call to repent and the suggestion that salvation is still possible (4:14). It is characteristic of the book of Jeremiah that in the midst of the announcement of overwhelming and unavoidable devastation, hope is still to be found.

> in a flash, my shelters.
> ²¹How long must I see the signal,
> hear the blast of the horn!
> ²²My people are fools,
> they do not know me;
> They are senseless children,
> without understanding;
> They are wise at evil,
> but they do not know how to do
> good.
> ²³I looked at the earth—it was waste
> and void;
>
> at the heavens—their light had
> gone out!
> ²⁴I looked at the mountains—they
> were quaking!
> All the hills were crumbling!
> ²⁵I looked—there was no one;
> even the birds of the air had
> flown away!
> ²⁶I looked—the garden land was a
> wilderness,
> with all its cities destroyed
> before the Lord, before his
> blazing anger.

It seems that there is a shift from the Lord's judgment against the people to Jeremiah's response to the coming devastation (4:23-26) and then a return to the Lord's voice in verses 27-31. The ambiguity with reference to speaker may result from the close identity of the prophet with God. The anguish of God over the judgment decreed because of the wickedness of the people is experienced by the prophet himself and finds expression in the prophetic word. The sheer physicality of the prophet's response suggests not only the passionate nature of Jeremiah but also his extreme sensitivity to the suffering that is to come. Using the language of the wisdom tradition, Jeremiah speaks of the foolishness of a people who are wise with respect to evil but without sense when it comes to knowing how to do good.

In terms reminiscent of the creation accounts of Genesis 1 and 2, Jeremiah presents a vision of the uncreation of the world (4:23-26). The word of God resulted in the creation of the world in Genesis 1, but now that world is undone as God's anger is unleashed in judgment. Gone are the light, the mountains, humanity; even the birds have disappeared. The world has returned to the chaos (*tōhû wābōhû*, "waste and void," 4:23) that preceded creation (*tōhû wābōhû*, "without form or shape," Gen 1:2); the garden of Genesis 2:8 returns to its wilderness state as at the beginning of creation. This is a powerful and rhetorically sophisticated passage that confronts the people with the horror of their actions; what they are doing will lead to the undoing of the world.

The Lord's voice reemerges with another announcement of judgment. It is a judgment that is said to be a total destruction (4:27b, 28cd), but the totality of that destruction is offset by a mitigation of that judgment (4:27c). This "total yet not total announcement of destruction" occurs elsewhere in Jeremiah (e.g., 5:18) and may reflect a tendency to hyperbole on Jeremiah's part, but it may also reflect a qualification upon Jeremiah's original state-

²⁷For thus says the LORD:
The whole earth shall be waste,
   but I will not wholly destroy it.
²⁸Because of this the earth shall
      mourn,
   the heavens above shall darken;
I have spoken, I will not change my
      mind,
   I have decided, I will not turn
      back.
²⁹At the shout of rider and archer
   each city takes to flight;
They shrink into the thickets,
   they scale the rocks:
All the cities are abandoned,
   no one lives in them.
³⁰You now who are doomed, what
      are you doing
   dressing in purple,
   bedecking yourself with gold,
Enlarging your eyes with kohl?
   You beautify yourself in vain!
Your lovers reject you,
   they seek your life.
³¹Yes, I hear the cry, like that of a
      woman in labor,
   like the anguish of a mother
      bearing her first child—
The cry of daughter Zion gasping,
   as she stretches out her hands:
"Ah, woe is me! I sink exhausted
   before my killers!"

Universal Corruption

5 ¹Roam the streets of Jerusalem,
   look about and observe,
Search through her squares,
   to find even one
Who acts justly
   and seeks honesty,
   and I will pardon her!
²They say, "As the LORD lives,"
   but in fact they swear falsely.
³LORD, do your eyes not search
   for honesty?
You struck them, but they did not
      flinch;
   you laid them low, but they
      refused correction;
They set their faces harder than
      stone,
   and refused to return.
⁴I thought: These are only the lowly,
   they behave foolishly;
For they do not know the way of
      the LORD,
   the justice of their God.
⁵Let me go to the leaders
   and speak with them;
For they must know the way of the
      LORD,
   the justice of their God.
But, one and all, they have broken
      the yoke,
   torn off the harness.

---

ment inserted by later editors who are writing on the other side of survival. The passage returns to the imagery of war, but now focuses on the people's response to the invasion: they take flight, shrink, dress up, and moan in anguish. Yet in the midst of it all Zion is still referred to in personal terms: *daughter* Zion.

5:1-31 Universal corruption

The voices of the Lord, Jeremiah, and the people are found in this passage, but it is not always possible to identify each voice with certainty. The entire chapter is a series of indictments (5:1-5, 10-13, 20-28) that justify the Lord's judgment (5:6-9, 14-17, 29-31) against the people. As is characteristic of Jeremiah's prophetic message, these indictments are in general and specific

⁶Therefore, lions from the forest
slay them,
wolves of the desert ravage
them,
Leopards keep watch round their
cities:
all who come out are torn to
pieces,
For their crimes are many,
their rebellions numerous.
⁷Why should I pardon you?
Your children have forsaken me,
they swear by gods that are no
gods.
I fed them, but they commit
adultery;
to the prostitute's house they
throng.
⁸They are lustful stallions,
each neighs after the other's wife.
⁹Should I not punish them for
this?—oracle of the LORD;
on a nation like this should I not
take vengeance?
¹⁰Climb her terraces, and ravage
them,
destroy them completely.
Tear away her tendrils,
they do not belong to the LORD.
¹¹For they have openly rebelled
against me,
both the house of Israel and the
house of Judah—
oracle of the LORD.
¹²They denied the LORD,
saying, "He is nothing,
No evil shall come to us,
neither sword nor famine shall
we see.
¹³The prophets are wind,

and the word is not with them.
Let it be done to them!"
¹⁴Therefore, thus says the LORD, the
God of hosts,
because you have said this—
See! I make my words
a fire in your mouth,
And this people the wood
that it shall devour!—
¹⁵Beware! I will bring against you
a nation from far away,
O House of Israel—oracle of the
LORD;
A long-lived nation, an ancient
nation,
a people whose language you
do not know,
whose speech you cannot
understand.
¹⁶Their quivers are like open graves;
all of them are warriors.
¹⁷They will devour your harvest
and your bread,
devour your sons and your
daughters,
Devour your sheep and cattle,
devour your vines and fig trees;
With their swords they will beat
down
the fortified cities in which you
trust.

¹⁸Yet even in those days—oracle of the LORD—I will not completely destroy you. ¹⁹And when they ask, "Why has the LORD our God done all these things to us?" say to them, "As you have abandoned me to serve foreign gods in your own land, so shall you serve foreigners in a land not your own."

terms: unjust (5:1), dishonest (5:1), "swear falsely" (5:2) or by other gods (5:7), refuse to repent (5:3), act "foolishly" (5:4), "have broken the yoke" (5:5), commit many crimes (5:6, 25-26), have "rebelled" (5:7, 11, 23), have forsaken the Lord (5:7, 19), "commit adultery" (5:7), are dismissive of the Lord and the prophets (5:12-13), serve other gods (5:19), stubborn (5:23), refuse to fear the

²⁰Announce this to the house of
 Jacob,
   proclaim it in Judah:
²¹Pay attention to this,
   you foolish and senseless people,
Who have eyes and do not see,
   who have ears and do not hear.
²²Should you not fear me—oracle of
 the LORD—
   should you not tremble before
     me?
I made the sandy shore the sea's
 limit,
   which by eternal decree it may
     not overstep.
Toss though it may, it is to no avail;
   though its billows roar, they
     cannot overstep.
²³But this people's heart is stubborn
 and rebellious;
   they turn and go away,
²⁴And do not say in their hearts,
   "Let us fear the LORD, our God,
Who gives us rain
   early and late, in its time;
Who watches for us
   over the appointed weeks of
     harvest."
²⁵Your crimes have prevented these
 things,

your sins have turned these
   blessings away from you.
²⁶For criminals lurk among my
 people;
   like fowlers they set traps,
   but it is human beings they
     catch.
²⁷Their houses are as full of
 treachery
   as a bird-cage is of birds;
Therefore they grow powerful and
 rich,
²⁸fat and sleek.
They pass over wicked deeds;
   justice they do not defend
By advancing the claim of the
 orphan
   or judging the cause of the poor.
²⁹Shall I not punish these things?—
   oracle of the LORD;
   on a nation such as this shall I
     not take vengeance?
³⁰Something shocking and horrible
   has happened in the land:
³¹The prophets prophesy falsely,
   and the priests teach on their
     own authority;
Yet my people like it this way;
   what will you do when the end
     comes?

Lord (5:24), and neither prophets nor priests do as they should (5:31). Judgment takes the form of attacks by wild animals (5:6), the destruction of the produce of the land (5:10), fire as a metaphor for the Lord's word and for the devastation wrought by war (5:14), war (5:15-17), and exile (5:19). Throughout these indictments and announcements of judgment the passage speaks of a God who tried to discipline the people (5:3), to find anyone among the people and its leaders who was just (5:1, 4-5), and who provided for them in creation (5:22) and harvest (5:24), but nothing has worked. The people continue to deny the Lord (5:12) and ignore the prophets (5:13). The prose of verses 18-19 interrupts the poetic oracles that make up this chapter. These verses serve two functions: to indicate that the destruction of the people is not total and to reiterate a justification for the exile. The Lord's punishment is justified, for the people refuse to worship the Lord and the Lord alone.

The Enemy at the Gates

6 ¹Seek refuge, Benjaminites,
  from the midst of Jerusalem!
Blow the trumpet in Tekoa,
  raise a signal over Beth-
    haccherem;
For disaster threatens from the
  north,
  and mighty destruction.
²Lovely and delicate
  daughter Zion, you are ruined!
³Against her, shepherds come with
  their flocks;
  all around, they pitch their tents
    against her;
  each one grazes his portion.
⁴"Prepare for war against her,
  Up! let us rush upon her at
    midday!"
"Woe to us! the day is waning,
  evening shadows lengthen!"
⁵"Up! let us rush upon her by night,
  destroy her palaces!"
⁶For thus says the LORD of hosts:
Hew down her trees,
  throw up a siege mound against
    Jerusalem.
Woe to the city marked for punish-
    ment;
  there is nothing but oppression
    within her!
⁷As a well keeps its waters fresh,
  so she keeps fresh her wicked-
    ness.
Violence and destruction resound
  in her;

ever before me are wounds and
  blows.
⁸Be warned, Jerusalem,
  or I will be estranged from you,
And I will turn you into a wilder-
    ness,
  a land where no one dwells.
⁹Thus says the LORD of hosts:
Glean, glean like a vine
  the remnant of Israel;
Pass your hand, like a vintager,
  repeatedly over the tendrils.
¹⁰To whom shall I speak?
  whom shall I warn, and be
    heard?
See! their ears are uncircumcised,
  they cannot pay attention;
See, the word of the LORD has
  become for them
  an object of scorn, for which
    they have no taste.
¹¹But the wrath of the LORD brims
  up within me,
  I am weary of holding it in.
I will pour it out upon the child in
  the street,
  upon the young men gathered
    together.
Yes, husband and wife will be
    taken,
  elder with ancient.
¹²Their houses will fall to others,
  their fields and their wives as
    well;
For I will stretch forth my hand
  against those who dwell in the
    land—oracle of the LORD.

6:1-30 The enemy at the gates

The theme of judgment continues in this chapter by focusing on the imminence of an invasion from the north, an invasion that can no longer be held off. An ominous tone pervades this passage as the people prepare for war. From the blowing of the trumpet that announces the coming of war to the siege and destruction of Jerusalem and its people, the passage is dominated by the horror that is to come. The Lord warns the people time

¹³Small and great alike, all are
    greedy for gain;
  prophet and priest, all practice
      fraud.
¹⁴They have treated lightly
    the injury to my people:
  "Peace, peace!" they say,
      though there is no peace.
¹⁵They have acted shamefully,
    committing abominations,
  yet they are not at all ashamed,
    they do not know how to blush.
Therefore they will fall among the
    fallen;
  in the time of their punishment
      they shall stumble,
  says the LORD.
¹⁶Thus says the LORD:
Stand by the earliest roads,
  ask the pathways of old,
"Which is the way to good?" and
    walk it;
  thus you will find rest for
      yourselves.
  But they said, "We will not walk
    it."
¹⁷I raised up watchmen for them:
  "Pay attention to the sound of
    the trumpet!"
  But they said, "We will not pay
    attention!"
¹⁸Therefore hear, O nations,
  and know, O earth,
  what I will do with them:
¹⁹See, I bring evil upon this people,
  the fruit of their own schemes,
Because they did not pay attention
    to my words,
  because they rejected my law.
²⁰Of what use to me is incense that
  comes from Sheba,

or sweet cane from far-off lands?
Your burnt offerings find no favor
    with me,
  your sacrifices do not please me.
²¹Therefore, thus says the LORD:
See, I will place before this people
  obstacles to trip them up;
Parents and children alike,
  neighbors and friends shall
      perish.
²²Thus says the LORD:
See, a people comes from the land
    of the north,
  a great nation, rising from the
      very ends of the earth.
²³Bow and javelin they wield;
  cruel and pitiless are they.
They sound like the roaring sea
  as they ride forth on horses,
Each in his place for battle
  against you, daughter Zion.
²⁴We hear news of them;
  our hands hang helpless,
Anguish takes hold of us,
  pangs like a woman in childbirth.
²⁵Do not go out into the field,
  do not step into the street,
For the enemy has a sword;
  terror on every side!
²⁶Daughter of my people, dress in
    sackcloth,
  roll in the ashes.
Mourn as for an only child
  with bitter wailing:
"How suddenly the destroyer
  comes upon us!"
²⁷A tester for my people I have
    appointed you,
  to search and test their way.
²⁸Arch-rebels are they all,
  dealers in slander,

and again, but they refuse to pay attention to the prophets or to be obedient to the law. There is no call for the people to mend their ways; indeed their continued refusal to do good seals their fate. The passage ends with the Lord's word directed specifically to Jeremiah. Jeremiah is said to be a "tester"

bronze and iron, all of them,
  destroyers they are.
[29]The bellows are scorched,
  the lead is consumed by the fire;
In vain has the refiner refined,
  the wicked are not drawn off.
[30]"Silver rejected" they shall be
  called,
  for the LORD has rejected them.

II. Oracles Primarily from the Days of Jehoiakim

7 The Temple Sermon. [1]The word came to Jeremiah from the LORD: [2]Stand at the gate of the house of the LORD and proclaim this message there: Hear the word of the LORD, all you of Judah who enter these gates to worship the LORD! [3]Thus says the LORD of hosts, the God of Israel: Reform your ways and your deeds so that I may dwell with you in this place. [4]Do not put your trust in these deceptive words: "The temple of the LORD! The temple of the LORD! The temple of the LORD!" [5]Only if you thoroughly reform your ways and your deeds; if each of you deals justly with your neighbor; [6]if you no longer oppress the alien, the orphan, and the widow; if you no longer shed innocent blood in this place or follow after other gods to your own harm, [7]only then will I let you continue to dwell in this place, in the land I gave your ancestors long ago and forever.

[8]But look at you! You put your trust in deceptive words to your own loss! [9]Do you think you can steal and murder, commit adultery and perjury, sacrifice to Baal, follow other gods that you do not know, [10]and then come and stand in

---

for my people. This is a role that is given to the Lord elsewhere (9:6; 17:10) in the book of Jeremiah. As a refiner tests metal, so Jeremiah is appointed to search and test the way of the people, but here the Lord indicates that the refining process has failed. The people persist in turning away from the Lord; their destruction is inevitable.

ORACLES PRIMARILY FROM THE DAYS OF JEHOIAKIM

Jeremiah 7:1–20:18

This section is a rather eclectic collection of oracles of indictment and judgment against Judah and Jerusalem. The language of lament is drawn into these often harsh oracles, but now and then a brief reference to hope finds expression. Many of the themes of the first six chapters continue to dominate Jeremiah's message in these chapters, but Jeremiah's response to his own suffering receives greater focus as well.

7:1-15 The temple sermon

The temple sermon, which runs from 7:1 to 8:3, is clearly set off from its context as a prose insert into a series of poetic oracles. The entire sermon is most probably a composite work, but taken as a whole the sermon is a

my presence in this house, which bears my name, and say: "We are safe! We can commit all these abominations again!"? [11]Has this house which bears my name become in your eyes a den of thieves? I have seen it for myself!—oracle of the Lord. [12]Go to my place at Shiloh, where I made my name dwell in the beginning. See what I did to it because of the wickedness of my people Israel. [13]And now, because you have committed all these deeds—oracle of the Lord—because you did not listen, though I spoke to you untiringly, and because you did not answer, though I called you, [14]I will do to this house, which bears my name, in which you trust, and to the place which I gave you and your ancestors, exactly what I did to Shiloh. [15]I will cast you out of my sight, as I cast away all your kindred, all the offspring of Ephraim.

Abuses in Worship. [16]You, now, must not intercede for this people! Do not raise a cry or prayer in their behalf! Do

---

series of indictments against the people and the announcement of judgment against them. The sermon betrays the thought and language of the Deuteronomic school, but the core of the chapter reflects a prophetic message similar to that of Jeremiah. All the people of Judah coming to the temple are addressed in verses 1-15. They are coming to worship the Lord of Hosts, but by the end of the sermon it is made clear that in actuality they are worshiping the "host of heaven" (8:2). There are a series of demands made upon the people: "reform your ways," "do not put your trust in . . . deceptive words," "[deal] justly with your neighbor," don't "oppress the alien, the orphan, and the widow," don't "shed innocent blood" (7:3-6). Only by obedience to these demands will the people remain secure in the land given to their ancestors. Attention is drawn to the shocking behavior of the people: "But look at you!" (7:8). By means of rhetorical questions Jeremiah exposes the absurdity of their behavior; they do the opposite of what the Lord has commanded. They "trust in deceptive words," "steal and murder, commit adultery and perjury, sacrifice to Baal," and "follow other gods" (7:8-9). The perverse nature of their actions is seen, not simply in their disobedience, but also by their coming into the temple to worship after sinning, as if temple services alone can make them safe. This section concludes with the announcement of judgment: the fate of Shiloh bears witness that the Lord will destroy the city of Jerusalem and its temple.

7:16–8:3 Abuses in worship

The word of the Lord up to this point in the temple sermon had been directed to the people of Judah, but now the addressee is the prophet himself. Jeremiah is commanded not to intercede on behalf of the people. It is too late. They failed to listen (7:13); now the Lord will not listen. The Lord points to their behavior and speaks of all family members, fathers, mothers,

not press me, for I will not listen to you! [17]Do you not see what they are doing in the cities of Judah, in the streets of Jerusalem? [18]The children gather wood, their fathers light the fire, and the women knead dough to make cakes for the Queen of Heaven, while libations are poured out to other gods—all to offend me! [19]Are they really offending me—oracle of the LORD—or rather themselves, to their own disgrace? [20]Therefore, thus says the Lord GOD: my anger and my wrath will pour out upon this place, upon human being and beast, upon the trees of the field and the fruits of the earth; it will burn and not be quenched.

[21]Thus says the LORD of hosts, the God of Israel: Heap your burnt offerings upon your sacrifices; eat up the meat! [22]In speaking to your ancestors on the day I brought them out of the land of Egypt, I gave them no command concerning burnt offering or sacrifice. [23]This rather is what I commanded them: Listen to my voice; then I will be your God and you shall be my people. Walk exactly in the way I command you, so that you may prosper.

[24]But they did not listen to me, nor did they pay attention. They walked in the stubbornness of their evil hearts and turned their backs, not their faces, to me. [25]From the day that your ancestors left the land of Egypt even to this day, I kept on sending all my servants the prophets to you. [26]Yet they have not listened to me nor have they paid attention; they have stiffened their necks and done worse than their ancestors. [27]When you speak all these words to them, they will not listen to you either. When you call to them, they will not answer you. [28]Say to them: This is the nation which does not listen to the voice of the LORD, its God, or take correction. Faithfulness has disappeared; the word itself is banished from their speech.

---

and children, engaged in the worship of the Queen of Heaven and other gods. The description of the worship of this goddess is drawn out at length in contrast to the Decalogue-like listing of 7:8. The focus shifts from a violation of many commandments to the violation of the first commandment: do not worship other gods; for this they stand under judgment. Though verses 21-22 are sometimes taken as a repudiation of the whole sacrificial system, it seems that only certain sacrifices are dismissed. What the Lord requires is obedience, but the history of Israel has been one of a stubborn refusal to faithfully worship the Lord and walk in the ways commanded. Rather than worship the Lord, the people prefer the high places of Topheth, where they sacrifice their own children by fire in the Valley of Ben-hinnom. The horror of their actions is matched by the horror of what will happen to them on the Day of Judgment. They will be slaughtered, become food for birds of prey, and there will be no burial of their bones. The note of finality in this passage will be countered by hope found in chapters 30–33, but the harsh vehemence of this sermon is meant to awaken the people to repent. Unfortunately it does not do so.

²⁹Cut off your hair and throw it
    away!
on the heights raise a lament;
The LORD has indeed rejected and
    cast off
    the generation that draws down
        his wrath.

³⁰The people of Judah have done what is evil in my eyes—oracle of the LORD. They have set up their detestable things in the house which bears my name, thereby defiling it. ³¹In the Valley of Ben-hinnom they go on building the high places of Topheth to sacrifice their sons and daughters by fire, something I never commanded or considered. ³²Be assured! Days are coming—oracle of the LORD—when they will no longer say "Topheth" or "Valley of Ben-hinnom" but "Valley of Slaughter." For want of space, Topheth will become burial ground. ³³The corpses of this people will be food for the birds of the sky and beasts of the earth, which no one will drive away. ³⁴I will silence the cry of joy, the cry of gladness, the voice of the bridegroom and the voice of the bride, in the cities of Judah and in the streets of Jerusalem; for the land will be turned to rubble.

8 ¹At that time—oracle of the LORD— the bones of the kings and princes of Judah, the bones of the priests and the prophets, and the bones of the inhabitants of Jerusalem will be brought out of their graves ²and spread out before the sun, the moon, and the whole host of heaven, which they loved and served, which they followed, consulted, and worshiped.

They will not be gathered up for burial, but will lie like dung upon the ground. ³Death will be preferred to life by all the survivors of this wicked people who remain in any of the places to which I banish them—oracle of the LORD of hosts.

Israel's Conduct Incomprehensible

⁴Tell them: Thus says the LORD:
When someone falls, do they not
    rise again?
    if they turn away, do they not
        turn back?
⁵Why then do these people resist
    with persistent rebellion?
Why do they cling to deception,
    refuse to turn back?
⁶I have listened closely:
    they speak what is not true;
No one regrets wickedness,
    saying, "What have I done?"
Everyone keeps on running their
    course,
    like a horse dashing into battle.
⁷Even the stork in the sky
    knows its seasons;
Turtledove, swift, and thrush
    observe the time of their return,
But my people do not know
    the order of the LORD.
⁸How can you say, "We are wise,
    we have the law of the LORD"?
See, that has been changed into
    falsehood
    by the lying pen of the scribes!
⁹The wise are put to shame,
    terrified, and trapped;
Since they have rejected the word
    of the LORD,
    what sort of wisdom do they
        have?

8:4-9 Israel's conduct incomprehensible

There is a pervasive tone of pathos in this indictment of the people. God's anguish over the inexplicable behavior of the people (8:5) is underscored

Shameless in Their Crimes

¹⁰Therefore, I will give their wives
to other men,
their fields to new owners.
Small and great alike, all are greedy
for gain,
prophet and priest, all practice
fraud.
¹¹They have treated lightly
the injury to the daughter of my
people:
"Peace, peace!" they say,
though there is no peace.
¹²They have acted shamefully; they
have done abominable
things,
yet they are not at all ashamed,
they do not know how to blush.

Hence they shall be among those
who fall;
in their time of punishment they
shall stumble,
says the LORD.

Threats of Punishment

¹³I will gather them all in—oracle of
the LORD:
no grapes on the vine,
No figs on the fig trees,
foliage withered!
Whatever I have given them is
gone.
¹⁴Why do we remain here?
Let us assemble and flee to the
fortified cities,
where we will meet our doom;

---

by the use of rhetorical questions (8:4, 5, 8, 9): How is it possible that the people will not repent? The repetition of the term *šûb* ("to turn/return/ repent") dominates the opening verses of chapter 8 (six times in vv. 4-6). "To return" gives expression to the hope that the people will repent, but more often it is used as it is here, to speak of the refusal of the people "to turn back" toward the Lord. Chapter 7 brought to the fore the failure of the people in relation to worship, but other areas of Israel's life, specifically law and instruction (8:7-9), have been distorted as well by falsehood and lies. With the refusal of the people to worship properly, to be obedient to the law, and to be truthful in instruction, it is inevitable that they will not know the Lord (8:7) and what the Lord requires of them.

8:10-12 Shameless in their crimes

A severe sentence follows upon the indictment of 8:4-9. Women will be raped, as often happens in war, land will be confiscated (8:10), and all will be lost because everyone, "small and great," has pursued greed. Priest and prophet are singled out for their failure to treat the sins of the people with seriousness and for speaking falsely that peace was at hand (8:11). They have acted shamefully and yet are impervious to feeling shame. Their actions will result in their inevitable punishment.

8:13-17 Threats of punishment

Judgment is announced in verse 13 in agricultural imagery, but this quickly gives way to war imagery (8:15-16). Instead of an abundant harvest

For the Lord our God has doomed
     us,
  he has given us poisoned water
     to drink,
  because we have sinned against
     the Lord.
¹⁵We wait for peace to no avail;
  for a time of healing, but terror
     comes instead.
¹⁶From Dan is heard
  the snorting of horses;
The neighing of stallions
  shakes the whole land.
They come to devour the land and
     everything in it,
  the city and its inhabitants.
¹⁷Yes, I will send against you
  poisonous snakes.
Against them no charm will work
  when they bite you—oracle of
     the Lord.

**The Prophet's Grief over
the People's Suffering**
¹⁸My joy is gone,
  grief is upon me,

  my heart is sick.
¹⁹Listen! the cry of the daughter of
     my people,
  far and wide in the land!
"Is the Lord no longer in Zion,
  is her King no longer in her
     midst?"
Why do they provoke me with their
     idols,
  with their foreign nonentities?
²⁰"The harvest is over, the summer
     ended,
  but we have not yet been
     saved!"
²¹I am broken by the injury of the
     daughter of my people.
  I am in mourning; horror has
     seized me.
²²Is there no balm in Gilead,
  no healer there?
Why does new flesh not grow
  over the wound of the daughter
     of my people?
²³Oh, that my head were a spring of
     water,
  my eyes a fountain of tears,

in the land, there will be no crops. This passage begins and ends as an "oracle of the Lord," but it is the voice of the people that is heard in verses 14-17. They realize the inevitability of their punishment as they await the arrival of the armies from the north that will devour everything in their path. These armies are moving across the land with war horses eager for battle. Words such as "doomed," "poisoned," no "peace," no "healing," "terror," "shakes," "devour," "no charm will work" suggest the relentless and all-consuming nature of this judgment (8:14-17).

8:18-23 The prophet's grief over the people's suffering

There is an interweaving of the voices of the Lord, Jeremiah, and the people in this passage. Moving away from the images of war, this lament responds to the sense of abandonment expressed by the people (8:19b, 20) and the grief of God or Jeremiah over the refusal of the people to repent and over the suffering the people endure on account of their sinfulness. It is not clear whether Jeremiah is speaking on behalf of God or in his own voice, but the prophet embodies the pathos of God in a way that God's

That I might weep day and night
over the slain from the daughter
of my people!

The Corruption of the People

9 ¹Oh, that I had in the wilderness
a travelers' lodging!
That I might leave my people
and depart from them.
They are all adulterers,
a band of traitors.
²They ready their tongues like a
drawn bow;
with lying, and not with truth,
they are powerful in the land.
They go from evil to evil,
and me they do not know—
oracle of the LORD.
³Be on your guard, everyone
against his neighbor;
put no trust in any brother.
Every brother imitates Jacob, the
supplanter,
every neighbor is guilty of
slander.

⁴Each one deceives the other,
no one speaks the truth.
They have accustomed their
tongues to lying,
they are perverse and cannot
repent.
⁵Violence upon violence,
deceit upon deceit:
They refuse to know me—
oracle of the LORD.
⁶Therefore, thus says the LORD of
hosts:
I will refine them and test them;
how else should I deal with the
daughter of my people?
⁷A murderous arrow is their tongue,
their mouths utter deceit;
They speak peaceably with their
neighbors,
but in their hearts they lay an
ambush!
⁸Should I not punish them for these
deeds—oracle of the LORD;
on a nation such as this should I
not take vengeance?

---

grief becomes his own. The deep pain that finds expression in this passage reveals a God/prophet who suffers with the people.

9:1-8 The corruption of the people

Lament, indictment, and judgment are intertwined, picking up earlier themes but reiterated in different terms. Though the voice of the Lord dominates in this passage, Jeremiah's voice may be evident in the opening verses. The Lord (and/or Jeremiah) longs to put some distance between them and their sinful people (9:1). The opening lament shifts into an indictment that centers on the people's lack of fidelity, expressed primarily as deception and lying and summed up by the phrases "me they do not know" (9:2) and "they refuse to know me" (9:5). The sinfulness of the people is unrelenting as they "go from evil to evil" (9:2) and thus judgment against them is unavoidable (9:6, 8).

9:9-21 Dirge over the ravaged land

The language of lament, picked up from 9:1, pervades these verses that include both indictment and judgment. The horror of the devastation of

Dirge over the Ravaged Land

⁹Over the mountains I shall break
  out in cries of lamentation,
  over the pastures in the wilder-
    ness, in a dirge:
They are scorched, and no one
  crosses them,
  no sound of lowing cattle;
Birds of the air as well as beasts,
  all have fled and are gone.
¹⁰I will turn Jerusalem into a heap
  of ruins,
  a haunt of jackals;
The cities of Judah I will make a
  waste,
  where no one dwells.

¹¹Who is wise enough to understand this? To whom has the mouth of the LORD spoken? Let him declare it!

Why is the land ravaged,
  scorched like a wilderness no
    one crosses?

¹²The LORD said: Because they have abandoned my law, which I set before them, and did not listen to me or follow it, ¹³but followed instead their stubborn hearts and the Baals, as their ancestors had taught them, ¹⁴therefore, thus says the LORD of hosts, the God of Israel: See now, I will give this people wormwood to eat and poisoned water to drink. ¹⁵I will scatter them among nations whom neither they nor their ancestors have known; I will send the sword to pursue them until I have completely destroyed them.

¹⁶Thus says the LORD of hosts:
Inquire, and call the wailing
    women to come;
  summon the most skilled of
    them.
¹⁷Let them come quickly
  and raise for us a dirge,
That our eyes may run with tears,
  our pupils flow with water.
¹⁸The sound of the dirge is heard
  from Zion:
  We are ruined and greatly
    ashamed;
We have left the land,
  given up our dwellings!

the land is reiterated over and over again: the land has been "scorched" (2x), is "a waste," and is "ravaged." From the land even the animals "have fled" and in the future Jerusalem will be "a heap of ruins, / a haunt of jackals" (9:9-11). The response to this overwhelming destruction is a call to professional mourners to sing a funeral song (dirge) to give full expression to the depth of the people's grief (9:16-21). Between the poetic oracles that make up this section, a prose explanation draws attention to the cause of this judgment: the people have abandoned the law, did not listen, were stubborn, and followed the Baals. The judgment itself is a reversal of the gifts of manna and water that the Lord bestowed upon the people in the wilderness (Exod 15:22-25; 16:1-35). Now they will eat "wormwood" and drink "poisoned water." The people will be "scatter[ed] among the nations" and killed, in stark contrast to the exodus where the Lord brought the people out of slavery into the Promised Land (9:14-15). The harshness of the punishment is set over against the persistence in sin by the people.

¹⁹Hear, you women, the word of the LORD,
  let your ears receive the word of his mouth.
Teach your daughters a dirge,
  and each other a lament:
²⁰Death has come up through our windows,
  has entered our citadels,
To cut down children in the street,
  young people in the squares.
²¹Corpses shall fall
  like dung in the open field,
Like sheaves behind the harvester,
  with no one to gather them.

True Glory

²²Thus says the LORD:
Let not the wise boast of his wisdom,
  nor the strong boast of his strength,
nor the rich man boast of his riches;
²³But rather, let those who boast, boast of this,
  that in their prudence they know me,
Know that I, the LORD, act with fidelity,
  justice, and integrity on earth.
How I take delight in these—oracle of the LORD.

False Circumcision. ²⁴See, days are coming—oracle of the LORD—when I will demand an account of all those circumcised in the foreskin: ²⁵Egypt and Judah, Edom and the Ammonites, Moab, and those who live in the wilderness and shave their temples. For all the nations are uncircumcised, even the whole house of Israel is uncircumcised at heart.

Though the Lord is behind their destruction, it is a destruction that causes the Lord grief (9:16-17) and would never have been sent, but for their sins.

9:22-23 True glory

In what may be a response to people who boast in their riches, strength, or wealth, these verses direct the reader to the proper basis for boasting: knowing that the Lord acts with fidelity, justice, and integrity. The locus of the Lord's action is "on earth" (9:23), thus underscoring that the judgment that has come or is coming upon the people is grounded in the actions of a just and faithful deity. Indeed acting with "fidelity, / justice, and integrity" is a "delight" to the Lord (9:23).

9:24-25 False circumcision

The theme of judgment continues in this passage, but judgment comes against even those who are circumcised. Circumcision of the flesh provides no exemption from divine judgment; all stand judged.

10:1-16 The folly of idolatry

With satiric tones the idols of the nations are mocked (10:2-5, 8-9, 11, 14-15) and set in sharp contrast to the incomparable God of Israel (10:6-7,10, 12-13, 16). The denigration of idols is found in Psalms 115:4-8; 135:15-18;

10 **The Folly of Idolatry.** ¹Hear the word the LORD speaks to you, house of Israel. ²Thus says the LORD:

Do not learn the ways of the nations,
    and have no fear of the signs in
        the heavens,
    even though the nations fear
        them.
³For the carvings of the nations are
        nonentities,
    wood cut from the forest,
Fashioned by artisans with the adze,
    ⁴adorned with silver and gold.
With nails and hammers they are
        fastened,
    so they do not fall.
⁵Like a scarecrow in a cucumber
        field are they,
    they cannot speak;
They must be carried about,
    for they cannot walk.
Do not fear them, they can do no
        harm,
    neither can they do good.
⁶No one is like you, LORD,
    you are great,
    great and mighty is your name.
⁷Who would not fear you,
    King of the nations,
    for it is your due!
Among all the wisest of the nations,
    and in all their domains,
    there is none like you.

⁸One and all they are stupid and
        senseless,
    the instruction from nonenti-
        ties—only wood!
⁹Silver plates brought from Tarshish,
    and gold from Ophir,
The work of the artisan
    and the handiwork of the smelter,
Clothed with violet and purple—
    all of them the work of skilled
        workers.
¹⁰The LORD is truly God,
    he is the living God, the eternal
        King,
Before whose anger the earth
        quakes,
    whose wrath the nations cannot
        endure.

¹¹Thus shall you say of them: The gods that did not make heaven and earth—let these perish from earth and from beneath heaven!

¹²The one who made the earth by
        his power,
    established the world by his
        wisdom,
    and by his skill stretched out the
        heavens.
¹³When he thunders, the waters in
        the heavens roar,
    and he brings up clouds from
        the end of the earth,

Isaiah 40:18-20; 41:6-7; 46:5-7, but the outright mocking of these idols is mainly represented in Isaiah 44:9-20 and this passage of Jeremiah. Israel is admonished not to fear omens, for the idols of the nations are the work of artisans; they are lifeless and inert, like scarecrows in a field, and they will perish. They cannot do harm or good; they are "nonentities." By way of contrast, the God of Israel is a living God, great and mighty, incomparable, eternal. The Lord is truly God, for God is the creator and the heavens and earth are under God's dominion and judgment. Israel's status as the Lord's elect is brought into the conclusion of this passage: Israel is the Lord's "very own tribe" (10:16).

Makes lightning flash in the rain,
and brings forth the wind from
his storehouses.
¹⁴Everyone is too stupid to know;
every artisan is put to shame by
his idol:
He has molded a fraud,
without breath of life.
¹⁵They are nothing, objects of
ridicule;
they will perish in their time of
punishment.
¹⁶Jacob's portion is nothing like
them:
for he is the maker of everything!
Israel is his very own tribe,
LORD of hosts is his name.

Abandonment of Judah

¹⁷Gather up your bundle from the
land,
City living under siege!
¹⁸For thus says the LORD:
Now, at this time
I will sling away the inhabitants
of the land;
I will hem them in,
that they may be taken.
¹⁹Woe is me! I am undone,
my wound is beyond healing.
Yet I had thought:
if I make light of my sickness, I
can bear it.
²⁰My tent is ruined,
all its cords are severed.
My children have left me, they are
no more:
no one to pitch my tent,
no one to raise its curtains.
²¹How stupid are the shepherds!
The LORD they have not sought;
For this reason they have failed,
and all their flocks scattered.

10:17-22 Abandonment of Judah

It is probably best to assume that Jeremiah is the speaker of this passage, but he brings to the fore the voices of God (10:18) and the people (10:19-20) by quoting them. With the city under siege Jeremiah commands the people to prepare for exile. The response of the prophet to the unleashing of the Lord's judgment against the people mirrors the reaction of the people to the unfolding of their judgment. They are in distress and pain for the loss of their children and thus the loss of their future. For Jeremiah the blame falls upon the behavior of the leaders of the land. They failed to lead the flock and thus the flock has gone astray and will be sent into exile. The advancing armies from the north leave destruction in their path.

10:23-25 Prayer of Jeremiah

This prayer of Jeremiah does not seem to be related directly to the previous passage, but it may represent Jeremiah's response to the coming of the armies from the north. Jeremiah begins with an observation, drawn perhaps from the wisdom traditions of Israel, suggesting that humans are not able to shape their own destiny. Jeremiah petitions the Lord to correct him, that is, to guide his destiny, and to do so with justice, not anger. Then his peti-

²²Listen! a rumor! here it comes,
a great commotion from the
land of the north:
To make the cities of Judah a
desolation,
the haunt of jackals.

Prayer of Jeremiah

²³I know, LORD,
that no one chooses their way,
Nor determines their course
nor directs their own step.
²⁴Correct me, LORD, but with equity,
not in anger, lest you diminish
me.
²⁵Pour out your wrath on the
nations that
do not know you,
on the tribes that do not call
your name;
For they have utterly devoured
Jacob,
and laid waste his home.

11 **Plea for Fidelity to the Covenant.**
¹The word that came to Jeremiah
from the LORD: ²Speak to the people of
Judah and the inhabitants of Jerusalem,
³and say to them: Thus says the LORD,
the God of Israel: Cursed be anyone who
does not observe the words of this covenant, ⁴which I commanded your ancestors the day I brought them up out of the
land of Egypt, that iron furnace, saying:
Listen to my voice and do all that I command you. Then you shall be my people,
and I will be your God. ⁵Thus I will fulfill the oath I swore to your ancestors, to
give them a land flowing with milk and
honey, the one you have today. "Amen,
LORD," I answered.

⁶Then the LORD said to me: Proclaim
all these words in the cities of Judah and
in the streets of Jerusalem: Hear the
words of this covenant and obey them.
⁷I warned your ancestors unceasingly
from the day I brought them up out of
the land of Egypt even to this day: obey
my voice. ⁸But they did not listen or
obey. They each walked in the stubbornness of their evil hearts, till I brought
upon them all the threats of this covenant which they had failed to observe as
I commanded them.

⁹A conspiracy has been found, the
LORD said to me, among the people of
Judah and the inhabitants of Jerusalem:
¹⁰They have returned to the crimes of
their ancestors who refused to obey my
words. They also have followed and
served other gods; the house of Israel
and the house of Judah have broken the
covenant I made with their ancestors.
¹¹Therefore, thus says the LORD: See, I am
bringing upon them a disaster they cannot escape. Though they cry out to me,
I will not listen to them. ¹²Then the cities
of Judah and the inhabitants of Jerusalem will go and cry out to the gods to
whom they have been offering incense.
But these gods will give them no help
whatever in the time of their disaster.

---

tion shifts its focus to the nations who have destroyed Israel. Jeremiah wants
the Lord's anger not to be set against him but against Israel's enemies.

11:1-14 Plea for fidelity to the covenant

The indictments, announcements of judgment, and laments that have
been intermixed in the previous ten chapters continue in the next ten chapters,
but overtones of lament, particularly the laments of the prophet himself, are

¹³For as many as your cities
    are your gods, O Judah!
As many as the streets of Jerusalem
    are the altars for sacrifice to
        Baal.

¹⁴Now, you must not intercede for this
people; do not raise on their behalf a cry
or prayer! I will not listen when they call
to me in the time of their disaster.

Sacrifices of No Avail

¹⁵What right has my beloved in my
    house,
    while she devises her plots?
Can vows and sacred meat turn
    away
    your disaster from you?
Will you still be jubilant
    ¹⁶when you hear the great
        tumult?

---

more evident in this section. A frequent shift from poetry to prose character-izes these chapters. Symbolic actions of Jeremiah (13:1-11, 12-14; 16:1-9; 18:1-12; 19:1-15) receive attention in prose narratives that punctuate this section. Oracles of salvation (13:15-27; 14:10-16; 15:1-4; 16:10-13; 17:1-4; 18:13-17), wisdom sayings (17:5-13), and exhortation (17:19-27) are all represented in these ten chapters.

This first section of chapter 11 has often been identified as a Deutero-nomic composition because the language of the passage echoes the language found in writings attributed to Deuteronomic authors, such as, "com-manded your ancestors," "brought them up out of the land of Egypt," "you shall be my people," "followed and served other gods" (11:4, 10). This passage is often associated with Josiah's reform, but no explicit connection is drawn between Jeremiah's message and the reform of Josiah in the pas-sage itself. The themes that have dominated Jeremiah's message thus far are brought together in these verses and serve as an introduction to what will follow in subsequent chapters. The certainty of punishment grounds the laments from God, Jeremiah, and the people that are interspersed in the following chapters.

Israel's life as a nation is grounded in the covenant (11:3, 6, 8, 10). In formulaic language the relationship between deity and people is defined: "you shall be my people, and I will be your God" (11:4). It is a relationship that is lived by Israel's listening to and obeying the commands of the Lord. The Lord has shown graciousness to this people by redeeming them from a harsh slavery (Egypt as an "iron furnace," 11:4) and bringing them into a "land flowing with milk and honey" (11:5), but it is reiterated in this pas-sage that the people of Israel have failed to listen and obey. The people, like their ancestors, stubbornly persist in following and serving other gods and therefore the covenant curses are in effect. The threatened disaster will come upon them because of their infidelity; no intercession is now possible (11:14). The command to Jeremiah not to intercede on behalf of the people

The LORD has named you
    "a spreading olive tree, a plea-
        sure to behold";
Now he sets fire to it,
    its branches burn.

[17]The LORD of hosts who planted you has decreed disaster for you because of the evil done by the house of Israel and by the house of Judah, who provoked me by sacrificing to Baal.

The Plot Against Jeremiah. [18]I knew it because the LORD informed me: at that time you showed me their doings.

  [19]Yet I was like a trusting lamb led to slaughter, not knowing that they were hatching plots against me: "Let us destroy the tree in its vigor; let us cut him off from the land of the living, so that his name will no longer be remembered."

    [20]But, you, LORD of hosts, just Judge,
      searcher of mind and heart,
  Let me witness the vengeance you
      take on them,
    for to you I have entrusted my
      cause!

[21]Therefore, thus says the LORD concerning the men of Anathoth who seek your life and say, "Do not prophesy in the name of the LORD; otherwise you shall die by our hand." [22]Therefore, thus says the LORD of hosts: I am going to punish them. The young men shall die by the sword; their sons and daughters shall die by famine. [23]None shall be spared among them, for I will bring disaster upon the men of Anathoth, the year of their punishment.

12 [1]You would be in the right, O LORD,
    if I should dispute with you;
    even so, I must lay out the case
      against you.
Why does the way of the wicked
    prosper,
    why do all the treacherous live
      in contentment?
[2]You planted them; they have taken
    root,
    they flourish and bear fruit as
      well.
You are upon their lips,
    but far from their thoughts.

---

is a recurring theme in Jeremiah (7:16; 11:14; 14:11; 15:1) and it indicates that it is too late to turn back the punishment.

11:15-17 Sacrifices of no avail

Directly addressing the people, the Lord raises questions about the right of the people to worship in the temple when their actions do not align with their covenant relationship. Though Israel was to be full of life and a source of joy for the Lord ("a spreading olive tree, a pleasure to behold," 11:16), the nation has worshiped other gods, specifically Baal. There is no undoing of the disaster that has been decreed. Yet, in the opening verse of this section, the Lord addresses the people as "my beloved." That punishment is the only recourse left does not mean that the Lord ceases to love the people.

11:18–12:6 The plot against Jeremiah

Six passages (11:18–12:6; 15:10-21; 17:14-18; 18:18-23; 20:7-13; 20:14-18) in the book of Jeremiah have been labeled the "Confessions of Jeremiah."

³LORD, you know me, you see me,
  you have found that my heart is
    with you.
Pick them out like sheep for the
  butcher,
  set them apart for the day of
    slaughter.
⁴How long must the land mourn,
  the grass of the whole country-
    side wither?

Because of the wickedness of those
  who dwell in it
  beasts and birds disappear,
  for they say, "God does not care
    about our future."

⁵If running against men has wearied
  you,
  how will you race against horses?
And if you are safe only on a level
  stretch,

These are called "confessions," not in the sense that Jeremiah is confessing sins or even confessing his faith; they are "confessions" in the sense that Jeremiah is giving expression to his innermost feelings. These passages resemble "laments" and draw heavily from the language of the psalms of lament. There are laments of both God (12:7-13; 14:2-6, 17-18; 15:5-9; 18:13-17) and the people (14:7-9, 19-22) worked into chapters 11–20, but these laments of Jeremiah are unique in prophetic literature. There are no introductions to these six passages; they are set apart because in them we have the voice of the prophet raised in complaint against God and in two of the confessions we have God's response.

Interpretation of these "confessions" have ranged from seeing them as the prophet's personal prayer in response to the difficulties Jeremiah faced in carrying out his prophetic role to formulaic communal laments drawn from worship giving voice to the complaint of the people through the prophet's voice. While we cannot ignore the formulaic language drawn from the laments, there is a personal element in these "confessions" that must be taken into account. These prayers are situated in the life of a person who suffered persecution and rejection delivering God's message and so they are particularly suited to the circumstances of Jeremiah's life. There is no reason to assume that Jeremiah himself could not have voiced his complaint in the formal language of lament.

In the first confession Jeremiah responds to information given to him by the Lord. He had been unaware that some from his hometown of Anathoth were plotting against him (11:18, 21) and indeed that members of his own family were against him (12:6). He calls for vengeance against those who plot against his life. In Jeremiah's call to be prophet in chapter 1, the Lord had assured Jeremiah that the Lord would be with him to defend him and Jeremiah calls upon the Lord to take vengeance upon those who persecute him. Two things are to be noted here: vengeance is the Lord's ven-

what will you do in the jungle of
the Jordan?

⁶Your kindred and your father's
house, even they betray you; they have
recruited a force against you. Do not believe them, even when they speak fair
words to you.

The Lord's Complaint

⁷I have abandoned my house,
cast off my heritage;
The beloved of my soul I have
delivered
into the hand of her foes.
⁸My heritage has become for me
like a lion in the thicket;
She has raised her voice against me,
therefore she has incurred my
hatred.
⁹My heritage is a prey for hyenas,
is surrounded by vultures;

geance and the integrity of the Lord's word is at stake here. Jeremiah does
not himself exact vengeance against his enemies; it is up to the Lord to do
so. For the integrity of the Lord's word to stand, Jeremiah's enemies must
not be allowed to triumph. The Lord responds to Jeremiah, assuring him
that those who plot to take his life will be punished, but Jeremiah continues
his complaint, raising the issue of why the wicked prosper. In a reversal of
Psalm 1, Jeremiah maintains that it is the wicked who are like trees that are
planted and flourish, and, even more stridently, Jeremiah says that it is the
Lord who plants and nurtures them. Jeremiah is seemingly impatient for
justice because the land suffers. The Lord's response is surprising both in
form and content. The Lord confronts Jeremiah with rhetorical questions
that imply Jeremiah's situation will get worse. If he complains at minor
difficulties, how will he manage when the situation gets worse? It is at this
point that the Lord reveals to Jeremiah that not only is the town against
him but his own family is not to be trusted.

12:7-13 The Lord's complaint

After responding to Jeremiah's lament, the Lord gives expression to
sorrow at the condition of the people and their land. The frequent use of
"my" (12:7 [3x], 8, 9, 10 [3x]), and terms like "house," "beloved" (12:7),
"heritage" (12:7, 8, 9, 10), "vineyard," and "delightful portion" (12:10) lend
a certain poignancy to the passage. The Lord's own people, God's own
possession, have turned against the Lord who grieves for them and yet
must punish them. Throughout much of the book of Jeremiah there is an
unrelenting doom that awaits the people, but it is a doom that is brought
about by their own actions. The land has been and will be "ravaged,"
"trampled," "turned into a desert" (12:10) and "a mournful waste" (12:11);
there is "no peace" (12:12) or fruitful harvest (12:13). This damage has been
caused as punishment for people turning against the Lord, but the Lord is
not a cold executioner; rather, the Lord mourns for the land and its people.

Come, gather together, all you wild
 animals,
  come and eat!
¹⁰Many shepherds have ravaged my
 vineyard,
  have trampled down my
   heritage;
My delightful portion they have
 turned
  into a desert waste.
¹¹They have made it a mournful
 waste,
  desolate before me,
Desolate, the whole land,
  because no one takes it to heart.
¹²Upon every height in the wilder-
 ness
  marauders have appeared.
The LORD has a sword that
 consumes
  the land from end to end:
  no peace for any living thing.
¹³They have sown wheat and
 reaped thorns,
  they have tired themselves out
   for no purpose;
They are shamed by their harvest,
  the burning anger of the LORD.

Judah's Neighbors. ¹⁴Thus says the LORD,
against all my evil neighbors who plun-
der the heritage I gave my people Israel
as their own: See, I will uproot them
from their land; the house of Judah I will
uproot in their midst.

¹⁵But after uprooting them, I will
have compassion on them again and
bring them back, each to their heritage,
each to their land. ¹⁶And if they truly
learn my people's custom of swearing
by my name, "As the LORD lives," just
as they taught my people to swear by
Baal, then they shall be built up in the
midst of my people. ¹⁷But if they do not
obey, I will uproot and destroy that nation entirely—oracle of the LORD.

13 **Judah's Corruption.** ¹The LORD said
to me: Go buy yourself a linen
loincloth; wear it on your loins, but do
not put it in water. ²I bought the loincloth, as the LORD commanded, and put
it on. ³A second time the word of the
LORD came to me thus: ⁴Take the loincloth which you bought and are wear-
ing, and go at once to the Perath; hide it
there in a cleft of the rock. ⁵Obedient to
the LORD's command, I went to the Per-
ath and buried the loincloth. ⁶After a
long time, the LORD said to me: Go now

12:14-17 Judah's neighbors

The element of hope in these verses contrasts sharply with the harsh
judgment that characterizes much of Jeremiah's prophecy. The Lord's
people have been uprooted by invading armies as punishment, but those
armies will not have the last word. The Lord's judgment will give way to
compassion and an uprooted people will be returned to their land and their
enemies will be uprooted in turn, but even that uprooting will not be forever, for Israel's enemies will be given the opportunity to learn the ways
of the Lord and be restored to their lands.

13:1-11 Judah's corruption

This chapter opens with the first of several symbolic acts of Jeremiah.
These symbolic acts add a dramatic element to the proclamation of the

to the Perath and fetch the loincloth which I told you to hide there. ⁷So I went to the Perath, looked for the loincloth and took it from the place I had hidden it. But it was rotted, good for nothing! ⁸Then the word came to me from the LORD: ⁹Thus says the LORD: So also I will allow the pride of Judah to rot, the great pride of Jerusalem. ¹⁰This wicked people who refuse to obey my words, who walk in the stubbornness of their hearts and follow other gods, serving and worshiping them, will be like this loincloth, good for nothing. ¹¹For, as the loincloth clings to a man's loins, so I made the whole house of Israel and the whole house of Judah cling to me—oracle of the LORD—to be my people, my fame, my praise, my glory. But they did not listen.

The Broken Wineflask. ¹²Now speak to them this word: Thus says the LORD, the God of Israel: Every wineflask should be filled with wine. If they reply, "Do we not know that every wineflask should be filled with wine?" ¹³say to them: Thus says the LORD: Beware! I am making all the inhabitants of this land drunk, the kings who sit on David's throne, the priests and prophets, and all the inhabitants of Jerusalem. ¹⁴I will smash them against each other, parents and children together—oracle of the LORD—showing no compassion, I will neither spare nor pity, but I will destroy them.

A Last Warning
¹⁵Listen and give ear, do not be arrogant,
for the LORD speaks.

prophetic word. The details of what Jeremiah actually does are debated, for he is commanded to go to Babylon twice and it is difficult to see how that could have been accomplished in a three-to-four-month period, given the distance and slow means of travel available at the time. What is clear, however, is the meaning of the symbolic act: the loincloth is a metaphor for the people. The closeness of the loincloth to the body suggests an intimacy between the Lord and the people (13:11), but the rotting of the loincloth represents the judgment that will come upon the people (13:9) because of their refusal to obey the Lord, especially in their persistent worship of other gods (13:10).

13:12-14 The broken wineflask

The proverb regarding a wineflask (13:12) becomes the basis for an announcement of judgment. Wine is often seen as a blessing from the Lord, thus the proverb suggests that Israel should be "filled with" the Lord's blessings, but their actions lead, rather, to their destruction. It is the ill effects of wine (drunkenness) that they experience, rather than its blessing. The harshness of the judgment is characteristic of Jeremiah's prophecy, but it is mitigated to some extent by announcements of hope found later in the book (chaps. 30–33).

¹⁶Give glory to the LORD, your God,
    before he brings darkness;
Before your feet stumble
    on mountains at twilight;
Before the light you look for turns
        to darkness,
    changes into black clouds.
¹⁷If you do not listen to this in your
        pride,
    I will weep many tears in secret;
My eyes will run with tears
    for the LORD's flock, led away to
        exile.

Exile

¹⁸Say to the king and to the queen
        mother:
    come down from your throne;
From your heads
    your splendid crowns will fall.
¹⁹The cities of the Negeb are besieged,
    with no one to relieve them;
Judah is taken into exile—all of it—
    in total exile.

Jerusalem's Disgrace

²⁰Lift up your eyes and see
    those coming in from the north.
Where is the flock entrusted to you,
    your splendid sheep?
²¹What will you say when rulers are
        appointed over you,
    those you taught to be allies?
Will not pains seize you
    like those of a woman giving birth?
²²If you say to yourself:
    "Why have these things
        happened to me?"
For your great guilt your skirts are
        stripped away
    and you are violated.
²³Can Ethiopians change their skin,
    leopards their spots?
As easily would you be able to do
        good,
    accustomed to evil as you are.
²⁴I will scatter them like chaff that
        flies
    on the desert wind.

13:15-17 The last warning

The message of these verses is clear: return to the Lord before it is too late. The complete destruction announced in 13:14 and picked up again in verses 20-27 stands in tension with this call for repentance, but hope may emerge even as darkness begins to descend. It may well be that some of the people will respond and repent, thus sowing the seeds upon which a better future can be built. Jeremiah's own grief is given expression in verse 17.

13:18-19 Exile

The king and queen mother of verse 18 are most likely Jehoiachin and Nehushta (22:24-27; see also 2 Kgs 24:8). Their descent from the throne and the removal of their crowns signifies the end of the king's reign and the end of his mother's position as queen mother. The besieging of the cities of the Negeb suggests that the demise of Jerusalem is close at hand. Judah's rulers will be dethroned and its people forced into exile.

13:20-27 Jerusalem's disgrace

Jerusalem is addressed (13:27b) in this announcement of judgment, but it is a judgment that is intermixed with indictment and lament. The indict-

²⁵This is your lot, the portion I have
measured out to you—
oracle of the LORD.
Because you have forgotten me,
and trusted in deception,
²⁶I now will strip away your skirts,
so that your shame is visible.
²⁷Your adulteries, your neighings,
your shameless prostitutions:
On the hills, in the fields
I see your detestable crimes.
Woe to you, Jerusalem! How long
will it be
before you are clean?

14 **The Great Drought.** ¹The word of
the LORD that came to Jeremiah
concerning the drought:

²Judah mourns,
her gates are lifeless;

They are bowed to the ground,
and the outcry of Jerusalem goes
up.
³The nobles send their servants for
water,
but when they come to the
cisterns
They find no water
and return with empty jars.
Confounded, despairing, they
cover their heads
⁴because of the ruined soil;
Because there is no rain in the land
the farmers are confounded,
they cover their heads.
⁵Even the doe in the field deserts
her young
because there is no grass.
⁶The wild donkeys stand on the
bare heights,
gasping for breath like jackals;

---

ment draws upon graphic and offensive sexual imagery to speak of Jerusalem's infidelity to the Lord, and the announcement of judgment borrows the language of sexual violence. This intense rhetoric is presumably aimed at shocking the people into recognizing their sinfulness and repenting, but the passage suggests, rather, that the people of Jerusalem won't change and so there is no other option than a punishment that "fits the crime."

14:1–15:4 The great drought

This section is characterized by a dialogic interplay of the voices of the Lord, Jeremiah, and the people in both poetry and prose. Set against the background of a drought, this prophetic word is dominated by laments from the people (14:7-9, 19-22), the prophet (14:13), and God (14:1-6, 17-18). These laments sometimes merge as in 14:1-6, where the lament of the people is the lament of the Lord. Jeremiah's voice recedes into the background, allowing the voices of God and people to come to the fore. At issue is the anguish of the people who turn to the Lord as their salvation in times of need, but the Lord insists that it is too late. Nothing can turn aside the destruction that will overtake them; it is the inevitable result of their apostasy. The intercession, even of Moses and Samuel, notable prophets of the past, will not work. Offering sacrifice and confessing sin will not be effective. Jeremiah's attempt to excuse the people and blame false prophets is

Their eyes grow dim;
  there is no grass.
⁷Even though our crimes bear wit-
    ness against us,
  act, LORD, for your name's
    sake—
Even though our rebellions are
    many,
  and we have sinned against you.
⁸Hope of Israel, LORD,
  our savior in time of need!
Why should you be a stranger in
    the land,
  like a traveler stopping only for
    a night?
⁹Why are you like someone
    bewildered,
  a champion who cannot save?
You are in our midst, LORD,
  your name we bear:
  do not forsake us!
¹⁰Thus says the LORD about this
    people:
They so love to wander
  that they cannot restrain their
    feet.
The LORD takes no pleasure in
    them;
  now he remembers their guilt,
  and will punish their sins.

¹¹Then the LORD said to me: Do not intercede for the well-being of this people. ¹²If they fast, I will not listen to their supplication. If they sacrifice burnt offerings or grain offerings, I will take no pleasure in them. Rather, I will destroy them with the sword, famine, and plague. ¹³"Ah! Lord GOD," I replied, "it is the prophets who say to them, 'You shall not see the sword; famine shall not befall you. Indeed, I will give you lasting peace in this place.'"

¹⁴These prophets utter lies in my name, the LORD said to me: I did not send them; I gave them no command, nor did I speak to them. They prophesy to you lying visions, foolish divination, deceptions from their own imagination. ¹⁵Therefore, thus says the LORD: Concerning the prophets who prophesy in my name, though I did not send them, and who say, "Sword and famine shall not befall this land": by sword and famine shall these prophets meet their end. ¹⁶The people to whom they prophesy shall be thrown out into the streets of Jerusalem because of famine and the sword. No one shall bury them, their wives, their sons, or their daughters, for I will pour out upon them their own wickedness. ¹⁷Speak to them this word:

Let my eyes stream with tears
  night and day, without rest,
Over the great destruction which
    overwhelms
  the virgin daughter of my
    people,
  over her incurable wound.
¹⁸If I walk out into the field,
  look! those slain by the sword;
If I enter the city,
  look! victims of famine.
Both prophet and priest ply their
    trade
  in a land they do not know.
¹⁹Have you really cast Judah off?
  Is Zion loathsome to you?

---

dismissed by the Lord, even though the Lord acknowledges that these false prophets were not personally sent by God; nevertheless the people are accountable. There is no turning the heart of the Lord away from punishment (15:1-4). The vehemence in the description of the devastation to come upon

Why have you struck us a blow
  that cannot be healed?
We wait for peace, to no avail;
  for a time of healing, but terror
    comes instead.
²⁰We recognize our wickedness,
  Lord,
  the guilt of our ancestors:
  we have sinned against you.
²¹Do not reject us, for your name's
    sake,
  do not disgrace your glorious
    throne.
  Remember! Do not break your
    covenant with us.
²²Among the idols of the nations are
    there any that give rain?
  Or can the mere heavens send
    showers?
Is it not you, Lord,
  our God, to whom we look?
  You alone do all these things.

15 ¹The Lord said to me: Even if Moses and Samuel stood before me, my heart would not turn toward this people. Send them away from me and let them go. ²If they ask you, "Where should we go?" tell them, Thus says the Lord: Whoever is marked for death, to death; whoever is marked for the sword, to the sword; whoever is marked for famine, to famine; whoever is marked for captivity, to captivity. ³Four kinds of scourge I have decreed against them— oracle of the Lord—the sword to kill them; dogs to drag them off; the birds of the sky and the beasts of the earth to devour and destroy them. ⁴And I will make them an object of horror to all the kingdoms of the earth because of what Manasseh, son of Hezekiah, king of Judah, did in Jerusalem.

Scene of Tragedy

⁵Who will pity you, Jerusalem,
  who will grieve for you?
Who will stop to ask
  about your welfare?
⁶It is you who have disowned me—
    oracle of the Lord—
  turned your back upon me;
I stretched out my hand to destroy
    you,
  because I was weary of relenting.
⁷I winnowed them with a winnow-
    ing fork
  at the gates of the land;
I have bereaved, destroyed my
    people;
  they have not turned from their
    evil ways.
⁸Their widows were more numerous
    before me
  than the sands of the sea.
I brought against the mother of
    youths
  the destroyer at midday;
Suddenly I struck her
  with anguish and terror.
⁹The mother of seven faints away,
  breathing out her life;

---

the people is offset by the recognition that the suffering of the people, however much deserved, is a personal source of grief to God (14:17).

15:5-9 Scene of tragedy

The themes of the previous passage continue: the punishment of the people has come about because the people refused to turn from their evil ways. The metaphors of destruction are drawn from farming with its winnowing of the wheat to remove the chaff, and from family life with its cycle

Her sun sets in full day,
  she is ashamed, abashed.
Their survivors I will give to the
    sword
  in the presence of their
      enemies—oracle of the
      LORD.

Jeremiah's Complaint

¹⁰Woe to me, my mother, that you
    gave me birth!
  a man of strife and contention to
    all the land!
I neither borrow nor lend,
  yet everyone curses me.
¹¹Tell me, LORD, have I not served
    you for their good?
  Have I not interceded with you
    in time of misfortune and
    anguish?

¹²Can one break iron,
  iron from the north, and bronze?
¹³Your wealth and your treasures
  I give as plunder, demanding no
    payment,
  because of all your sins,
    throughout all your
    territory.
¹⁴And I shall enslave you to your
    enemies
  in a land you do not know,
For fire has broken out from my
    anger,
  it is kindled against you.
¹⁵You know, LORD:
Remember me and take care of
    me,
  avenge me on my persecutors.
Because you are slow to anger, do
    not banish me;

---

of life and death where the death of the young is the source of great grief. There is a sense of finality that pervades this oracle.

15:10-21 Jeremiah's complaint

This is the second of Jeremiah's confessions and, as with the first confession, the Lord responds. It is unusual that Jeremiah addresses his opening words to his mother, but he quickly shifts address to the Lord. Jeremiah's complaint is related to his call to be a prophet, a prophet who has to proclaim the unleashing of the Lord's wrath against the people. It is not Jeremiah who has willed the destruction of his people; indeed he has interceded on their behalf, yet conflict follows him wherever he goes. The Lord responds to Jeremiah's outburst, but the translation of verses 12-13 is not certain. The gist seems to be that the Lord will be with Jeremiah to deliver him. The first "iron" (v. 12) may refer to the "stiff-necked" people of Judah who will not break the "iron from the north," that is, Babylon, and the "bronze" may refer to Jeremiah who will stand firm in the face of opposition from the people (cf. 1:18; 15:20). If the "you" of verses 13-14 refers to Jeremiah, then the Lord informs Jeremiah that he too will suffer loss in the future, but these verses are often taken as directed to the people as an announcement of judgment against them.

Jeremiah's lament continues by drawing the Lord's attention to the suffering he endures in carrying out his prophetic commission. He embraced

know that for you I have borne
  insult.
¹⁶When I found your words, I
  devoured them;
  your words were my joy, the
    happiness of my heart,
Because I bear your name,
  Lord, God of hosts.
¹⁷I did not sit celebrating
  in the circle of merrymakers;
Under the weight of your hand I sat
  alone
  because you filled me with rage.
¹⁸Why is my pain continuous,
  my wound incurable, refusing
    to be healed?
To me you are like a deceptive
  brook,
  waters that cannot be relied on!
¹⁹Thus the Lord answered me:
If you come back and I take you
  back,
  in my presence you shall stand;
If you utter what is precious and
  not what is worthless,
  you shall be my mouth.
Then they will be the ones who
  turn to you,

not you who turn to them.
²⁰And I will make you toward this
  people
  a fortified wall of bronze.
Though they fight against you,
  they shall not prevail,
For I am with you,
  to save and rescue you—oracle
    of the Lord.
²¹I will rescue you from the hand of
  the wicked,
  and ransom you from the power
    of the violent.

16 **Jeremiah's Life a Warning.** ¹This word
came to me from the Lord: ²Do not
take a wife and do not have sons and
daughters in this place, ³for thus says the
Lord concerning the sons and daughters
born in this place, the mothers who give
them birth, the fathers who beget them in
this land: ⁴Of deadly disease they shall
die. Unlamented and unburied they will
lie like dung on the ground. Sword and
famine will make an end of them, and
their corpses will become food for the
birds of the sky and the beasts of the earth.

his role as messenger of God, but because of his vocation, he has borne insult
and was set apart from his people and their celebrations, holding within
himself the Lord's rage. From his anguish Jeremiah raises the question, why
does he know constant pain? In a stinging reproach Jeremiah even accuses
the Lord of failing him as water that cannot be found when needed. The
Lord again responds to Jeremiah, but the first part of the response ignores
Jeremiah's pain. Rather, the Lord focuses Jeremiah on his task as prophet.
He is to come back to the Lord and once again to be the Lord's mouth. Only
then does the Lord assure Jeremiah that he will be delivered, reaffirming
the promise made at the time of his call (1:18-19).

16:1-13 Jeremiah's life a warning

Jeremiah not only speaks the word of the Lord but he is also called upon
by the Lord to embody that word in his life. He is given three commands:
do not marry and have children, do not join in mourning, and do not join

⁵Thus says the LORD: Do not go into a house of mourning; do not go there to lament or grieve for them. For I have withdrawn my peace from this people—oracle of the LORD—my love and my compassion. ⁶They shall die, the great and the lowly, in this land, unburied and unlamented. No one will gash themselves or shave their heads for them. ⁷They will not break bread with the bereaved to offer consolation for the dead; they will not give them the cup of consolation to drink over the death of father or mother.

⁸Do not enter a house of feasting to sit eating and drinking with them. ⁹For thus says the LORD of hosts, the God of Israel: Before your eyes and in your lifetime, I will silence in this place the song of joy and the song of gladness, the song of the bridegroom and the song of the bride.

¹⁰When you proclaim all these words to this people and they ask you: "Why has the LORD pronounced all this great disaster against us? What is our crime? What sin have we committed against the LORD, our God?"— ¹¹you shall answer them: It is because your ancestors have forsaken me—oracle of the LORD—and followed other gods that they served and worshiped; but me they have forsaken, and my law they did not keep. ¹²And you have done worse than your ancestors. Here you are, every one of you, walking in the stubbornness of your evil heart instead of listening to me. ¹³I will throw you out of this land into a land that neither you nor your ancestors have known; there you can serve other gods day and night because I will not show you mercy.

Return from Exile. ¹⁴Therefore, days are coming—oracle of the LORD—when it will no longer be said, "As the LORD lives, who brought the Israelites out of Egypt"; ¹⁵but rather, "As the LORD lives, who brought the Israelites out of the

in celebrations. Each of these commands relates to Jeremiah's message. The command not to marry and have children will protect Jeremiah from grief at the death of his children when children will die of disease, famine, and the violence of war at the time of punishment. Jeremiah is not to express grief, for the Lord has withdrawn peace from the people and Jeremiah is to do likewise. He is not to participate in joyful celebrations, for there will be no cause for joy in the future. The devastation that is coming is so overwhelming that the normal routines of life will be disrupted. Once again when it is asked why this punishment has come upon the people, the answer is the same: the people have abandoned the Lord and turned to other gods in service and worship.

16:14-15 Return from exile

Interrupting the indictments and punishments of the previous and following passages, this passage resounds with hope and counters the unrelenting sense of doom that permeates these chapters. The exodus has been the

land of the north and out of all the countries to which he had banished them." I will bring them back to the land I gave their ancestors.

Double Punishment. ¹⁶Look!—oracle of the LORD—I will send many fishermen to catch them. After that, I will send many hunters to hunt them out from every mountain and hill and rocky crevice. ¹⁷For my eyes are upon all their ways; they are not hidden from me, nor does their guilt escape my sight. ¹⁸I will at once repay them double for their crime and their sin because they profaned my land with the corpses of their detestable idols, and filled my heritage with their abominations.

Conversion of the Nations

¹⁹LORD, my strength, my fortress,
  my refuge in the day of distress!
To you nations will come
  from the ends of the earth, and
  say,
"Our ancestors inherited mere
  frauds,
  empty, worthless."
²⁰Can human beings make for
  themselves gods?
  But these are not gods at all!
²¹Therefore, I will indeed give them
  knowledge;
  this time I will make them
  acknowledge
My strength and my power:
  they shall know that my name is
  LORD.

---

paradigm for the Lord's gracious act of deliverance, but this passage elevates the rescue and return of the exiles to the Promised Land as the act of the Lord's salvific power that future generations will confess. These verses may represent a later addition drawn from a nearly identical passage in 23:7-8.

16:16-18 Double punishment

Following upon the hopeful statement in verses 14-15, this announcement of punishment may be tempered by the suggestion that the Lord is aware of the people wherever they may be and so will be able to find them and return them to their land, but verse 18 indicates that first they must be held accountable for their sins.

16:19-21 Conversion of the nations

Jeremiah's response opens this section and the Lord's word closes it. After addressing the Lord in conventional language that we find in the psalms (Ps 46:1; see also Pss 27:1; 37:39-40), Jeremiah introduces the notion that the nations will come to the Lord, a notion not foreign to the prophets (Isa 2:3/Mic 4:2; Zech 8:20-23; 14:16-19). Even the nations will see in what has happened to Judah, both in its punishment and its deliverance, the hand of the Lord. They will recognize that their gods are nothing and will come to know the Lord. A characteristic tenet of Old Testament theology is that Israel comes to know the Lord in what the Lord does. This is now extended to the other nations; they too will come to know the Lord in what is done.

The Sin of Judah and Its Punishment

17 ¹The sin of Judah is written
with an iron stylus,
Engraved with a diamond point
upon the tablets of their hearts,

And the horns of their altars, ²when their children remember their altars and their asherahs, beside the green trees, on the high hills, ³the peaks in the country.

Your wealth and all your treasures
I give as plunder,
As payment for all your sins
throughout your territory,
⁴You will relinquish your hold on
your heritage
which I have given you.
I will enslave you to your enemies
in a land you do not know:

For a fire has broken out from my
anger,
burning forever.

True Wisdom

⁵Thus says the LORD:
Cursed is the man who trusts in
human beings,
who makes flesh his strength,
whose heart turns away from
the LORD.
⁶He is like a barren bush in the
wasteland
that enjoys no change of season,
But stands in lava beds in the
wilderness,
a land, salty and uninhabited.
⁷Blessed are those who trust in the
LORD;
the LORD will be their trust.

17:1-4 The sin of Judah and its punishment

Judah is indicted for the worship of other gods (17:1-3a) and its punishment is the loss of its wealth and land, enslavement, and exile (17:3b-4). That sin is written with an "iron stylus"/"diamond point" suggests the permanence of the people's sin; it is carved into their being and passed on to the next generation ("when their children remember"). The reference to the "horns of their altars" is not clear. The horns of an altar are the projections on the four corners of an altar, but their significance is unknown. A person could claim sanctuary by holding onto the horns of an altar and the passage may suggest that the people will find no sanctuary because of the depth of their sin.

17:5-11 True wisdom

Moving away from indictment and sentence, this passage consists of a collection of wisdom sayings that contrast the fate of those who trust in the Lord with those who trust in human beings or wealth (17:5-8, 10-11). The wisdom tradition is characterized by setting out a choice between two ways: the way of wisdom or the way of folly, but this can also be expressed as a choice between obedience or disobedience, righteousness or wickedness, and, as here, trust in the Lord or trust in humans. Consequences inevitably flow from one's choice and that is the focus of these wisdom sayings. In images drawn from nature those who do not trust in the Lord are like

55

"Cursed is the man . . . whose heart turns away from the LORD. He is like a barren bush in the wasteland" (Jer 17:5-6).

⁸They are like a tree planted beside
the waters
that stretches out its roots to the
stream:
It does not fear heat when it comes,
its leaves stay green;
In the year of drought it shows no
distress,
but still produces fruit.
⁹More tortuous than anything is the
human heart,
beyond remedy; who can understand it?
¹⁰I, the LORD, explore the mind
and test the heart,
Giving to all according to their
ways,
according to the fruit of their
deeds.
¹¹A partridge that broods but does
not hatch
are those who acquire wealth
unjustly:

In midlife it will desert them;
in the end they are only fools.

The Source of Life

¹²A throne of glory, exalted from the
beginning,
such is our holy place.
¹³O Hope of Israel, LORD!
all who forsake you shall be put
to shame;
The rebels shall be enrolled in the
netherworld;
they have forsaken the LORD,
source of living waters.

Prayer for Vengeance

¹⁴Heal me, LORD, that I may be
healed;
save me, that I may be saved,
for you are my praise.
¹⁵See how they say to me,
"Where is the word of the
LORD?

---

withered shrubs in a barren land, but those who trust in the Lord flourish like well-watered trees. Verse 9 presents a negative reflection upon the nature of the human heart, but it is consistent with Jeremiah's emphasis on the stubborn refusal of the people to return to the Lord. The human heart is open before the Lord and every person is requited in accordance with his or her deeds.

17:12-13 The source of life

In a hymnic interlude these verses reiterate the consequences of forsak-ing the Lord, the hope of Israel. As in 2:13 the Lord is identified as the source of living waters.

17:14-18 Prayer of vengeance

This third confession of Jeremiah is a prayer for healing and a call for vengeance against those who persecute him. The Lord has promised Jeremiah salvation (15:20) and in confidence Jeremiah petitions the Lord for that salvation. He declares his own innocence, for he has not been the one who has desired the destruction of his people. Indeed, he has interceded on their behalf. The depth of Jeremiah's anguish breaks forth when he cries out that the Lord should not be a terror to him, but his refuge. Jeremiah's

Let it come to pass!"
¹⁶Yet I did not press you to send
disaster;
the day without remedy I have
not desired.
You know what passed my lips;
it is present before you.
¹⁷Do not become a terror to me,
you are my refuge in the day of
disaster.
¹⁸Let my persecutors be con-
founded—not me!
let them be terrified—not me!
Bring upon them the day of disaster,
crush them with double
destruction.

Observance of the Sabbath. ¹⁹Thus said the Lord to me: Go, stand at the Gate of Benjamin, where the kings of Judah enter and leave, and at the other gates of Jerusalem. ²⁰There say to them: Hear the word of the Lord, you kings of Judah, and all Judah, and all you inhabitants of Jerusalem who enter these gates! ²¹Thus says the Lord: As you love your lives, take care not to carry burdens on the sabbath, to bring them in through the gates of Jerusalem. ²²Bring no burden from your homes on the sabbath. Do no work whatever, but keep holy the sabbath day, as I commanded your ancestors, ²³though they did not listen or give ear, but stiffened their necks so they could not hear or take correction. ²⁴If you truly obey me—oracle of the Lord—and carry no burden through the gates of this city on the sabbath, keeping the sabbath day holy and abstaining from all work on it, ²⁵then, through the gates of this city, kings who sit upon the throne of David will continue to enter, riding in their chariots or upon their horses, along with their princes, and the people of Judah, and the inhabitants of Jerusalem. This city will remain inhabited forever. ²⁶To it people will come from the cities of Judah and the neighborhood of Jerusalem, from the land of Benjamin and from the Shephelah, from the hill country and the Negeb, to bring burnt offerings and sacrifices, grain offerings, incense, and thank offerings to the house of the Lord. ²⁷But if you do not obey me and keep holy the sabbath day, if you carry burdens and come through the gates of Jerusalem on the sabbath, I will

call for vengeance may be disconcerting, but what is at stake is Jeremiah's role as prophet. If the word that Jeremiah proclaims is the Lord's word, then those who mock and persecute him are obstructing the Lord's word. For the Lord's word to go forth, Jeremiah's enemies must be stopped.

17:19-27 Observance of the sabbath

It is not clear how this prose sermon fits in its present context. Previous indictments have been focused on the people's turning to other gods, but here the issue is the proper observance of the sabbath. Also, there has been a ring of finality in previous announcements of punishment, but here punishment is not inevitable; the people still have the opportunity to live in accordance with the laws against working on the sabbath. The future is open-ended and will be shaped by what the people do.

set fire to its gates—a fire never to be extinguished—and it will consume the palaces of Jerusalem.

18 **The Potter's Vessel.** ¹This word came to Jeremiah from the LORD: ²Arise and go down to the potter's house; there you will hear my word. ³I went down to the potter's house and there he was, working at the wheel. ⁴Whenever the vessel of clay he was making turned out badly in his hand, he tried again, making another vessel of whatever sort he pleased. ⁵Then the word of the LORD came to me: ⁶Can I not do to you, house of Israel, as this potter has done?—oracle of the LORD. Indeed, like clay in the hand of the potter, so are you in my hand, house of Israel. ⁷At one moment I may decree concerning a nation or kingdom that I will uproot and tear down and destroy it; ⁸but if that nation against whom I have decreed turns from its evil, then I will have a change of heart regarding the evil which I have decreed. ⁹At another moment, I may decree concerning a nation or kingdom that I will build up and plant it; ¹⁰but if that nation does what is evil in my eyes, refusing to obey my voice, then I will have a change of heart regarding the good with which I planned to bless it.

¹¹And now, tell this to the people of Judah and the inhabitants of Jerusalem: Thus says the LORD: Look, I am fashioning evil against you and making a plan. Return, all of you, from your evil way; reform your ways and your deeds. ¹²But they will say, "No use! We will follow our own devices; each one of us will behave according to the stubbornness of our evil hearts!"

Unnatural Apostasy

¹³Therefore thus says the LORD:
Ask among the nations—
who has ever heard the like?
Truly horrible things
virgin Israel has done!
¹⁴Does the snow of Lebanon
desert the rocky heights?
Do the gushing waters dry up
that flow fresh down the
mountains?
¹⁵Yet my people have forgotten me:
they offer incense in vain.

18:1-12 The potter's vessel

Jeremiah is commanded to observe a potter at work. The way a potter shapes a pot and reshapes the clay when the pot turns out badly symbolizes the Lord's treatment of Israel. In drawing out the meaning of what Jeremiah observes, the Lord states that all nations are as clay in the hands of the Lord. As bad pots are destroyed and remade, so the nations are destroyed and remade by the Lord when they pursue evil. Jeremiah is commanded to bring this message to Judah and Jerusalem with a call to repentance, but any hope that the people will change is overridden by Jeremiah's insistence that the people will stubbornly refuse.

18:13-17 Unnatural apostasy

A tone of divine lament permeates this announcement of judgment. Through a series of rhetorical questions addressed to the nations, the

"[L]ike clay in the hand of the potter, so are you in my hand, house of Israel"
(Jer 18:6).

They stumble off their paths,
the ways of old,
Traveling on bypaths,
not the beaten track.
¹⁶Their land shall be made a waste,
an object of endless hissing:
All passersby will be horrified,
shaking their heads.
¹⁷Like the east wind, I will scatter
them
before their enemies;
I will show them my back, not my
face,
in their day of disaster.

Another Prayer for Vengeance. ¹⁸"Come,"
they said, "let us devise a plot against Jeremiah, for instruction will not perish from
the priests, nor counsel from the wise, nor
the word from the prophets. Come, let us
destroy him by his own tongue. Let us
pay careful attention to his every word."

¹⁹Pay attention to me, O LORD,
and listen to what my
adversaries say.

²⁰Must good be repaid with evil
that they should dig a pit to take
my life?
Remember that I stood before you
to speak on their behalf,
to turn your wrath away from
them.
²¹So now, give their children to
famine,
deliver them to the power of the
sword.
Let their wives be childless and
widows;
let their husbands die of pestilence,
their youths be struck down by
the sword in battle.
²²May cries be heard from their
homes,
when suddenly you send plunderers against them.
For they have dug a pit to capture
me,
they have hidden snares for my
feet;

---

impossibility of nature to act "unnaturally" is underscored; and yet, Israel
has acted "unnaturally" in forgetting the Lord (18:15). The "horrible things"
that Israel has inexplicably done will result in the ruin of the land and the
exile of the people. Passersby will recognize what has happened and be
horrified at the destruction. The severity of the Lord's judgment is suggested by the image of turning the Lord's back to the people.

18:18-23 Another prayer for vengeance

Verse 18 sets the context for the fourth confession of Jeremiah. Three
groups are singled out as plotting against Jeremiah: priests, sages, and
prophets. They are attentive to Jeremiah's words in order to use his words
against him. In response Jeremiah turns to the Lord with another call for
vengeance against his adversaries. Jeremiah calls upon the Lord to remember that he has interceded on their behalf, but they repay him with evil.
Then Jeremiah unleashes his wrath in a relentless list of horrors that God
should bring upon the prophet's enemies. Though Jeremiah's words are
particularly harsh, they match the language of judgment found throughout

²³But you, Lord, know
    all their planning for my death.
Do not forgive their crime,
    and their sin do not blot out
        from your sight!
Let them stumble before you,
    in the time of your anger act
        against them.

19 **Symbol of the Potter's Flask.** ¹Thus said the Lord: Go, buy a potter's earthenware flask. Take along some of the elders of the people and some of the priests, ²and go out toward the Valley of Ben-hinnom, at the entrance of the Potsherd Gate; there proclaim the words which I will speak to you: ³You shall say, Listen to the word of the Lord, kings of Judah and inhabitants of Jerusalem: Thus says the Lord of hosts, the God of Israel: I am going to bring such evil upon this place that the ears of all who hear of it will ring. ⁴All because they have forsaken me and profaned this place by burning incense to other gods which neither they nor their ancestors knew; and because the kings of Judah have filled this place with innocent blood, ⁵building high places for Baal to burn their children in fire as offerings to Baal—something I never considered or said or commanded. ⁶Therefore, days are coming—oracle of the Lord—when this place will no longer be called Topheth, or the Valley of Ben-hinnom, but rather, the Valley of Slaughter. ⁷In this place I will foil the plan of Judah and Jerusalem; I will make them fall by the sword before their enemies, at the hand of those who seek their lives. Their corpses I will give as food to the birds of the sky and the

---

the book of Jeremiah and are similar to the curses upon one's enemies found in laments psalms (Pss 35:4-6, 8; 58:7-11; 109:6-13).

19:1–20:6 Symbol of the potter's flask

The themes of chapter 18 are continued in this prose narrative, which presents another symbolic act that the Lord commanded Jeremiah to perform. After buying an earthenware flask from a potter, Jeremiah is to deliver three announcements of judgment; two are to be given in the presence of some elders and priests (19:3-9, 10-13) and one to the people in the temple courtyard (19:14-15). The first announcement of judgment is delivered near the Valley of Ben-hinnom or Topheth. This valley was the scene of the sacrifice or ritualized initiation of children to the god Molech (2 Kgs 23:10). Jeremiah speaks of it as the valley in which the people burned incense to other gods; the kings of Judah filled the valley with the innocent blood of children sacrificed to Baal. The horror of these actions is matched by the harshness of the judgment. The second announcement of judgment accompanies the breaking of the flask. As the flask has been shattered, so shall the people and their city be shattered. The third announcement of judgment is directed more generally against the people for their stubbornness and disobedience.

beasts of the earth. ⁸I will make this city a waste and an object of hissing. Because of all its wounds, every passerby will be horrified and hiss. ⁹I will have them eat the flesh of their sons and daughters; they shall eat one another's flesh during the harsh siege under which their enemies and those who seek their lives will confine them.

¹⁰And you shall break the flask in the sight of the men who went with you, ¹¹and say to them: Thus says the LORD of hosts: Thus will I smash this people and this city, as one smashes a clay pot so that it cannot be repaired. And Topheth shall be its burial place, for there will be no other place for burial. ¹²Thus I will do to this place and to its inhabitants—oracle of the LORD; I will make this city like Topheth. ¹³And the houses of Jerusalem and the houses of the kings of Judah shall be defiled like the place of Topheth, all the houses upon whose roofs they burnt incense to the whole host of heaven and poured out libations to other gods.

¹⁴When Jeremiah returned from Topheth, where the LORD had sent him to prophesy, he stood in the court of the house of the LORD and said to all the people: ¹⁵Thus says the LORD of hosts, the God of Israel: I will bring upon this city all the evil I have spoken against it, because they have become stubborn and have not obeyed my words.

20 ¹Now the priest Pashhur, son of Immer, chief officer in the house of the LORD, heard Jeremiah prophesying these things. ²So he struck the prophet and put him in the stocks at the upper Gate of Benjamin in the house of the LORD. ³The next morning, after Pashhur had released Jeremiah from the stocks, the prophet said to him: "Instead of Pashhur, the LORD names you 'Terror on every side.' ⁴For thus says the LORD: Indeed, I will hand you over to terror, you and all your friends. Your own eyes

---

The persecution of Jeremiah, which has been a recurring theme in these chapters, is concretized in the actions of Pashhur, the chief officer in the temple. He strikes Jeremiah and puts him in stocks overnight. Jeremiah does not rescind the judgment that he declared the previous day. Rather, he reiterates it, adding that Pashhur himself will bear the name "Terror on every side" because of the "terror" he will experience and witness. "Terror on every side" was a phrase that summarized Jeremiah's word of judgment and it is the phrase with which Jeremiah himself is mocked (20:10). Babylon is identified as the nation through whom the Lord's judgment will be carried out (20:4). On the basis of this verse it is likely that Babylon is to be identified as the unnamed foe "from the north" (1:14; 4:6; 6:1, 22; 10:22; 13:20).

20:7-18 Jeremiah's interior crisis

The fifth and sixth confessions of Jeremiah draw this section of the book of Jeremiah to a close. The intensity of the language with which Jeremiah

shall see them fall by the sword of their enemies. All Judah I will hand over to the power of the king of Babylon, who shall take them captive to Babylon or strike them down with the sword. ⁵All the wealth of this city, all its resources and its valuables, all the treasures of the kings of Judah, I will hand over to their enemies, who will plunder it and carry it away to Babylon. ⁶You, Pashhur, and all the members of your household shall go into exile. To Babylon you shall go; there you shall die and be buried, you and all your friends, because you have prophesied lies to them."

Jeremiah's Interior Crisis

⁷You seduced me, LORD, and I let
　　myself be seduced;
　　you were too strong for me, and
　　　　you prevailed.
All day long I am an object of
　　　　laughter;
　　everyone mocks me.
⁸Whenever I speak, I must cry out,
　　violence and outrage I proclaim;
The word of the LORD has brought
　　me
　　reproach and derision all day
　　　　long.

⁹I say I will not mention him,
　　I will no longer speak in his
　　　　name.
But then it is as if fire is burning in
　　my heart,
　　imprisoned in my bones;
I grow weary holding back,
　　I cannot!
¹⁰Yes, I hear the whisperings of
　　many:
　　"Terror on every side!
　　Denounce! let us denounce
　　　　him!"
All those who were my friends
　　are on the watch for any misstep
　　　　of mine.
"Perhaps he can be tricked; then we
　　will prevail,
　　and take our revenge on him."
¹¹But the LORD is with me, like a
　　mighty champion:
　　my persecutors will stumble,
　　　　they will not prevail.
In their failure they will be put to
　　utter shame,
　　to lasting, unforgettable
　　　　confusion.
¹²LORD of hosts, you test the just,
　　you see mind and heart,
Let me see the vengeance you take
　　on them,

---

addresses the Lord in the fifth confession (20:7-13) is striking. He accuses the Lord of seducing or deceiving him (the Hebrew root *pth* carries both meanings) and overpowering him. This strong language suggests that Jeremiah did not realize what he was getting into when he accepted his prophetic role. His life is now defined by mockery and violence precisely because of the message he must proclaim. Jeremiah is caught between the people who persecute him for that message and the Lord who will not allow him to withhold that message. In spite of Jeremiah's bitter outcry against the Lord, he trusts that the Lord will champion his cause against those who persecute him. The abrupt shift from complaint to trust and praise is typical of the form of a lament and so it is not surprising to find a hymn of praise at the end of this confession.

for to you I have entrusted my
cause.
¹³Sing to the LORD,
praise the LORD,
For he has rescued the life of the
poor
from the power of the evildoers!

¹⁴Cursed be the day
on which I was born!
May the day my mother gave me
birth
never be blessed!
¹⁵Cursed be the one who brought
the news
to my father,
"A child, a son, has been born to
you!"
filling him with great joy.
¹⁶Let that man be like the cities
which the LORD relentlessly
overthrew;

Let him hear war cries in the
morning,
battle alarms at noonday,
¹⁷because he did not kill me in
the womb!
Then my mother would have been
my grave,
her womb confining me forever.
¹⁸Why did I come forth from the
womb,
to see sorrow and pain,
to end my days in shame?

III. Oracles in the Last Years of Jerusalem

21 Fate of Zedekiah and Jerusalem. ¹The word which came to Jeremiah from the LORD when King Zedekiah sent Pashhur, son of Malchiah, and the priest Zephaniah, son of Maaseiah, to him with this request: ²Inquire

Though the sixth confession (20:14-18) is included among the confessions of Jeremiah, it stands apart from them. There is no address to the Lord or petition here; it echoes the anguish characteristic of laments, but it opens with the curse of the day of his birth. Jeremiah has not only proclaimed the word of the Lord but he has also embodied that word in his life and suffered because of it. It is because of the sorrow and pain he has endured that he cries out against the day of his birth.

ORACLES IN THE LAST YEARS OF JERUSALEM

Jeremiah 21:1–25:38

Prose narratives and prophetic statements are intermixed with poetic oracles in this section, which is thought to be an appendix to the previous chapters. The collection of oracles in chapters 21–23 focus mainly on the kings of Judah, Jerusalem, and the false prophets, and chapters 24–25 look to the future of Judah and the nations.

21:1-10 Fate of Zedekiah and Jerusalem

King Zedekiah consults Jeremiah four times in the book of Jeremiah (21:1-10; 37:3-10, 17-21; 38:14-28), but each time the prophet speaks a message that is unfavorable. The historical context of this first consultation is

for us of the LORD, because Nebuchadnezzar, king of Babylon, is attacking us. Perhaps the LORD will act for us in accord with his wonderful works by making him withdraw from us. ³But Jeremiah answered them: This is what you shall report to Zedekiah: ⁴Thus says the LORD, the God of Israel: I will turn against you the weapons with which you are fighting the king of Babylon and the Chaldeans who besiege you outside the walls. These weapons I will pile up in the midst of this city, ⁵and I myself will fight against you with outstretched hand and mighty arm, in anger, wrath, and great rage! ⁶I will strike down the inhabitants of this city, human being and beast; they shall die in a great pestilence. ⁷After that—oracle of the LORD—I will hand over Zedekiah, king of Judah, and his ministers and the people in this city who survive pestilence, sword, and famine, to Nebuchadnezzar, king of Babylon, to their enemies and those who seek their lives. He shall strike them down with the edge of the sword, without quarter, without mercy or compassion. ⁸And to this people you shall say: Thus says the LORD: See, I am giving you a choice between the way to life and the way to death. ⁹Whoever remains in this city shall die by the sword or famine or pestilence. But whoever leaves and surrenders to the Chaldeans who are besieging you shall live and escape with his life. ¹⁰I have set my face against this city, for evil and not for good—oracle of the LORD. It shall be given into the power of the king of Babylon who shall set it on fire.

Oracles Regarding the Kings

¹¹To the royal house of Judah:
Hear the word of the LORD,
¹²house of David!
Thus says the LORD:
Each morning dispense justice,
    rescue the oppressed from the
        hand of the oppressor,
Or my fury will break out like fire
    and burn with no one to quench
        it
    because of your evil deeds.
¹³Beware! I am against you, Ruler of
    the Valley,
    Rock of the Plain—oracle of the
        LORD.
You say, "Who will attack us,
    who can storm our defenses?"

---

the siege of Nebuchadnezzar, king of Babylon, against Jerusalem in 588–587 B.C. King Zedekiah asks Jeremiah to intercede in the hopes that the Lord will cause Nebuchadnezzar to end the siege, but Jeremiah's response is particularly harsh: the Lord will fight against Jerusalem and King Zedekiah will be handed over to the Babylonian king. The only choice that the Lord gives to the people is to remain in the city and die, or leave the city, surrender to the Babylonians, and live. The fall of Jerusalem is certain, for the Lord is firmly against the city.

21:11–22:9 Oracles regarding the kings

Without referring to any specific king, this section is addressed to the royal line of David commanding the king to dispense justice daily. It is

¹⁴I will punish you—oracle of the LORD—
as your deeds deserve!
I will kindle a fire in its forest
that shall devour all its surroundings.

22 ¹Thus says the LORD: Go down to the palace of the king of Judah and there deliver this word: ²You shall say: Listen to the word of the LORD, king of Judah, who sit on the throne of David, you, your ministers, and your people who enter by these gates! ³Thus says the LORD: Do what is right and just. Rescue the victims from the hand of their oppressors. Do not wrong or oppress the resident alien, the orphan, or the widow, and do not shed innocent blood in this place. ⁴If you carry out these commands, kings who succeed to the throne of David will continue to enter the gates of this house, riding in chariots or mounted on horses, with their ministers, and their people. ⁵But if you do not obey these commands, I swear by myself—oracle of the LORD: this house shall become rubble. ⁶For thus says the LORD concerning the house of the king of Judah:

Though you be to me like Gilead,
like the peak of Lebanon,
I swear I shall turn you into a waste,
with cities uninhabited.
⁷Against you I will send destroyers,
each with their tools:
They shall cut down your choice cedars,
and cast them into the fire.

⁸Many nations will pass by this city and ask one another: "Why has the LORD done this to so great a city?" ⁹And they will be told: "Because they have deserted their covenant with the LORD, their God, by worshiping and serving other gods."

Jehoahaz

¹⁰Do not weep for him who is dead,
nor mourn for him!
Weep rather for him who is going away;

---

implied that the kings did not secure justice for the oppressed (21:12) and they arrogantly dismiss the possibility that this city can be defeated (21:13). However, the Lord's fury will be unleashed against them; the city will fall. A second word (22:1-9) is mediated by Jeremiah to the king and his officials, but this word is conditional. It reiterates the demand for justice, especially for the resident alien, the orphan, and the widow, but the future is open-ended. If they pursue justice, they will continue to rule in Jerusalem; but if they fail in justice, then the city will be destroyed. A short oracle describes this destruction (22:6-7). Consistent with previous passages, the cause of the destruction of Jerusalem is that the people worship other gods, but here this is said to be a desertion of their covenant with the Lord.

22:10-12 Jehoahaz

The command is given not to mourn one who is dead but to mourn one who is going into exile (22:10), but it is not clear who these individuals are

never again to see
the land of his birth.

¹¹Thus says the LORD concerning Shallum, son of Josiah, king of Judah, his father's successor, who left this place: He shall never return, ¹²but in the place where they exiled him, there he shall die; he shall never see this land again.

Jehoiakim

¹³Woe to him who builds his house
on wrongdoing,
his roof-chambers on injustice;
Who works his neighbors without
pay,
and gives them no wages.
¹⁴Who says, "I will build myself a
spacious house,
with airy rooms,"
Who cuts out windows for it,
panels it with cedar,
and paints it with vermilion.
¹⁵Must you prove your rank among
kings
by competing with them in
cedar?

Did not your father eat and drink,
And act justly and righteously?
Then he prospered.
¹⁶Because he dispensed justice to
the weak and the poor,
he prospered.
Is this not to know me?—
oracle of the LORD.
¹⁷But your eyes and heart are set on
nothing
except your own gain,
On shedding innocent blood
and practicing oppression and
extortion.

¹⁸Therefore, thus says the LORD concerning Jehoiakim, son of Josiah, king of Judah:

They shall not lament him,
"Alas! my brother"; "Alas!
sister."
They shall not lament him,
"Alas, Lord! alas, Majesty!"
¹⁹The burial of a donkey he shall be
given,
dragged forth and cast out
beyond the gates of Jerusalem.

until verses 11-12. The one who is dead is presumably King Josiah, and the one who will be exiled is King Jehoahaz (Shallum). It may be that the time for mourning King Josiah is past and whatever hopes were associated with his reign are gone.

22:13-19 Jehoiakim

The oracle concerning Jehoiakim, king of Judah, is an indictment against him for injustice. The specific instance of injustice is that he had built for himself a lavish palace but did not pay the laborers for their work. The indictment is drawn out at length, highlighting the opulence of Jehoiakim's palace built to reflect his exalted status as king. This attention to his palace is set over against his lack of concern for justice, especially to the weak and poor. It is also set over against the justice and righteousness of his father, King Josiah. The prosperity that Josiah enjoyed was the result of his concern for the weak and poor, but Jehoiakim's arrogant disregard for the poor earns him a severe punishment: no one will mourn his death and his corpse

Jeconiah

²⁰Climb Lebanon and cry out,
in Bashan lift up your voice;
Cry out from Abarim,
for all your lovers are crushed.
²¹I spoke to you when you were
secure,
but you answered, "I will not
listen."
This has been your way from your
youth,
not to listen to my voice.
²²The wind shall shepherd all your
shepherds,
your lovers shall go into exile.
Surely then you shall be ashamed
and confounded
because of all your wickedness.
²³You who dwell on Lebanon,
who nest in the cedars,
How you shall groan when pains
come upon you,
like the pangs of a woman in
childbirth!

²⁴As I live—oracle of the LORD—even
if you, Coniah, son of Jehoiakim, king of
Judah, were a signet ring on my right
hand, I would snatch you off. ²⁵I will
hand you over to those who seek your
life, to those you dread: Nebuchadnezzar, king of Babylon, and the Chaldeans.
²⁶I will cast you out, you and the mother
who bore you, into a land different from
the land of your birth; and there you will
die. ²⁷Neither shall return to the land for
which they yearn.

²⁸Is this man Coniah a thing
despised, to be broken,
a vessel that no one wants?
Why are he and his offspring cast
out?
why thrown into a land they do
not know?
²⁹O land, land, land,
hear the word of the LORD—
³⁰Thus says the LORD:

---

will be treated as that of a donkey, that is, it will be discarded and left as food for scavengers.

22:20-30 Jeconiah

The judgment against King Jehoiachin (Jeconiah/Coniah) is preceded by an indictment and judgment against Jerusalem. The oracle against Jerusalem is to be announced upon a mountain for all to hear. It reiterates themes that pervade the book of Jeremiah. Jerusalem is unfaithful and has always been so. The "wind" is used as an agent of judgment against the leaders of the people. They lived in comfort in a palace and temple built with the cedars of Lebanon, but now they will cry out in pain when judgment comes upon them.

There are two oracles that announce judgment against King Jehoiachin, one in prose (22:24-27) and the other in poetry (22:28-30). That the judgment against Jehoiachin is unalterable is underscored by presenting the first oracle as an oath taken by the Lord: Jehoiachin will go into exile and there he will die. No reason is given for this judgment and the severity of this judgment is puzzling in light of the fact that Jehoiachin reigned only three

"I will raise up shepherds for them who will shepherd them so that they need no longer fear or be terrified" (Jer 23:4).

Write this man down as childless,
    a man who will never prosper in
        his life!
Nor shall any of his descendants
    prosper,
    to sit upon the throne of David,
    to rule again over Judah.

23 **A Just Shepherd.** ¹Woe to the shepherds who destroy and scatter the flock of my pasture—oracle of the Lord. ²Therefore, thus says the Lord, the God of Israel, against the shepherds who shepherd my people: You have scattered my sheep and driven them away. You have not cared for them, but I will take care to punish your evil deeds. ³I myself will gather the remnant of my flock from all the lands to which I have banished them and bring them back to their folds; there they shall be fruitful and multiply. ⁴I will raise up shepherds for them who will shepherd them so that they need no longer fear or be terrified; none shall be missing—oracle of the Lord.

⁵See, days are coming—oracle of
    the Lord—
    when I will raise up a righteous
        branch for David;
As king he shall reign and govern
    wisely,
    he shall do what is just and right
        in the land.
⁶In his days Judah shall be saved,
    Israel shall dwell in security.
This is the name to be given him:
    "The Lord our justice."

⁷Therefore, the days are coming—oracle of the Lord—when they shall no longer say, "As the Lord lives, who brought the Israelites out of the land of Egypt"; ⁸but rather, "As the Lord lives, who brought the descendants of the

---

months. The second judgment reinforces the judgment of the prose oracle. Not only has Jehoiachin been cast out and exiled but there will also be no future kings from his line. The question as to why this is so is raised in the opening lines, but it remains unanswered.

23:1-8 A just shepherd

This section consists of brief oracles. The first oracle (23:1-4) is an indictment and judgment that is followed by an announcement of salvation. The indictment is against the leaders of the nation for misleading the people. The failure of the leader results in the destruction of Judah and the exile of the people. The metaphors of kings as shepherds and Israel as the Lord's flock are found frequently in the Old Testament. The metaphor continues in the announcement of the return and restoration of the people. The Lord will be shepherd to the people, gathering and leading them back to the land where they will be fruitful and multiply. This announcement of salvation borrows from the language of the creation story and the patriarchal promises (Gen 1:28; 17:1-8, 20; 28:3-4; 48:4). Additionally, the Lord will raise up shepherds who will care for the flock.

Another oracle of salvation is introduced in verses 5-6, but here the focus is on one ruler from the line of David. This future king is referred to

house of Israel up from the land of the north"—and from all the lands to which I banished them; they shall again live on their own soil.

The False Prophets

⁹Concerning the prophets:
My heart is broken within me,
    all my bones tremble;
I am like a drunk,
    like one overcome by wine,
Because of the LORD,
    because of his holy words.
¹⁰The land is filled with adulterers;
    because of the curse the land
        mourns,
    the pastures of the wilderness
        are withered.
Theirs is an evil course,
    theirs is unjust power.
¹¹Both prophet and priest are
        godless!

In my very house I find their
        wickedness—
    oracle of the LORD.
¹²Hence their way shall become for
        them
    slippery ground.
Into the darkness they shall be
        driven,
    and fall headlong;
For I will bring disaster upon them,
    the year of their punishment—
        oracle of the LORD.
¹³Among Samaria's prophets
    I saw something unseemly:
They prophesied by Baal
    and led my people Israel astray.
¹⁴But among Jerusalem's prophets
    I saw something more shocking:
Adultery, walking in deception,
    strengthening the power of the
        wicked,
    so that no one turns from evil;

---

as a "righteous branch" (23:5; see also 33:15; Zech 3:8; 6:12). The term "branch" will take on messianic overtones in the postexilic period, but here it indicates that the future king will be a legitimate heir to the throne of David. This king will rule with justice and righteousness, that is, he will rule as the Lord rules. The result of his rule will be salvation for Israel and peace in their land. The name of the future king, "The LORD our justice" (23:6), may play off the name Zedekiah, which means "The Lord is my justice." The rule of this future king will be the just rule of the Lord.

A final oracle of salvation (23:7-8) concludes this section. It is an oracle that is nearly identical to 16:14-15, but here it seems to reinforce the hopeful elements of verses 1-6. The return of the people of Israel from exile and their restoration on the land becomes a new salvific action of the Lord to be proclaimed by future generations.

23:9-40 The false prophets

The various poetic and prose oracles in this section are united by a common interest in the topic of false prophets. How does one determine who truly speaks the Lord's word when prophets issue conflicting statements? The book of Deuteronomy attempts to resolve the conflict (Deut 13:1-6; 18:9-22), but looking to the future fulfillment of the prophetic word

To me they are all like Sodom,
its inhabitants like Gomorrah.

¹⁵Therefore, thus says the LORD of hosts
against the prophets:

Look, I will give them wormwood
to eat,
and poisoned water to drink;
For from Jerusalem's prophets
ungodliness has gone forth into
the whole land.
¹⁶Thus says the LORD of hosts:
Do not listen to the words of your
prophets,
who fill you with emptiness;
They speak visions from their own
fancy,
not from the mouth of the LORD.
¹⁷They say to those who despise the
word of the LORD,
"Peace shall be yours";

And to everyone who walks in
hardness of heart,
"No evil shall overtake you."
¹⁸Now, who has stood in the council
of the LORD,
to see him and to hear his word?
Who has heeded his word so as
to announce it?
¹⁹See, the storm of the LORD!
His wrath breaks forth
In a whirling storm
that bursts upon the heads of
the wicked.
²⁰The anger of the LORD shall not
abate
until he has carried out
completely
the decisions of his heart.
In days to come
you will understand fully.
²¹I did not send these prophets,
yet they ran;

---

does not help at the time the word is announced. Jeremiah insists that he is speaking a message on behalf of the Lord, a message that is primarily one of future disaster unless the people repent and surrender to Babylon, but he is countered by prophets who preach "peace." The issue of false prophecy is critical for Jeremiah because false prophets give the people a false hope that will ultimately lead to their destruction.

It seems likely that Jeremiah is the speaker of the opening verse (23:9), but very quickly it becomes difficult to separate the divine voice from the voice of the prophet. As in the confessions, we see into Jeremiah's inner struggle because of the word he must proclaim, a struggle that impacts him both emotionally and physically. Because of infidelity to the Lord and an evil way of life, seen even among the prophets and priests (23:11, 14), disaster will come upon all the people. Verses 13-14 focus on the infidelity of both the prophets of Israel and the prophets of Judah, with the prophets of Judah receiving the harshest judgment; it is judgment as bitter food and poisoned water. The people are likened to the inhabitants of Sodom and Gomorrah who merited only punishment. The failure of the prophets impacts the whole land because the prophets have led the people into ungodliness.

I did not speak to them,
  yet they prophesied.
²²Had they stood in my council,
  they would have proclaimed my
    words to my people,
They would have brought them
    back from their evil ways
  and from their wicked deeds.
²³Am I a God near at hand only—
    oracle of the LORD—
  and not a God far off?
²⁴Can anyone hide in secret
  without my seeing them?—
    oracle of the LORD.
Do I not fill
  heaven and earth?—oracle of
    the LORD.

²⁵I have heard the prophets who prophesy lies in my name say, "I had a dream! I had a dream!" ²⁶How long? Will the hearts of the prophets who prophesy lies and their own deceitful fancies ever turn back? ²⁷By the dreams they tell each other, they plan to make my people forget my name, just as their ancestors forgot my name for Baal. ²⁸Let the prophets who have dreams tell their dreams; let those who have my word speak my word truthfully!

What has straw to do with wheat?
  —oracle of the LORD.
²⁹Is not my word like fire—oracle of
    the LORD—
  like a hammer shattering rock?

³⁰Therefore I am against the prophets—oracle of the LORD—those who steal my words from each other. ³¹Yes, I am against the prophets—oracle of the LORD—those who compose their own speeches and call them oracles. ³²Yes, I am against the prophets who tell lying dreams—oracle of the LORD—those who lead my people astray by recounting their reckless lies. It was not I who sent them or commanded them; they do this people no good at all—oracle of the LORD.

³³And when this people or a prophet or a priest asks you, "What is the burden of the LORD?" you shall answer, "You are the burden, and I cast you off"—oracle of the LORD. ³⁴If a prophet or a priest or anyone else mentions "the burden of the LORD," I will punish that man and his household. ³⁵Thus you shall ask, when speaking to one another, "What answer did the LORD give?" or "What did the LORD say?" ³⁶But "the burden of the LORD" you shall mention no more. For each of you, your own word becomes the burden so that you pervert the words of the living God, the LORD of hosts, our God. ³⁷Thus shall you ask the prophet, "What answer did the LORD give?" or "What did the LORD say?" ³⁸But if you ask about "the burden of the LORD," then thus says the LORD: Because you use this phrase, "the burden of the

---

The next oracle (23:16-22) warns the people against false prophets. The people should recognize as false the word of prophets who proclaim a word of peace to those who persist in evil. It was thought that the prophet had access to the council of the Lord. This council was composed of divine beings over whom the Lord presided. The function of the council was to advise the high God (23:18, 22). It was thought that prophets had access to the divine council and thus their words were true. Jeremiah contends that the false prophets have not stood in the Lord's council (23:22) and consequently their

LORD," though I forbade you to use it, ³⁹therefore I will lift you on high and cast you from my presence, you and the city which I gave to you and your ancestors. ⁴⁰And I will bring upon you eternal reproach, eternal shame, never to be forgotten.

24 **The Two Baskets of Figs.**¹The LORD showed me two baskets of figs placed before the temple of the LORD. This was after Nebuchadnezzar, king of Babylon, had exiled from Jerusalem Jeconiah, son of Jehoiakim, king of Judah, and the princes of Judah, the artisans and smiths, and brought them to Babylon. ²One basket contained excellent figs, those that ripen early. But the other basket contained very bad figs, so bad they could not be eaten. ³Then the LORD said to me: What do you see, Jeremiah? "Figs," I replied; "the good ones are very good, but the bad ones very

bad, so bad they cannot be eaten." ⁴Thereupon this word of the LORD came to me: ⁵Thus says the LORD, the God of Israel: Like these good figs, I will also regard with favor Judah's exiles whom I sent away from this place into the land of the Chaldeans. ⁶I will look after them for good and bring them back to this land, to build them up, not tear them down; to plant them, not uproot them. ⁷I will give them a heart to know me, that I am the LORD. They shall be my people and I will be their God, for they shall return to me with their whole heart. ⁸But like the figs that are bad, so bad they cannot be eaten—yes, thus says the LORD—even so will I treat Zedekiah, king of Judah, and his princes, the remnant of Jerusalem remaining in this land and those who have settled in the land of Egypt. ⁹I will make them an object of horror to all the kingdoms of the earth,

---

words are false. The announcement of judgment (23:19) draws upon imagery of a storm to indicate that the Lord is coming as a warrior against the people. The three rhetorical questions of verses 23-24 make the claim that God is in touch with every sphere of creation.

The final section of this chapter (23:25-40) continues the focus on false prophecy. Jeremiah insists that the way one receives a prophetic word is not as important as the content of that word. Claims to visionary experiences and dreams carry no weight if the Lord did not send the prophet. The words of the false prophets are like straw to wheat; the Lord's word is as a fire. The key to understanding the question of verse 33 is in the word *maśśā'*, which means both "burden" and "oracle." Verses 34-40 attempt to say who is authorized to speak the word of the Lord, but they do not actually give one a way to distinguish true from false prophecy. It simply says that one is not to use "burden/oracle" for any claimed revelation.

24:1-10 The two baskets of figs

Two baskets of figs, one containing good figs and the other bad, provide the controlling metaphor to prophesy concerning the future of two groups: those who had been exiled to Babylon in 597 B.C. and those who remained

a reproach and a byword, a taunt and a curse, in all the places to which I will drive them. ¹⁰I will send upon them sword, famine, and pestilence, until they have disappeared from the land which I gave them and their ancestors.

25 **Seventy Years of Exile.** ¹The word that came to Jeremiah concerning all the people of Judah, in the fourth year of Jehoiakim, son of Josiah, king of Judah (the first year of Nebuchadnezzar, king of Babylon). ²This word the prophet Jeremiah spoke to all the people of Judah and all the inhabitants of Jerusalem: ³Since the thirteenth year of Josiah, son of Amon, king of Judah, to this day— that is, twenty-three years—the word of the Lord has come to me and I spoke to you untiringly, but you would not listen. ⁴The Lord kept sending you all his servants the prophets, but you refused to listen or pay attention ⁵to this message: Turn back, each of you, from your evil way and from your evil deeds; then you shall remain in the land which the Lord gave you and your ancestors, from of old and forever. ⁶Do not follow other gods to serve and bow down to them; do not provoke me with the works of your hands, or I will bring evil upon you. ⁷But you would not listen to me— oracle of the Lord—and so you provoked me with the works of your hands to your own harm. ⁸Hence, thus says the Lord of hosts: Since you would not listen to my words, ⁹I am about to send for and fetch all the tribes from the north— oracle of the Lord—and I will send for Nebuchadnezzar, king of Babylon, my servant; I will bring them against this land, its inhabitants, and all these neighboring nations. I will doom them, making them an object of horror, of hissing, of everlasting reproach. ¹⁰Among them I will put to an end the song of joy and the song of gladness, the voice of the bridegroom and the voice of the bride, the sound of the millstone and the light of the lamp. ¹¹This whole land shall be a ruin and a waste. Seventy years these nations shall serve the king of Babylon; ¹²but when the seventy years have elapsed, I will punish the king of Babylon and that nation and the land of the Chaldeans for their guilt—oracle of the Lord. Their land I will turn into everlasting waste. ¹³Against that land I will fulfill all the words I have spoken

in the land or escaped to Egypt. The former are the good figs and the Lord will look with favor upon them, return them to the land, and they will flourish. The bad figs represent those who remained in the land, including King Zedekiah and his princes, and those who settled in Egypt. A particularly harsh punishment awaits them in the future. The future of Israel rests with the exiles according to Jeremiah and, indeed, it is the exiles who will lay the foundation for the future of the people.

25:1-14 Seventy years of exile

A summary of twenty-three years of Jeremiah's prophetic message is inserted at this point in the book. It reiterates the main message contained in the oracles of Jeremiah: the people are remiss in worshiping the Lord

against it, all that is written in this book, which Jeremiah prophesied against all the nations. [14]They also shall serve many nations and great kings, and thus I will repay them according to their own deeds and according to the works of their hands.

The Cup of Judgment on the Nations. [15]For thus said the LORD, the God of Israel, to me: Take this cup of the wine of wrath from my hand and have all the nations to whom I will send you drink it. [16]They shall drink, and retch, and go mad, because of the sword I will send among them. [17]I took the cup from the hand of the LORD and gave it as drink to all the nations to whom the LORD sent me: [18]to Jerusalem, the cities of Judah, its kings and princes, to make them a ruin and a waste, an object of hissing and cursing, as they are today; [19]to Pharaoh, king of Egypt, and his servants, princes, all his people [20]and those of mixed ancestry; all the kings of the land of Uz; all the kings of the land of the Philistines: Ashkelon, Gaza, Ekron, and the remnant of Ashdod; [21]Edom, Moab, and the Ammonites; [22]all the kings of Tyre, of Sidon, and of the shores beyond the sea; [23]Dedan and Tema and Buz, all the desert dwellers who shave their temples; [24]all the kings of Arabia; [25]all the kings of Zimri, of Elam, of the Medes; [26]all the kings of the north, near and far, one after the other; all the kingdoms upon the face of the earth and after them the king of Sheshach shall drink.

[27]Tell them: Thus says the LORD of hosts, the God of Israel: Drink! Get drunk and vomit! Fall, never to rise, before the sword that I will send among you! [28]If they refuse to take the cup from your hand and drink, say to them: Thus says the LORD of hosts: You must drink! [29]Now that I am inflicting evil on this city, called by my name, how can you possibly escape? You shall not escape! I am calling down the sword upon all the inhabitants of the earth—oracle of the LORD of hosts. [30]As for you, prophesy against them all these words and say to them:

---

and the Lord alone, they refuse to change their ways, and thus they stand under judgment. There is surprisingly no reference to the Lord's saving actions of the past; there is only a focus on sin and its inevitable punishment. The only additional element is that seventy years after punishment the Babylonian Empire itself will be the focus of the Lord's judgment. In 29:10 it is the exile itself that is set at seventy years. It is simply not possible, despite some creative attempts, to get seventy years as the period of time that the Babylonian Empire was dominant in the region or that the exile lasted seventy years. It is most likely that the number is simply a round number suggesting a normal life span (cf. Ps 90:10).

25:15-38 The cup of judgment on the nations

It is not clear whether this section is intended as a report of a symbolic act, the expansion of a vivid metaphor, or the explanation of a vision, but

The LORD roars from on high,
    from his holy dwelling he raises
        his voice;
Mightily he roars over his sheepfold,
    a shout like that of vintagers
        echoes
    over all the inhabitants of the
        earth.
[31]The uproar spreads
    to the end of the earth;
For the LORD has an indictment
    against the nations,
    he enters into judgment against
        all flesh:
The wicked shall be given to the
    sword—
    oracle of the LORD.
[32]Thus says the LORD of hosts:
Look! disaster stalks
    nation after nation;
A violent storm surges
    from the recesses of the earth.

[33]On that day, those whom the LORD has slain will be strewn from one end of the earth to the other. They will not be mourned, they will not be gathered, they will not be buried; they shall lie like dung upon the ground.

[34]Howl, you shepherds, and wail!
    roll on the ground, leaders of
        the flock!
The time for your slaughter has
    come;
    like choice rams you shall fall.
[35]There is no flight for the shepherds,
    no escape for the leaders of the
        flock.
[36]Listen! Wailing from the shepherds,
    howling from the leaders of the
        flock!
For the LORD lays waste their
    grazing place;
[37]desolate are the peaceful
    pastures,
    from the burning wrath of the
        LORD.
[38]Like a lion he leaves his lair,
    and their land is made desolate

---

the prophetic message itself is clear. The drinking of the cup of wine of wrath sets the context for a severe judgment against the nations. There is no indictment in this section, only an announcement of punishment. The nations will experience the devastation brought by Babylon's armies; they have no choice but to drink the wine of wrath. The Babylonian Empire is bent on conquest and every nation will be defeated by the Babylonian armies, but in the end Babylon itself will fall to the sword. The cryptic reference to Babylon as Sheshach (25:26) is an example of an *atbash* cipher in which the Hebrew letters are substituted in reverse alphabetical order, that is, the first letter of the alphabet is replaced by the last letter, the second letter is replaced by the second last letter, and so forth. Thus Babel (*bbl*) becomes Sheshach (*ššk*). The list of nations is similar to that found in the oracles against the nations (chs. 46–51). Jeremiah had been commissioned as "prophet to the nations" (1:5, 10) and in this passage Jeremiah receives a message from the Lord that is directed to the other nations. It is more likely that Jeremiah carried out the command he is given in a symbolic way than that he traveled from nation to nation carrying a cup of wine for each nation to drink.

By the sweeping sword,
   and the burning wrath of the
      Lord.

IV. The Temple Sermon

26 **Jeremiah Threatened with Death.** ¹In the beginning of the reign of Jehoiakim, son of Josiah, king of Judah, this word came from the Lord: ²Thus says the Lord: Stand in the court of the house of the Lord and speak to the inhabitants of all the cities of Judah who come to worship in the house of the Lord; whatever I command you, tell them, and hold nothing back. ³Perhaps they will listen and turn, all of them from their evil way, so that I may repent of the evil I plan to inflict upon them for their evil deeds. ⁴Say to them: Thus says the Lord: If you do not obey me, by walking according to the law I set before you ⁵and listening to the words of my servants the prophets, whom I kept sending you, even though you do not listen to them, ⁶I will treat this house like Shiloh, and make this city a curse for all the nations of the earth.

⁷Now the priests, the prophets, and all the people heard Jeremiah speaking these words in the house of the Lord. ⁸When Jeremiah finished speaking all that the Lord commanded him to speak to all the people, then the priests, the prophets, and all the people laid hold of him, crying, "You must die! ⁹Why do you prophesy in the name of the Lord: 'This house shall become like Shiloh,' and 'This city shall be desolate, without inhabitant'?" And all the people crowded around Jeremiah in the house of the Lord.

¹⁰When the princes of Judah heard about these things, they came up from the house of the king to the house of the Lord and convened at the New Gate of the house of the Lord. ¹¹The priests and prophets said to the princes and to all

---

Of the two poetic oracles that conclude the chapter, the first (25:30-32) continues the announcement of judgment against the nations. The Lord is imaged as a roaring lion that ravages his flock in stark contrast to the Lord as a protective shepherd. The Lord is also spoken of as a vintager treading grapes and a judge rendering a verdict. The judgment is likened to a storm that has been unleashed against the whole earth. After a prose interlude that speaks of the vast number of the slain who will not be mourned and buried, the second poetic oracle (25:34-38) calls for a lament over the slaughter from which there is no escape. The final verse leads us back to the image of the Lord as a lion on the prowl wreaking devastation across the land.

THE TEMPLE SERMON

Jeremiah 26:1-24; cf. 7:1-15

26:1-19 Jeremiah threatened with death

The negative response to Jeremiah's preaching is no more dramatically presented than in chapter 26 when Jeremiah is put on trial for speaking of

the people, "Sentence this man to death! He has prophesied against this city! You heard it with your own ears." [12]Jeremiah said to the princes and all the people: "It was the LORD who sent me to prophesy against this house and city everything you have heard. [13]Now, therefore, reform your ways and your deeds; listen to the voice of the LORD your God, so that the LORD will have a change of heart regarding the evil he has spoken against you. [14]As for me, I am in your hands; do with me what is good and right in your eyes. [15]But you should certainly know that by putting me to death, you bring innocent blood on yourselves, on this city and its inhabitants. For in truth it was the LORD who sent me to you, to speak all these words for you to hear."

[16]Then the princes and all the people said to the priests and the prophets, "This man does not deserve a death sentence; it is in the name of the LORD, our God, that he speaks to us." [17]At this, some of the elders of the land arose and said to the whole assembly of the people, [18]"Micah of Moresheth used to prophesy in the days of Hezekiah, king of Judah, and he said to all the people of Judah: Thus says the LORD of hosts:

> Zion shall be plowed as a field,
> Jerusalem, a heap of ruins,
> and the temple mount,
> a forest ridge.

[19]Did Hezekiah, king of Judah, and all Judah condemn him to death? Did he not fear the LORD and entreat the favor of the LORD, so that the LORD had a change of heart regarding the evil he had spoken against them? We, however, are about to do great evil against ourselves."

The Fate of Uriah. [20]There was another man who used to prophesy in the name

---

the destruction of the temple. A fuller version of the temple sermon is given in chapter 7; the focus of this chapter is the reaction of the religious leaders, specifically the priests and prophets, and the people who hear Jeremiah's announcement of the judgment against the temple.

The substance of the temple sermon is summarized in verses 2-6: if the people turn away from evil, their punishment will be averted; but if they continue to disobey the Lord and not listen to the prophets, then the temple and city will be destroyed. Jeremiah is seized and an impromptu trial begins. The priests, prophets, and people demand a death sentence, which was the punishment for a false prophet (Deut 18:20); the princes of Judah convene to hear the evidence and render a verdict. Jeremiah's defense is to affirm that he was sent by the Lord; the message he speaks is the Lord's message and thus he does not deserve death. The princes of Judah and the people, who seem to have shifted sides, agree that Jeremiah should not be put to death. Some of the elders support this verdict by citing precedent. Micah had prophesied the destruction of Jerusalem and the temple (Mic 3:12), but the king and the people responded to Micah's prophecy by repenting and so the Lord relented.

of the LORD, Uriah, son of Shemaiah, from Kiriath-jearim; he prophesied against this city and this land the same message as Jeremiah. ²¹When King Jehoiakim and all his officers and princes heard his words, the king sought to have him killed. But Uriah heard of it and fled in fear to Egypt. ²²Then King Jehoiakim sent Elnathan, son of Achbor, and others with him into Egypt, ²³and they brought Uriah out of Egypt and took him to Jehoiakim the king, who struck him down with the sword and threw his corpse into the common burial ground. ²⁴But the hand of Ahikam, son of Shaphan, protected Jeremiah, so they did not hand him over to the people to be put to death.

V. Controversies with the False Prophets

27 **Serve Babylon or Perish.** ¹In the beginning of the reign of Zedekiah, son of Josiah, king of Judah, this word came to Jeremiah from the LORD: ²The LORD said to me: Make for yourself thongs and yoke bars and put them on your shoulders. ³Send them to the kings of Edom, Moab, the Ammonites, Tyre, and Sidon, through the ambassadors who have come to Jerusalem to Zedekiah, king of Judah, ⁴and command them to tell their lords: Thus says the LORD of hosts, the God of Israel, Thus shall you say to your lords: ⁵It was I who made the earth, human being and beast on the face of the earth, by my great power, with my outstretched arm; and I can give them to whomever I think fit. ⁶Now I have given all these lands into the hand of Nebuchadnezzar, king of Babylon, my servant; even the wild animals I have given him to serve him. ⁷All nations shall serve him and his son and his grandson, until the time comes for

26:20-24 The fate of Uriah

The trial of Jeremiah continues with a counterprecedent. Another prophet, Uriah, announced the destruction of Jerusalem and the temple, but he was executed by King Jehoiakim. No further report of the proceedings of the trial is given. The passage ends rather abruptly with the notice that Jeremiah was protected by Ahikam, son of Shaphan who had been an official in King Josiah's court. Though Ahikam's office is never given in the Old Testament, it is possible that he was a high-ranking official of the court.

CONTROVERSIES WITH THE FALSE PROPHETS

Jeremiah 27:1–29:32

These three chapters continue to develop the theme of conflict between true and false prophets (14:13-16; 23:9-40). Prophets speak a message regarding the present behavior of the people and the future consequences of such behavior. As prophets claim to be speaking a message from God, a problem arises when prophets make conflicting claims regarding that message. Jeremiah's message was not simply unpopular, but there were

him and his land; then many nations and great kings will enslave him. ⁸Meanwhile, the nation or the kingdom that will not serve him, Nebuchadnezzar, king of Babylon, or bend its neck under the yoke of the king of Babylon, I will punish that nation with sword, famine, and pestilence—oracle of the LORD—until I finish them by his hand.

⁹You, however, must not listen to your prophets, to your diviners and dreamers, to your soothsayers and sorcerers, who say to you, "Do not serve the king of Babylon." ¹⁰For they prophesy lies to you, so as to drive you far from your land, making me banish you so that you perish. ¹¹The people that bends the neck to the yoke of the king of Babylon to serve him, I will leave in peace on its own land—oracle of the LORD—to cultivate it and dwell on it.

¹²To Zedekiah, king of Judah, I spoke the same words: Bend your necks to the yoke of the king of Babylon; serve him and his people, so that you may live. ¹³Why should you and your people die by sword, famine, and pestilence, in ac-

cordance with the word the LORD has spoken to the nation that will not serve the king of Babylon? ¹⁴Do not listen to the words of the prophets who say to you, "Do not serve the king of Babylon." They prophesy lies to you! ¹⁵I did not send them—oracle of the LORD—but they prophesy falsely in my name. As a result I must banish you, and you will perish, you and the prophets who are prophesying to you.

¹⁶To the priests and to all the people I said: Thus says the LORD: Do not listen to the words of your prophets who prophesy to you: "The vessels of the house of the LORD will soon be brought back from Babylon," for they prophesy lies to you. ¹⁷Do not listen to them! Serve the king of Babylon that you may live. Why should this city become rubble? ¹⁸If they were prophets, if the word of the LORD were with them, then they would intercede with the LORD of hosts, that the vessels remaining in the house of the LORD and in the house of the king of Judah and in Jerusalem should not also go to Babylon. ¹⁹For thus says the LORD

---

prophets who called its validity into question. In the previous chapter Jeremiah was put on trial for the message he proclaimed. In these three chapters Jeremiah insists that his message is authentic and that the prophets who oppose him are lying.

27:1-22 Serve Babylon or perish

The oracles that comprise this chapter are set in the reign of Zedekiah (597–587 B.C.) and are addressed to the kings of the nations surrounding Israel, to King Zedekiah of Judah, and to the priests and all the people. The point of contention is whether or not the nations, including Judah, should rebel against or submit to Babylon. Jeremiah is insistent in calling for submission to Babylon and thus he comes into conflict with those who foment rebellion, especially other prophets. The yoke that Jeremiah is commanded to wear and then to send to the nations is accompanied by the exhortation

of hosts concerning the pillars, the sea, the stands, and the rest of the vessels remaining in this city, ²⁰which Nebuchadnezzar, king of Babylon, did not take when he exiled Jeconiah, son of Jehoiakim, king of Judah, from Jerusalem to Babylon, along with all the nobles of Judah and Jerusalem— ²¹thus says the LORD of hosts, the God of Israel, concerning the vessels remaining in the house of the LORD, in the house of the king of Judah, and in Jerusalem: ²²To Babylon they shall go, and there they shall remain, until the day I look for them—oracle of the LORD; then I will bring them back and restore them to this place.

28 **The Two Yokes.** ¹That same year, in the beginning of the reign of Zedekiah, king of Judah, in the fifth month of the fourth year, Hananiah the prophet, son of Azzur, from Gibeon, said to me in the house of the LORD in the sight of the priests and all the people: ²"Thus says the LORD of hosts, the God of Israel: I have broken the yoke of the king of Babylon. ³Within two years I will restore to this place all the vessels of the house of the LORD which Nebuchadnezzar, king of Babylon, took from this place and carried away to Babylon. ⁴And Jeconiah, son of Jehoiakim, king of Judah, and all the exiles of Judah who went to Babylon, I will bring back to this place— oracle of the LORD—for I will break the yoke of the king of Babylon."

⁵Jeremiah the prophet answered the prophet Hananiah in the sight of the priests and all the people standing in the house of the LORD, ⁶and said: Amen! thus may the LORD do! May the LORD fulfill your words that you have prophesied, by bringing back the vessels of the house of the LORD and all the exiles from Babylon to this place! ⁷But now, listen to the word I am about to speak in your hearing and the hearing of all the people. ⁸In the past, the prophets who came before you and me prophesied war, disaster, and pestilence against many lands and mighty kingdoms. ⁹But the prophet who prophesies peace is recognized as the prophet whom the LORD has truly sent only when his word comes to pass.

---

to serve Babylon, for this is what the Lord wills. The prophets, diviners, dreamers, soothsayers, and sorcerers of these nations are singled out by Jeremiah as prophesying lies, for they encourage the people not to submit to Babylon. The same message is delivered to King Zedekiah, the priests, and all the people. Only in submission to Babylon will they be spared; rebellion will result in further pilfering of the vessels of the temple and the destruction of the city.

28:1-17 The two yokes

Chapter 28 is linked to chapter 27 by being set in the same year. It also echoes the previous chapter in its reference to yokes, temple vessels, and conflicting prophetic messages regarding submission to Babylon. The dramatic character of the confrontation between prophets is heightened by means of symbolic actions done by both prophets in the presence of an

¹⁰Thereupon Hananiah the prophet took the yoke bar from the neck of Jeremiah the prophet and broke it. ¹¹He said in the sight of all the people: "Thus says the LORD: Like this, within two years I will break the yoke of Nebuchadnezzar, king of Babylon, from the neck of all the nations." At that, the prophet Jeremiah went on his way.

¹²After Hananiah the prophet had broken the yoke bar off the neck of the prophet Jeremiah, the word of the LORD came to Jeremiah: ¹³Go tell Hananiah this: Thus says the LORD: By breaking a wooden yoke bar, you make an iron yoke! ¹⁴For thus says the LORD of hosts, the God of Israel: A yoke of iron I have placed on the necks of all these nations serving Nebuchadnezzar, king of Babylon, and they shall serve him; even the wild animals I have given him. ¹⁵And Jeremiah the prophet said to Hananiah the prophet: Listen to this, Hananiah! The LORD has not sent you, and you have led this people to rely on deception. ¹⁶For this, says the LORD, I am sending you from the face of the earth; this very year you shall die, because you have preached rebellion against the LORD. ¹⁷Hananiah the prophet died in that year, in the seventh month.

29 Letter to the Exiles in Babylon. ¹These are the words of the scroll which Jeremiah the prophet sent from Jerusalem to the remaining elders among the exiles, to the priests, the prophets, and all the people whom Nebuchadnezzar exiled from Jerusalem to Babylon. ²This was after King Jeconiah and the queen mother, the court officials,

audience. Hananiah announces the return of the temple vessels and of the exiles of 597 B.C. Jeremiah responds with the hope that Hananiah's word will come to pass, but he notes that prophets of the past prophesied war and disaster. According to Jeremiah an announcement of peace is to be trusted only if that word is fulfilled. Hananiah then takes the wooden yoke from around Jeremiah's neck and breaks it, reiterating his prophecy of liberation from Babylon. In a kind of prophetic one-upmanship, Jeremiah returns the next day with an iron yoke to confirm his message that the Lord wills that Judah and the surrounding nations serve Babylon. Jeremiah follows up his encounter with Hananiah with an oracle specifically directed against Hananiah. It is rare to find an announcement of judgment against an individual in the prophetic books and this announcement is particularly harsh: Hananiah will be dead before the year is up. There is a succinct and sober announcement of the fulfillment of this prophecy that concludes the chapter.

29:1-23 Letter to the exiles in Babylon

Those exiled to Babylon in 597 B.C. were not completely cut off from those who remained in Jerusalem. In spite of the distance between the two groups, letters passed between them, as exemplified by the letters sent by

the princes of Judah and Jerusalem, the artisans and smiths had left Jerusalem. ³Delivered in Babylon by Elasah, son of Shaphan, and by Gemariah, son of Hilkiah, whom Zedekiah, king of Judah, sent to the king of Babylon, the letter read:

⁴Thus says the LORD of hosts, the God of Israel, to all the exiles whom I exiled from Jerusalem to Babylon: ⁵Build houses and live in them; plant gardens and eat their fruits. ⁶Take wives and have sons and daughters; find wives for your sons and give your daughters to husbands, so that they may bear sons and daughters. Increase there; do not decrease. ⁷Seek the welfare of the city to which I have exiled you; pray for it to the LORD, for upon its welfare your own depends. ⁸For thus says the LORD of hosts, the God of Israel: Do not be deceived by the prophets and diviners who are among you; do not listen to those among you who dream dreams, ⁹for they prophesy lies to you in my name; I did not send them—oracle of the LORD.

¹⁰For thus says the LORD: Only after seventy years have elapsed for Babylon will I deal with you and fulfill for you my promise to bring you back to this place. ¹¹For I know well the plans I have in mind for you—oracle of the LORD—plans for your welfare and not for woe, so as to give you a future of hope. ¹²When you call me, and come and pray to me, I will listen to you. ¹³When you look for me, you will find me. Yes, when you seek me with all your heart, ¹⁴I will let you find me—oracle of the LORD—and I will change your lot; I will gather you together from all the nations and all the places to which I have banished you—oracle of the LORD—and bring you back to the place from which I have exiled you. ¹⁵As for your saying, "The LORD has raised up for us prophets here in Babylon"—

¹⁶Thus says the LORD concerning the king sitting on David's throne and all the people living in this city, your kinsmen who did not go with you into exile; ¹⁷thus says the LORD of hosts: I am sending against them sword, famine, and pestilence. I will make them like rotten figs, so spoiled that they cannot be eaten. ¹⁸I will pursue them with sword, famine,

---

Jeremiah to the leaders of the exiles found in this chapter. The occasion for these letters continues the theme of the preceding chapters: conflicting prophetic messages. Jeremiah opposes those prophets who maintain that the period of exile will be short. In a series of oracles relayed by Jeremiah, the Lord commands the people to settle down in the land of exile since they will be there a long time. After seventy years, Babylon will be dealt with, the Lord will favor the people and will return them to their land. (See comments above on 25:14 regarding seventy years.) Jeremiah's letter includes a harsh judgment against King Zedekiah and those remaining in Jerusalem for their failure to listen to the true prophets. A death sentence is given for two false prophets, Ahab, son of Kolaiah, and Zedekiah, son of Maaseiah, who are accused of adultery as well as prophesying falsely.

and pestilence, and make them an object of horror to all the kingdoms of the earth, a curse, a desolation, a hissing, and a reproach to all the nations among which I have banished them, [19]because they did not listen to my words—oracle of the LORD—even though I kept sending them my servants the prophets, but they would not listen to them—oracle of the LORD.

[20]As for you, listen to the word of the LORD, all you exiles whom I sent away from Jerusalem to Babylon. [21]This is what the LORD of hosts, the God of Israel, says about Ahab, son of Kolaiah, and Zedekiah, son of Maaseiah, who prophesy lies to you in my name: I am handing them over to Nebuchadnezzar, king of Babylon, who will kill them before your eyes. [22]And because of them this curse will be used by all the exiles of Judah in Babylon: "May the LORD make you like Zedekiah and Ahab, whom the king of Babylon roasted in fire," [23]because they have committed an outrage in Israel, committing adultery with their neighbors' wives, and alleging in my name things I did not command. I know, I am witness—oracle of the LORD.

The False Prophet Shemaiah. [24]To Shemaiah, the Nehelamite, say: [25]Thus says the LORD of hosts, the God of Israel: Because you sent documents in your own name to all the people in Jerusalem, to Zephaniah, the priest, son of Maaseiah, and to all the priests saying: [26]"It is the LORD who has appointed you priest in place of the priest Jehoiada, to provide officers for the house of the LORD, that you may confine in stocks or pillory any madman who poses as a prophet. [27]Why, then, have you not rebuked Jeremiah of Anathoth who poses as a prophet among you? [28]For he sent this message to us in Babylon: It will be a long time; build houses to live in; plant gardens and eat their fruit. . . ."

[29]When the priest Zephaniah read this letter to Jeremiah the prophet, [30]the word of the LORD came to Jeremiah: [31]Send to all the exiles: Thus says the LORD concerning Shemaiah, the Nehelamite: Because Shemaiah prophesies to you, although I did not send him, and has led you to rely on a lie, [32]therefore thus says the LORD, I will punish Shemaiah, the Nehelamite, and his descendants. None of them shall dwell among this people to see the good I will do for this people— oracle of the LORD—because he preached rebellion against the LORD.

VI. Oracles of the Restoration of Israel and Judah

The Restoration [1]This word came 30 to Jeremiah from the LORD: [2]Thus says the LORD, the God of Israel: Write down on a scroll all the words I have

---

29:24-32 The false prophet Shemaiah

Jeremiah responds to a letter Shemaiah sent to the priest Zephaniah demanding that Jeremiah be rebuked and confined in stocks for the letter he sent to the exiles. At contention is the length of the exile, which Jeremiah insists will be long (seventy years). Jeremiah denounces Shemaiah as a false prophet and prophesies that he and his descendants will not see the positive future for the people that the Lord has planned.

spoken to you. ³For indeed, the days are coming—oracle of the LORD—when I will restore the fortunes of my people Israel and Judah—oracle of the LORD. I will bring them back to the land which I gave to their ancestors, and they shall take possession of it.

⁴These are the words the LORD spoke to Israel and to Judah: ⁵Thus says the LORD:

> We hear a cry of fear:
>   terror, not peace.
> ⁶Inquire and see:
>   does a male give birth?
> Why, then, do I see all these men,
>   their hands on their loins
> Like women in labor,
>   all their faces drained of color?
> ⁷Ah! How mighty is that day—
>   there is none like it!

> A time of distress for Jacob,
>   though he shall be saved from
>   it.

⁸On that day—oracle of the LORD of hosts—I will break his yoke off your neck and snap your bonds. Strangers shall no longer enslave them; ⁹instead, they shall serve the LORD, their God, and David, their king, whom I will raise up for them.

> ¹⁰But you, my servant Jacob, do not
>   fear!—oracle of the LORD—
>   do not be dismayed, Israel!
> For I will soon deliver you from
>   places far away,
>   your offspring from the land of
>   their exile;
> Jacob shall again find rest,
>   secure, with none to frighten
>   him,

ORACLES OF THE RESTORATION OF ISRAEL AND JUDAH

Jeremiah 30:1–35:19

Oracles of salvation have been gathered together in chapters 30–33 of the book of Jeremiah. These chapters are often referred to as "the book of consolation" because of the pervasive note of hope that is present. They give evidence of later additions, but the core of these chapters may have originated with Jeremiah. Some of the oracles are addressed to the exiles of the northern kingdom, but in 30:3 the audience is both Israel and Judah. Thus far the book of Jeremiah has been dominated by severe indictments against the people, followed by announcements of a harsh and relentless judgment. It is not clear why the oracles and narratives of hope have been gathered together and inserted at this point in the book of Jeremiah, but it is a welcome respite in the midst of an overwhelmingly negative message. In chapters 34–35 we return to the more negative side of Jeremiah's message.

30:1-24 The restoration

Jeremiah is commanded by the Lord to write down all his past words, for now the fortunes of the people will change. The judgment of the past

¹¹for I am with you—oracle of
the LORD—to save you.
I will bring to an end all the nations
among whom I have scattered
you;
but you I will not bring to an
end.
I will chastise you as you deserve,
I will not let you go unpunished.
¹²For thus says the LORD:
Incurable is your wound,
grievous your injury;
¹³There is none to plead your case,
no remedy for your running sore,
no healing for you.
¹⁴All your lovers have forgotten you,
they do not seek you out.
I struck you as an enemy would
strike,
punishing you cruelly.
¹⁵Why cry out over your wound?
There is no relief for your pain.
Because of your great guilt,
your numerous sins,
I have done this to you.

¹⁶Yet all who devour you shall be
devoured,
all your enemies shall go into
exile.
All who plunder you shall become
plunder,
all who pillage you I will hand
over to be pillaged.
¹⁷For I will restore your health;
I will heal your injuries—oracle
of the LORD.
"The outcast" they have called you,
"whom no one looks for."
¹⁸Thus says the LORD:
See! I will restore the fortunes of
Jacob's tents,
on his dwellings I will have
compassion;
A city shall be rebuilt upon its own
ruins,
a citadel restored where it
should be.
¹⁹From them will come praise,
the sound of people rejoicing.

---

will give way to the return from exile and restoration on the land that was given to their ancestors. This action is based entirely on the Lord's initiative. The words of hope for the future are in response to the experience of fear and terror of the people. The day of distress is so great that no other day compares with it, but salvation is coming. As the chapter unfolds, the future promise is set against the necessity of the judgment the people have endured. They have sinned grievously; they deserved their punishment, but the God who judges is also the God who saves. The announcement of hope for the future is the undoing of the judgment of the past. Homes and cities will be rebuilt, fortunes will be restored, the population will increase, the people will be ruled by one of their own, and they will rejoice. Once again they will be known as the Lord's people and the Lord will be their God (30:22). The time of their punishment is at an end, but those who have oppressed them will now experience the Lord's wrath. The final two verses (30:23-24) duplicate 23:19-20, but in the context of chapter 23 the object of the Lord's wrath is Judah. In chapter 30 the wrath of the Lord has already been experienced by Judah, so the object of the Lord's wrath must be the enemies of Judah.

I will increase them, they will not
decrease,
I will glorify them, they will not
be insignificant.
²⁰His children shall be as of old,
his assembly shall stand firm in
my presence,
I will punish all his oppressors.
²¹His leader shall be one of his own,
and his ruler shall emerge from
his ranks.
He shall approach me when I
summon him;
Why else would he dare
approach me?—oracle of the
LORD.
²²You shall be my people,
and I will be your God.
²³Look! The storm of the LORD!
His wrath breaks out
In a whirling storm
that bursts upon the heads of
the wicked.
²⁴The anger of the LORD will not
abate
until he has carried out
completely
the decisions of his heart.
In days to come
you will fully understand it.

31 **Good News of the Return.** ¹At that ▶
time—oracle of the LORD—
I will be the God of all the
families of Israel,
and they shall be my people.
²Thus says the LORD:
The people who escaped the sword
find favor in the wilderness.
As Israel comes forward to receive
rest,
³from afar the LORD appears: ▶
With age-old love I have loved you;
so I have kept my mercy toward
you.
⁴Again I will build you, and you
shall stay built,
virgin Israel;
Carrying your festive tambourines,
you shall go forth dancing with
merrymakers.
⁵You shall again plant vineyards
on the mountains of Samaria;
those who plant them shall
enjoy their fruits.
⁶Yes, a day will come when the
watchmen
call out on Mount Ephraim:
"Come, let us go up to Zion,
to the LORD, our God."

31:1-6 Good news of the return

All the families of Israel are addressed in this oracle of salvation. It draws connections between Israel's past and its future. The wilderness period following upon the time of the exodus becomes a metaphor for the exile, but now the Lord's favor will come upon them. Based on the Lord's love, which is characterized as enduring ("age-old") and constant ("mercy" translates *hesed*, which is a love that is characterized by constancy and fidelity), the promises of the past will be realized in the future. Echoing the terminology associated with Jeremiah's call (31:4-5), the time has come for a reversal of judgment. The Lord will "build" up the people and "plant" the land so that it will produce in abundance. The call to go up to Zion indicates that Jerusalem will be rebuilt and it will become the center of worship for Israel.

The Road of Return

⁷For thus says the LORD:
Shout with joy for Jacob,
    exult at the head of the nations;
    proclaim your praise and say:
The LORD has saved his people,
    the remnant of Israel.
⁸Look! I will bring them back
    from the land of the north;
I will gather them from the ends of
    the earth,
    the blind and the lame in their
      midst,
Pregnant women, together with
    those in labor—
    an immense throng—they shall
      return.
⁹With weeping they shall come,
    but with compassion I will
      guide them;

I will lead them to streams of water,
    on a level road, without
      stumbling.
For I am a father to Israel,
    Ephraim is my firstborn.
¹⁰Hear the word of the LORD, you
    nations,
    proclaim it on distant coasts,
      and say:
The One who scattered Israel, now
    gathers them;
    he guards them as a shepherd
      his flock.
¹¹The LORD shall ransom Jacob,
    he shall redeem him from a
      hand too strong for him.
¹²Shouting, they shall mount the
    heights of Zion,
    they shall come streaming to the
      LORD's blessings:

31:7-14 The road of return

The hymnic language of this oracle suits its message of hope. It calls for a celebration of the deliverance of those who have been exiled. It is to be proclaimed that the Lord has saved the people by bringing them back, not simply from Babylon, "the land of the north" (31:8), but also from all nations. The gathering of those exiled is inclusive: the blind and lame, pregnant women and those about to give birth (31:8), young and old, men and women (31:13). Though this remnant of the people may weep over what has been lost (31:9), that mourning will be turned into joy (31:13). Israel's return to the land will be a time to rejoice because the Lord will guide them and do so with compassion (31:9, 13). Images of the Lord as father (31:9) and shepherd (31:10) replace the image of the Lord as a wrathful judge. The ransoming of Israel will include the fertility of the land and a return to worship (31:12, 14); it will be a time filled with blessings.

31:15-20 End of Rachel's mourning

The mourning of both Rachel (31:15) and Ephraim (31:18-19) at the devastating effects of the judgment against Israel receives a response from the Lord (31:16-17, 20-22). Rachel personifies all the mothers of Israel who grieve over the loss of their children and the loss of the future represented by those children (31:17). Ephraim personifies Rachel's children through

The grain, the wine, and the oil,
  flocks of sheep and cattle;
They themselves shall be like
    watered gardens,
    never again neglected.
[13]Then young women shall make
    merry and dance,
  young men and old as well.
I will turn their mourning into joy,
  I will show them compassion
    and have them rejoice
    after their sorrows.
[14]I will lavish choice portions on the
    priests,
  and my people shall be filled
    with my blessings—
  oracle of the LORD.

End of Rachel's Mourning

[15]Thus says the LORD:
In Ramah is heard the sound of
    sobbing,
  bitter weeping!
Rachel mourns for her children,
  she refuses to be consoled
  for her children—they are no
    more!
[16]Thus says the LORD:
Cease your cries of weeping,
  hold back your tears!
There is compensation for your
    labor—

oracle of the LORD—
  they shall return from the
    enemy's land.
[17]There is hope for your future—
  oracle of the LORD—
  your children shall return to
    their own territory.
[18]Indeed, I heard Ephraim rocking
    in grief:
You chastised me, and I was
    chastised;
  I was like an untamed calf.
Bring me back, let me come back,
  for you are the LORD, my God.
[19]For after I turned away, I repented;
  after I came to myself, I struck
    my thigh;
I was ashamed, even humiliated,
  because I bore the disgrace of
    my youth.
[20]Is Ephraim not my favored son,
  the child in whom I delight?
Even though I threaten him,
  I must still remember him!
My heart stirs for him,
  I must show him compassion!—
    oracle of the LORD.

Summons To Return Home

[21]Set up road markers,
  put up signposts;
Turn your attention to the highway,

Joseph, but probably represents Israel as a whole. Ephraim was one of the major tribes of Israel and it is used often as a synonym for Israel itself (e.g., Hos 5:3, 9). Ephraim's grief is caused by the destruction of Israel, but he acknowledges that the punishment was deserved. He confesses his guilt and repents. To both Rachel and Ephraim the Lord announces a word of hope. Rachel should be comforted, for her children are not wholly lost; they will return from exile. Ephraim/Israel is still the Lord's favored son in whom the Lord delights. The Lord's love remains constant even when forced to punish a disobedient child. The Lord's remembrance of this child is assured and leads to compassion.

the road you walked.
Turn back, virgin Israel,
   turn back to these your cities.
[22]How long will you continue to
   hesitate,
   rebellious daughter?
The Lord has created a new thing
   upon the earth:
   woman encompasses man.

[23]Thus says the Lord of hosts, the God of Israel: When I restore their fortunes in the land of Judah and in its cities, they shall again use this greeting: "May the Lord bless you, Tent of Justice, Holy Mountain!" [24]Judah and all its cities, the farmers and those who lead the flock shall dwell there together. [25]For I will slake the thirst of the faint; the appetite of all the weary I will satisfy. [26]At this I awoke and opened my eyes; my sleep was satisfying.

[27]See, days are coming—oracle of the Lord—when I will sow the house of Israel and the house of Judah with the seed of human beings and the seed of animals. [28]As I once watched over them to uproot and tear down, to demolish, to destroy, and to harm, so I will watch over them to build and to plant—oracle of the Lord. [29]In those days they shall no longer say,

"The parents ate unripe grapes,
   and the children's teeth are set
     on edge,"

[30]but all shall die because of their own iniquity: the teeth of anyone who eats unripe grapes shall be set on edge.

31:21-30 Summons to return home

Israel is called upon to begin the journey home (31:21-22). The time for hesitation and rebellion is past, for the Lord is creating a new thing. Only God is the subject of the verb "create" (*bārā'*) in the Old Testament; it is the same term that is used in the opening chapters of Genesis (Gen 1:1). The "new" thing that the Lord is about to do is thus placed on a par with the very act of creation at the beginning of time. It is difficult, however, to determine exactly what that "new" thing is, as the translation of the last phrase in verse 22 is uncertain. It may refer to a new kind of relationship between Israel (the woman) and the Lord (the man), but it may also simply be a reference to the embrace between a man and a woman that results in the conception of a child. The citing of this proverbial statement may then point to the repopulation of Israel in the future.

The next three oracles (31:23-26, 27-28, 29-30) refer to aspects of the restoration to the land. When the fortunes of the people are restored, the people will again refer to the Lord's blessing as a greeting; city folk, farmers, and shepherds, groups often in conflict will dwell in peace; and the Lord will renew the faint and weary (31:23-25). Verse 26 suggests that the content of this oracle was received in a pleasant dream presumably by Jeremiah. The next oracle announces the restoration of both people and animals to the land in language drawn from the call of Jeremiah (1:10). As

The New Covenant ³¹See, days are coming—oracle of the LORD—when I will make a new covenant with the house of Israel and the house of Judah. ³²It will not be like the covenant I made with their ancestors the day I took them by the hand to lead them out of the land of Egypt. They broke my covenant, though I was their master—oracle of the LORD. ³³But this is the covenant I will make with the house of Israel after those days—oracle of the LORD. I will place my law within them, and write it upon their hearts; I will be their God, and they shall be my people. ³⁴They will no longer teach their friends and relatives, "Know the LORD!" Everyone, from least to great-est, shall know me—oracle of the LORD—for I will forgive their iniquity and no longer remember their sin.

Certainty of God's Promise
³⁵Thus says the LORD,
Who gives the sun to light the day,
moon and stars to light the
night;
Who stirs up the sea so that its
waves roar,
whose name is LORD of hosts:
³⁶If ever this fixed order gives way
before me—oracle of the LORD—
Then would the offspring of Israel
cease
as a people before me forever.
³⁷Thus says the LORD:

---

the Lord "watched" over the word (1:12) to bring about judgment, so now God is "watching" over the word to bring salvation. The final oracle of this section includes a proverb that Jeremiah says will no longer apply. The proverb, "The parents ate unripe grapes, / and the children's teeth are set on edge" (31:29), has a fatalistic overtone, for it maintains every generation will suffer for the actions of the previous generation. That this proverb will no longer apply in the days to come is often interpreted as an introduction of individualistic judgment into Israel, but it is more likely that it simply means each generation will bear the consequences of its own actions.

31:31-34 The new covenant

The short oracle concerning the new covenant has had a considerable impact on the Dead Sea community, the New Testament (Luke 22:20; 1 Cor 11:25; 2 Cor 3:5-14; Heb 8:8-12; 10:16-17), and later Christian theology. It is tempting to read later theological development back into this passage, but here the focus will be on its meaning in its historical and literary context. Its immediate context is the announcement of the Lord's new salvific action on behalf of the people: God will bring them home from exile. This act of salvation is seen as a major event in Israel's history, an event as fundamental as the exodus, and it will issue in a new covenant. The repopulation of the land (31:27-28) and the rebuilding of Jerusalem (31:38-40) are part and parcel of the return from exile. Thus this new covenant is not spiritualized or universalized but is grounded in the Lord's actions on behalf of the people

If the heavens on high could be
measured,
or the foundations below the
earth be explored,
Then would I reject all the offspring
of Israel
because of all they have done—
oracle of the Lord.

Jerusalem Rebuilt. ³⁸See, days are coming—oracle of the Lord—when the city shall be rebuilt as the Lord's, from the Tower of Hananel to the Corner Gate. ³⁹A measuring line shall be stretched from there straight to the hill Gareb and then turn to Goah. ⁴⁰The whole valley of corpses and ashes, all the terraced slopes toward the Wadi Kidron, as far as the corner of the Horse Gate at the east, shall be holy to the Lord. Never again shall the city be uprooted or demolished.

at this time in their history and these actions will define their future. In spite of their unfaithfulness in the past, Israel's relationship to the Lord has never ceased. They are still "my people" and the Lord is "their God," but now they will be the Lord's people in a new way. The law remains, even in this new covenant, as an identifying characteristic of this people, but that law will no longer exist as an external reality; it will be "in the heart." The people will no longer need to be taught the law, as it will be a part of their being. Because the law is within, all will know the Lord. That "all know the Lord" renders obsolete distinctions between people: "Everyone, from least to greatest," will know the Lord (31:34). Furthermore, integral to this new covenant is that the Lord will forgive the iniquity of the people. Israel's history of sinfulness will be forgotten; it will be left in the past and play no role in the new covenant relationship between the Lord and the people. Knowledge of the Lord and forgiveness are constituent parts of the new covenant.

31:35-37 Certainty of God's promise

The focus of much of the book of Jeremiah is the Lord's actions in Israel's life as a nation, but now the prophet turns to nature to underscore the enduring character of the Lord's relationship to Israel. The Lord is identified as the creator and then, in two "if-then" sentences, impossible situations are imagined: the collapse of the fixed order of the world and measurability of the universe. Even if these impossibilities come to pass, never will Israel and its offspring cease to be the Lord's people. The faithfulness of the Lord and commitment to the people in spite of their sin provide a counterbalance to the many oracles of judgment throughout the book of Jeremiah.

31:38-40 Jerusalem rebuilt

The focus of the last verses of this chapter is the city of Jerusalem. It will be rebuilt and enlarged as the Lord's city, but no temple is mentioned.

32 Pledge of Restoration.

¹The word came to Jeremiah from the LORD in the tenth year of Zedekiah, king of Judah, the eighteenth year of Nebuchadnezzar. ²At that time the army of the king of Babylon was besieging Jerusalem, while Jeremiah the prophet was confined to the court of the guard, in the house of the king of Judah. ³Zedekiah, king of Judah, had confined him there, saying: "How dare you prophesy: Thus says the LORD: I am handing this city over to the king of Babylon that he may capture it. ⁴Zedekiah, king of Judah, shall not escape the hands of the Chaldeans: he shall indeed be handed over to the king of Babylon. He shall speak with him face to face and see him eye to eye. ⁵He shall take Zedekiah to Babylon. There he shall remain, until I attend to him—oracle of the LORD. If you fight against the Chaldeans, you cannot win!"

⁶Jeremiah said, This word came to me from the LORD: ⁷Hanamel, son of your uncle Shallum, will come to you with the offer: "Purchase my field in Anathoth, since you, as nearest relative, have the first right of purchase." ⁸And, just as the LORD had said, my cousin Hanamel came to me in the court of the guard and said, "Please purchase my field in Anathoth, in the territory of Benjamin; as nearest relative, you have the first right of possession—purchase it for yourself." Then I knew this was the word of the LORD. ⁹So I bought the field in Anathoth from my cousin Hanamel, weighing out for him the silver, seventeen shekels of silver.

¹⁰When I had written and sealed the deed, called witnesses and weighed out the silver on the scales, ¹¹I accepted the deed of purchase, both the sealed copy, containing title and conditions, and the open copy. ¹²I gave this deed of purchase to Baruch, son of Neriah, son of Mahseiah, in the presence of my cousin Hanamel and the witnesses who had signed the deed of purchase and before all the Judahites sitting around in the court of the guard.

¹³In their presence I gave Baruch this charge: ¹⁴Thus says the LORD of hosts,

---

Valleys and slopes previously contaminated by corpses and ashes will be rendered holy. Remarkably, an unconditional assurance is given that the city will never again be uprooted or demolished.

32:1-44 Pledge of restoration

Hope for the future continues to be the dominant theme as we move from poetic oracles of chapters 30–31 to prose narratives in chapters 32–33. The siege of Jerusalem has begun and Jeremiah has been confined in the "court of the guard," possibly as a result of his arrest for desertion when he attempted to leave Jerusalem to take care of family property in Benjamin (37:11-21). This confinement did allow for some freedom. The message of hope is concretized in a symbolic act that Jeremiah has been commanded by the Lord to perform: he is to purchase a field belonging to a relative. King Zedekiah raised the question of why Jeremiah prophesies as he does against the king and the city. Rather than answer the question directly,

the God of Israel: Take these deeds of purchase, both the sealed and the open deeds, and put them in an earthenware jar, so they can last a long time. ¹⁵For thus says the LORD of hosts, the God of Israel: They shall again purchase houses and fields and vineyards in this land.

¹⁶After I had given the deed of purchase to Baruch, son of Neriah, I prayed to the LORD: ¹⁷Ah, my Lord GOD! You made the heavens and the earth with your great power and your outstretched arm; nothing is too difficult for you. ¹⁸You continue your kindness through a thousand generations; but you repay the ancestors' guilt upon their children who follow them. Great and mighty God, whose name is LORD of hosts, ¹⁹great in counsel, mighty in deed, whose eyes are fixed on all the ways of mortals, giving to all according to their ways, according to the fruit of their deeds: ²⁰you performed signs and wonders in the land of Egypt and to this day, in Israel and among all peoples, you have made a name for yourself as on this day. ²¹You brought your people Israel out of the land of Egypt with signs and wonders, with a strong hand and an outstretched arm, and great terror. ²²And you gave them this land, as you had sworn to their ancestors to give them, a land flowing with milk and honey. ²³They went in and took possession of it, but they did not

listen to your voice. They did not live by your law; they did not do anything you commanded them to do. Then you made all this evil fall upon them. ²⁴See, the siegeworks have arrived at this city to capture it; the city is handed over to the Chaldeans who are attacking it, with sword, starvation, and disease. What you threatened has happened—you can see it for yourself. ²⁵Yet you told me, my Lord GOD: Purchase the field with silver and summon witnesses, when the city has already been handed over to the Chaldeans!

²⁶Then this word of the LORD came to Jeremiah: ²⁷I am the LORD, the God of all the living! Is anything too difficult for me? ²⁸Therefore the LORD says: I am handing over this city to the Chaldeans and to Nebuchadnezzar, king of Babylon, and he shall capture it. ²⁹The Chaldeans who are attacking this city shall go in and set the city on fire, burning it and the houses, on whose roofs incense was burned to Baal and libations were poured out to other gods in order to provoke me. ³⁰From their youth the Israelites and the Judahites have been doing only what is evil in my eyes; the Israelites have been provoking me with the works of their hands—oracle of the LORD. ³¹This city has so stirred my anger and wrath, from the day it was built to this day, that I must put it out of my

---

Jeremiah is commanded by the Lord to purchase the field in Anathoth, his hometown, and the response to Zedekiah's question comes later in the Lord's response to Jeremiah's prayer (32:26-44): Jeremiah's message of judgment is the Lord's response to the sinfulness of the people. The significance of Jeremiah's purchase is stipulated in verse 15. What Jeremiah has done testifies to a future beyond the time of destruction when life will return to normal and Israel will once again possess the land.

sight, ³²for all the evil the Israelites and Judahites have done to provoke me—they, their kings, their princes, their priests, and their prophets, the people of Judah and the inhabitants of Jerusalem. ³³They turned their backs to me, not their faces; though I taught them persistently, they would not listen or accept correction. ³⁴Instead they set up their abominations in the house which bears my name in order to defile it. ³⁵They built high places to Baal in the Valley of Ben-hinnom to sacrifice their sons and daughters to Molech; I never commanded them to do this, nor did it even enter my mind that they would practice this abomination, so as to bring sin upon Judah.

³⁶Now, therefore, thus says the Lord, the God of Israel, concerning this city, which you say is being handed over to the king of Babylon by means of the sword, starvation, and disease: ³⁷See, I am gathering them from all the lands to which I drove them in my rising fury and great anger; I will bring them back to this place and settle them here in safety. ³⁸They shall be my people, and I will be their God. ³⁹I will give them one heart and one way, that they may fear me always, for their own good and the good of their children after them. ⁴⁰With them I will make an everlasting covenant, never to cease doing good to them; I will put fear of me in their hearts so that they never turn away from me. ⁴¹I will take delight in doing good to them: I will plant them firmly in this land, with all my heart and soul.

⁴²For thus says the Lord: Just as I have brought upon this people all this great evil, so I will bring upon them all the good I have promised them. ⁴³Fields shall be purchased in this land, about which you say, "It is a wasteland, without human beings or animals, handed over to the Chaldeans." ⁴⁴They will purchase fields with silver, write up deeds, seal them, and have them witnessed in the land of Benjamin, in the neighborhood of Jerusalem, in the cities of Judah and of the hill country, in the cities of the Shephelah and the Negeb, when I restore their fortunes—oracle of the Lord.

Jeremiah lifts his voice in prayer recalling the Lord's wondrous deeds in creation and exodus, and God's enduring love. Jeremiah acknowledges that now the Lord has brought judgment against the people. He wonders if the hope for the future symbolized by the purchase of the field has any meaning when the city has already been handed over to the Babylonians (32:16-25). The Lord's answer balances the actions as judge against the people for their infidelity with the refusal to completely abandon the people. The Lord's relationship with Israel will continue, but now that relationship is defined as an everlasting covenant realized in the return of Israel from exile and their restoration in the land (32:26-44). The message of hope symbolized by the purchase of a field is given vivid expression by a God who envisions a future in which God delights in the people and never ceases doing good for them.

33 **Restoration of Jerusalem.** [1]The word of the LORD came to Jeremiah a second time while he was still confined in the court of the guard: [2]Thus says the LORD who made the earth, giving it shape and stability, LORD is his name: [3]Call to me, and I will answer you; I will tell you great things beyond the reach of your knowledge. [4]Thus says the LORD, the God of Israel, concerning the houses of this city and the houses of the kings of Judah, which are being torn down because of the siegeworks and the sword: [5]men come to battle the Chaldeans, and to fill these houses with the corpses of those whom I have struck down in my raging anger, when I hid my face from this city because of all their wickedness.

[6]Look! I am bringing the city recovery and healing; I will heal them and reveal to them an abundance of lasting peace. [7]I will restore the fortunes of Judah and Israel, and rebuild them as they were in the beginning. [8]I will purify them of all the guilt they incurred by sinning against me; I will forgive all their offenses by which they sinned and rebelled against me. [9]Then this city shall become joy for me, a name of praise and pride, before all the nations of the earth, as they hear of all the good I am doing for them. They shall fear and tremble because of all the prosperity I give it.

[10]Thus says the LORD: In this place, about which you say: "It is a waste without people or animals!" and in the cities of Judah, in the streets of Jerusalem now deserted, without people, without inhabitant, without animal, there shall yet be heard [11]the song of joy, the song of gladness, the song of the bridegroom, the song of the bride, the song of those bringing thank offerings to the house of the LORD: "Give thanks to the LORD of hosts, for the LORD is good; God's love

33:1-26 Restoration of Jerusalem

These oracles from Jeremiah are linked to the previous chapter, not only by being set in the same historical context, but they also carry forward the same themes of restoration and renewal while presenting them in greater detail. Verses 1-13 are filled with words of promise for the city and its people. The future will reverse the punishment that has decimated the land. There is a piling up of verbs referring to the Lord's actions: "heal," "reveal . . . lasting peace," "restore," "rebuild," "purify," "forgive" (33:6-8)—all images pointing to a glorious restoration. As before, notions of the Lord both as creator (33:2) and savior (33:6ff.) are brought together: the one who creates is the one who saves. This restoration, teeming with abundance, is a source of joy to the Lord and it is an expression of enduring love for the people. The exuberant rejoicing upon restoration is conveyed again by the piling up of songs: "of joy," "of gladness," "of the bridegroom," "of the bride," and "of those bringing thank offerings" (33:11). The second half of the chapter (33:14-26) shifts the focus of promise to the royal and priestly leaders of the land and its people. This section is missing from the LXX

endures forever." For I will restore the fortunes of this land as they were in the beginning, says the LORD.

¹²Thus says the LORD of hosts: In this place, now a waste, without people or animals, and in all its cities there shall again be sheepfolds for the shepherds to rest their flocks. ¹³In the cities of the hill country, of the Shephelah and the Negeb, in the land of Benjamin and the neighborhood of Jerusalem, and in the cities of Judah, flocks will again pass under the hands of the one who counts them, says the LORD.

¹⁴The days are coming—oracle of the LORD—when I will fulfill the promise I made to the house of Israel and the house of Judah. ¹⁵In those days, at that time, I will make a just shoot spring up for David; he shall do what is right and just in the land. ¹⁶In those days Judah shall be saved and Jerusalem shall dwell safely; this is the name they shall call her: "The LORD our justice." ¹⁷For thus says the LORD: David shall never lack a successor on the throne of the house of Israel, ¹⁸nor shall the priests of Levi ever be lacking before me, to sacrifice burnt offerings, to burn cereal offerings, and to make sacrifices.

¹⁹This word of the LORD also came to Jeremiah: ²⁰Thus says the LORD: If you can break my covenant with day and my covenant with night so that day and night no longer appear in their proper time, ²¹only then can my covenant with my servant David be broken, so that he will not have a descendant to act as king upon his throne, and my covenant with the priests of Levi who minister to me. ²²Just as the host of heaven cannot be numbered and the sands of the sea cannot be counted, so I will multiply the descendants of David my servant and the Levites who minister to me.

²³This word of the LORD came to Jeremiah: ²⁴Have you not noticed what these people are saying: "The LORD has rejected the two tribes he had chosen"? They hold my people in contempt as if it were no longer a nation in their eyes. ²⁵Thus says the LORD: If I have no covenant with day and night, if I did not establish statutes for heaven and earth, ²⁶then I will also reject the descendants of Jacob and of David my servant, no

---

and so may represent a later addition to the book of Jeremiah. It begins with the promise of a just and righteous king from the line of David, a passage (33:15-16) that is virtually identical to 23:5-6, but this restatement includes the promise that the Davidic dynasty will never end and the Levitical priests will always stand before the Lord, offering sacrifices. The enduring nature of dynasty and priesthood is grounded in the Lord's enduring covenant with day and night. This may be a reference to the covenant with Noah wherein the Lord guaranteed the order of the universe (Gen 8:21-22; 9:8-17). The passage draws to a close, connecting the permanence of the order of creation with the permanence of the relationship between the Lord and the people. In seeing these promises become reality, the nations who held Israel in contempt will now witness to the Lord's enduring love and mercy.

longer selecting from his descendants rulers for the offspring of Abraham, Isaac, and Jacob. Yes, I will restore their fortunes and show them mercy.

34 **Fate of Zedekiah.** ¹The word which came to Jeremiah from the LORD while Nebuchadnezzar, king of Babylon, and all his army and all the earth's kingdoms under his rule, and all the peoples were attacking Jerusalem and all her cities: ²Thus says the LORD, the God of Israel: Go to Zedekiah, king of Judah, and tell him: Thus says the LORD: I am handing this city over to the king of Babylon; he will burn it with fire. ³You yourself shall not escape his hand; rather you will be captured and fall into his hand. You shall see the king of Babylon eye to eye and speak to him face to face. Then you shall go to Babylon.

⁴Just hear the word of the LORD, Zedekiah, king of Judah! Then, says the LORD concerning you, you shall not die by the sword. ⁵You shall die in peace, and they will burn spices for you as they did for your ancestors, the earlier kings who preceded you, and they shall make lament over you, "Alas, Lord." I myself make this promise—oracle of the LORD.

⁶Jeremiah the prophet told all these things to Zedekiah, king of Judah, in Jerusalem, ⁷while the army of the king of Babylon was attacking Jerusalem and the remaining cities of Judah, Lachish, and Azekah. Only these fortified cities were left standing out of all the cities of Judah!

The Pact Broken. ⁸This is the word that came to Jeremiah from the LORD after King Zedekiah had made a covenant with all the people in Jerusalem to proclaim freedom: ⁹Everyone must free their Hebrew slaves, male and female, so that no one should hold another Judahite in servitude. ¹⁰All the princes and the people who entered this covenant agreed to set free their slaves, their male and female servants, so that they should no longer be in servitude. But even though they agreed and freed them, ¹¹afterward they took back their male and female servants whom they had set free and again forced them into servitude.

¹²Then this word of the LORD came to Jeremiah: ¹³Thus says the LORD, the God of Israel: I myself made a covenant with your ancestors the day I brought them out of the land of Egypt, out of the house

---

34:1-7 Fate of Zedekiah

In the midst of oracles of salvation there is a reiteration of the judgment against King Zedekiah similar to that found in 32:1-5. It is, however, difficult to reconcile verses 2-3, a prophecy of the capture and exile of Zedekiah, with the more positive note regarding his death and burial in verses 4-5. Zedekiah was captured, blinded, exiled, and died in prison (52:9-11; 2 Kgs 25:1-7). The details of the prophecy should not be pressed too far, for in general it came to pass.

34:8-22 The pact broken

This story of the unfaithfulness of the citizens of Jerusalem followed by an indictment and judgment stands in contrast to the story in chapter 35

of slavery: [14]Every seventh year each of you must set free all Hebrews who have sold themselves to you; six years they shall serve you, but then you shall let them go free. Your ancestors, however, did not listen to me or obey me. [15]As for you, today you repented and did what is right in my eyes by proclaiming freedom for your neighbor and making a covenant before me in the house which bears my name. [16]But then you again profaned my name by taking back your male and female slaves whom you had just set free for life; you forced them to become your slaves again. [17]Therefore, thus says the LORD: You for your part did not obey me by proclaiming freedom for your families and neighbors. So I now proclaim freedom for you—oracle of the LORD—for the sword, starvation, and disease. I will make you an object of horror to all the kingdoms of the earth. [18]Those who violated my covenant and did not observe the terms of the covenant they made in my presence—I will make them like the calf which they cut in two so they could pass between its parts— [19]the princes of Judah and of Jerusalem, the court officials, the priests, and all the people of the land, who passed between the parts of the calf. [20]These I will hand over to their enemies, to those who seek their lives: their corpses shall become food for the birds of the air and the beasts of the field.

[21]Zedekiah, king of Judah, and his princes, I will hand also over to their enemies, to those who seek their lives, to the army of the king of Babylon which is now withdrawing from you. [22]I am giving the command—oracle of the LORD—to bring them back to this city.

---

concerning the faithfulness of the Rechabites who receive a promise that their line will never end. In the oracles of Jeremiah the people have been frequently condemned for their unfaithfulness and this story functions as a concrete example of their fickle nature. The people bind themselves in a covenant with King Zedekiah to release their slaves, only to take them back into slavery later. Breaking this covenant is symptomatic of breaking the Lord's covenant. It may be that "freeing the slaves" was a belated attempt by the people to obey the laws of the Lord in the hopes that by their action they could stave off the destruction of the city. However, when the Babylonians seemed to have abandoned their siege of Jerusalem, the people were no longer motivated to keep the law and took back their slaves. There is no exact parallel to the freeing of all slaves in the law as requested by the king, but Deuteronomy 15:1-11 speaks of the release of slaves who have been in bondage for six years. It may be that this law had not been kept and King Zedekiah endorses freeing all slaves as a way to "catch up" on the law. The Lord affirms that the people did what was right in freeing their slaves (34:15), but their short-lived obedience betrays the lack of fidelity that has been characteristic of Israel throughout its history. The oracle brings in a reference to exodus and covenant (34:13-14). In the exodus the

They shall attack and capture it, and burn it with fire; the cities of Judah I will turn into a waste, where no one dwells.

35 The Faithful Rechabites.

¹The word that came to Jeremiah from the LORD in the days of Jehoiakim, son of Josiah, king of Judah: ²Go to the house of the Rechabites, speak to them, and bring them to the house of the LORD, to one of the rooms there, and give them wine to drink. ³So I took Jaazaniah, son of Jeremiah, son of Habazziniah, his brothers and all his sons—the whole house of the Rechabites— ⁴and I brought them to the house of the LORD, to the room of the sons of Hanan, son of Igdaliah, the man of God, next to the room of the princes above the room of Maaseiah, son of Shallum, the guard at the entrance. ⁵I set before the Rechabites bowls full of wine, and cups, and said to them, "Drink some wine."

⁶"We do not drink wine," they said to me; "Jonadab, Rechab's son, our father, commanded us, 'Neither you nor your children shall ever drink wine. ⁷Build no house and sow no seed; do not plant vineyards or own any. You must dwell in tents all your lives, so that you may live long on the land where you live as resident aliens.' ⁸We have obeyed Jonadab, Rechab's son, our father, in everything that he commanded us: not drinking wine as long as we live—neither we nor our wives nor our sons nor our daughters; ⁹not building houses to live in; not owning vineyards or fields or crops. ¹⁰We live in tents, doing everything our father Jonadab commanded us. ¹¹But when Nebuchadnezzar, king of Babylon, invaded this land, we said, 'Come, let us go into Jerusalem to escape the army of the Chaldeans and the army of the Arameans.' That is why we are now living in Jerusalem."

¹²Then the word of the LORD came to Jeremiah: ¹³Thus says the LORD of hosts, the God of Israel: Go, say to the people

---

Lord brings freedom to those who were enslaved; in the covenant the Lord is bound in faithful love (*hesed*) to Israel and Israel binds itself to the Lord in love and obedience. Against this history the true horror of the people's actions stands out: they enslave others and in doing so profane the name of the Lord (34:16), a God who is known for the liberation of slaves. The judgment against them fits their crime. They will not "release" their slaves, so they will be "released" to the "sword, starvation, and disease" (34:17); they "passed over" the covenant, so they will be cut apart as the animal they "passed through" was cut apart. The reference here is to part of the ritual that ratified the covenant (Gen 15:7-21). The judgment against the people is that the Babylonian army will return and lay siege again to the city, but this time the army will not leave until the city is destroyed.

35:1-19 The faithful Rechabites

The previous chapters were set in the time of King Zedekiah, but this chapter brings us back ten years earlier to the reign of King Jehoiakim.

of Judah and to the inhabitants of Jerusalem: Will you not take correction and obey my words?—oracle of the LORD. ¹⁴The words of Jonadab, Rechab's son, by which he commanded his children not to drink wine, have been upheld: to this day they have not drunk wine; they obeyed their ancestor's command. I, however, have spoken to you time and again. But you did not obey me! ¹⁵Time and again I sent you all my servants the prophets, saying: Turn away, each of you, from your evil way and reform your actions! Do not follow other gods to serve them that you may remain in the land which I gave you and your ancestors. But you did not pay attention. You did not obey me. ¹⁶Yes, the children of Jonadab, Rechab's son, upheld the command which their father laid on them. But this people has not obeyed me! ¹⁷Now, therefore, says the LORD God of hosts, the God of Israel: I will soon bring upon Judah and all the inhabitants of Jerusalem every evil with which I threatened them because I spoke but they did not obey, I called but they did not answer.

¹⁸But to the house of the Rechabites Jeremiah said: Thus says the LORD of hosts, the God of Israel: Since you have obeyed the command of Jonadab, your father, kept all his commands and done everything he commanded you, ¹⁹therefore, thus says the LORD of hosts, the God of Israel: Never shall there fail to be a descendant of Jonadab, Rechab's son, standing in my presence.

Though out of chronological sequence, Jeremiah's interaction with the Rechabites is probably placed here to draw a contrast between the unfaithfulness of the citizens of Jerusalem to the Lord's laws and the faithfulness of the Rechabites to the customs established by their founder, Jehonadab. Our knowledge of the Rechabites rests upon only a few passages of the Old Testament: 2 Kings 10:15-17; Jeremiah 35; 1 Chronicles 2:55; and possibly 1 Chronicles 4:11-12 if one accepts the LXX reading of Rechab for Recah of the Hebrew version. A son of Rechab, Jehonadab, called Jonadab in the book of Jeremiah, is presented as a supporter of the rebellion of Jehu, commander of the Israelite army (2 Kgs 10:15-17). Jehu is characterized as a religious zealot; Jehonadab rides in Jehu's chariot in support of Jehu who in a gruesome display of his "zeal for the Lord" has Baal worshipers burned to death in the course of ridding Israel of Baal worship (2 Kgs 10:15-28). Most of our information regarding the Rechabites comes from chapter 35 of the book of Jeremiah. Jonadab prohibited his community from drinking wine, building homes to live in, and owning vineyards or fields or crops. It has been suggested that this lifestyle represents a nomadic ideal whose adherents refused to adopt customs associated with settling in the land, but there is no evidence that such an ideal ever existed. The refusal of the Rechabites to drink wine, live in houses, and engage in agricultural pursuits fits with the lifestyle of ancient metallurgists. Their association with the

VII. Jeremiah and the Fall of Jerusalem

36 **Baruch, the Scribe of Jeremiah.** ¹In the fourth year of Jehoiakim, son of Josiah, king of Judah, this word came to Jeremiah from the LORD: ²Take a scroll and write on it all the words I have spoken to you about Israel, Judah, and all the nations, from the day I first spoke to you, from the days of Josiah, until today. ³Perhaps, if the house of Judah hears all the evil I have in mind to do to them, so that all of them turn from their evil way, then I can forgive their wickedness and their sin. ⁴So Jeremiah called Baruch, son of Neriah, and he wrote down on a scroll what Jeremiah said, all the words which the LORD had spoken to him. ⁵Then Jeremiah commanded Baruch: "I cannot enter the house of the LORD; I am barred from it. ⁶So you yourself must go. On a fast day in the hearing of the people in the LORD's house, read the words of the LORD from the scroll you wrote at my dictation; read them also to all the people of Judah who come up from their cities. ⁷Perhaps they will present their supplication before the LORD and will all turn back from their evil way; for great is the anger and wrath with which the LORD has threatened this people."

⁸Baruch, son of Neriah, did everything Jeremiah the prophet commanded; from the scroll he read the LORD's words in the LORD's house. ⁹In the ninth month,

---

Kenites (1 Chr 2:55), a tribe whose eponymous ancestor was Cain and whose descendants are noted for working with metal (Gen 4:22), suggests that their lifestyle grew out of the demands of their profession and not out of a nomadic ideal.

Jeremiah is commanded by the Lord to test the resolve of the Rechabites by inviting them to the temple and offering them wine. Their refusal to violate the commands given by their founder becomes an example of fidelity over against the infidelity of Israel. The Rechabites listen/obey (35:8, 10, 14), but Jeremiah's audience does not listen/obey (35:13, 14, 15, 16, 17) in spite of the many warnings they had received through the prophets. A final contrast between the citizens of Judah and Jerusalem and the Rechabites is drawn at the end of the chapter. Judah and Jerusalem stand under judgment, but the Rechabites will survive the destruction of the country. In language reminiscent of the promise given to David and the priestly families, the Rechabites will not "fail [to have] a descendant" (35:19); for all time they will stand in the presence of the Lord.

JEREMIAH AND THE FALL OF JERUSALEM

Jeremiah 36:1–45:5

These chapters continue with narratives reflecting upon the life of Jeremiah, but they focus on the suffering that Jeremiah endured as a prophet.

in the fifth year of Jehoiakim, son of Josiah, king of Judah, all the people of Jerusalem and all those who came from Judah's cities to Jerusalem proclaimed a fast before the LORD. [10]So Baruch read the words of Jeremiah from the scroll in the room of Gemariah, son of the scribe Shaphan, in the upper court of the LORD's house, at the entrance of the New Temple Gate, in the hearing of all the people.

[11]Now Micaiah, son of Gemariah, son of Shaphan, heard all the words of the LORD read from the scroll. [12]So he went down to the house of the king, into the scribe's chamber, where the princes were meeting in session: Elishama, the scribe; Delaiah, son of Shemaiah; Elnathan, son of Achbor; Gemariah, son of Shaphan; Zedekiah, son of Hananiah; and the other princes. [13]Micaiah reported to them all that he had heard Baruch read from his scroll in the hearing of the people. [14]The princes immediately sent Jehudi, son of Nethaniah, son of Shelemiah, son of Cushi, to Baruch with the order: "The scroll you read in the hearing of the people—bring it with you and come." Scroll in hand, Baruch, son of Neriah, went to them. [15]"Sit down," they said to him, "and read it in our hearing." Baruch read it in their hearing, [16]and when they had heard all its words, they turned to each other in alarm and said to Baruch, "We have to tell the king all these things." [17]Then they asked Baruch: "Tell us, please, how did you come to write down all these words? Was it at his dictation?" [18]"Yes, he would dictate all these words to me," Baruch answered them, "while I wrote them down with ink in the scroll." [19]The princes said to Baruch, "Go into hiding, you and Jeremiah; do not let anyone know where you are."

[20]They went in to the king, into the courtyard; they had deposited the scroll in the room of Elishama the scribe. When they told the king everything that had happened, [21]the king sent Jehudi to get the scroll. Jehudi brought it from the room of Elishama the scribe, and read it to the king and to all the princes who were attending the king. [22]Now the king was sitting in his winter house, since it was the ninth month, and a fire was burning in the brazier before him. [23]Each time Jehudi finished reading three or four columns, he would cut off the piece with a scribe's knife and throw it into the fire in the brazier, until the entire scroll was consumed in the fire in the brazier. [24]As they were listening to all

---

Elements of hope come to the fore (39:15-18; 40:7-12; 42:9-12; 45:5), but they are overshadowed by the imprisonment of Jeremiah and an attempt on his life. Traditionally, Baruch has been identified as the author of these chapters, but there is no evidence to support or refute this claim.

36:1-32 Baruch, the scribe of Jeremiah

The dictation of Jeremiah's oracles to Baruch is set in 605 B.C., when Nebuchadnezzar defeated Egypt at Carchemish. The threat that the Babylonian army posed to Judah may be behind the proclamation of a fast in verse 9, but the focus of the chapter is on the response of King Jehoiakim

these words the king and all his officials did not become alarmed, nor did they tear their garments. ²⁵And though Elnathan, Delaiah, and Gemariah urged the king not to burn the scroll, he would not listen to them. ²⁶He commanded Jerahmeel, a royal prince, and Seraiah, son of Azriel, and Shelemiah, son of Abdeel, to arrest Baruch, the scribe, and Jeremiah the prophet. But the LORD had hidden them away.

²⁷The word of the LORD came to Jeremiah, after the king burned the scroll and the words Jeremiah had dictated to Baruch: ²⁸Take another scroll, and write on it all the words in the first scroll, which Jehoiakim, king of Judah, burned. ²⁹And against Jehoiakim, king of Judah, say this: Thus says the LORD: You are the one who burned that scroll, saying,

"Why did you write on it: Babylon's king shall surely come and ravage this land, emptying it of every living thing"? ³⁰The LORD now says of Jehoiakim, king of Judah: No descendant of his shall sit on David's throne; his corpse shall be thrown out, exposed to heat by day, frost by night. ³¹I will punish him and his descendants and his officials for their wickedness; upon them, the inhabitants of Jerusalem, and the people of Judah I will bring all the evil threats to which they did not listen.

³²Then Jeremiah took another scroll and gave it to his scribe, Baruch, son of Neriah, who wrote on it at Jeremiah's dictation all the words contained in the scroll which Jehoiakim, king of Judah, had burned in the fire, adding many words like them.

---

to the reading of the scroll that Jeremiah had dictated to Baruch and commanded him to read to the people in the temple. Upon hearing the words of the scroll, court officials insist that the scroll be brought before the king, but they also advise Baruch and Jeremiah to go into hiding. King Jehoiakim destroyed the scroll by burning pieces of it as it was read to him. His rejection of Jeremiah's message is given dramatic representation and there is a note of finality in his burning of the scroll. The hope that the people would repent (36:3, 7) is closed off by the actions of the king. Jeremiah is commanded to dictate another scroll, perhaps signifying that the king's actions cannot silence the word of the Lord.

Of particular interest in this chapter are the insights it gives us into the role of scribes, the production of scrolls, and the development of prophetic books. There is considerable debate regarding the relationship of the second scroll that Jeremiah dictated and the book of Jeremiah itself. Many scholars hold that chapters 1–25 contain the contents of the second scroll in some form.

37:1-21 Jeremiah in the dungeon

This episode is the first of three encounters between Jeremiah and King Zedekiah after the Babylonian siege of Jerusalem had begun in 587 B.C.

37 **Jeremiah in the Dungeon.** ¹Zedekiah, son of Josiah, became king, succeeding Coniah, son of Jehoiakim; Nebuchadnezzar, king of Babylon, appointed him king over the land of Judah. ²Neither he, nor his officials, nor the people of the land would listen to the words which the LORD spoke through Jeremiah the prophet. ³Yet King Zedekiah sent Jehucal, son of Shelemiah, and Zephaniah, son of Maaseiah the priest, to Jeremiah the prophet with this request: "Please appeal to the LORD, our God, for us." ⁴At this time Jeremiah still came and went freely among the people; he had not yet been put into prison. ⁵Meanwhile, Pharaoh's army had set out from Egypt, and when the Chaldeans who were besieging Jerusalem heard this report, they withdrew from the city.

⁶Then the word of the LORD came to Jeremiah the prophet: ⁷Thus says the LORD, the God of Israel: Thus you must say to the king of Judah who sent you to consult me: Listen! Pharaoh's army, which has set out to help you, will return to Egypt, its own land. ⁸The Chaldeans shall return and attack this city; they shall capture it and destroy it by fire.

⁹Thus says the LORD: Do not deceive yourselves, saying: "The Chaldeans are surely leaving us forever." They are not! ¹⁰Even if you could defeat the whole Chaldean army that is now attacking you, and only the wounded remained, each in his tent, these would rise up and destroy the city with fire.

¹¹Now when the Chaldean army withdrew from Jerusalem because of the army of Pharaoh, ¹²Jeremiah set out from Jerusalem to go to the territory of Benjamin, to receive his share of property among the people. ¹³But at the Gate of Benjamin, the captain of the guard, by the name of Irijah, son of Shelemiah, son of Hananiah, arrested Jeremiah the prophet, saying, "You are deserting to the Chaldeans!" ¹⁴"That is a lie!" Jeremiah answered, "I am not deserting to the Chaldeans." Without listening to him, Irijah kept Jeremiah in custody and brought him to the princes.

¹⁵The princes were enraged at Jeremiah and had Jeremiah beaten and imprisoned in the house of Jonathan the scribe, for they were using it as a jail. ¹⁶And so Jeremiah went into a room in the dungeon, where he remained many days.

¹⁷Then King Zedekiah had him brought to his palace, and he asked him secretly, "Is there any word from the LORD?" "There is!" Jeremiah answered: "You shall be handed over to the king of Babylon." ¹⁸Jeremiah then asked King Zedekiah: "How have I wronged you or your officials or this people, that you should put me in prison? ¹⁹Where are your own prophets who prophesied for you, saying: 'The King of Babylon will

---

When the Egyptian army set out, possibly to come to the aid of Jerusalem, the Babylonian army withdrew from its assault on Jerusalem to engage the Egyptian army. It is not clear why King Zedekiah appeals to Jeremiah for prayers, for the king does not listen to Jeremiah, nor indeed does anyone else in Jerusalem (37:2). Jeremiah's response to the king underscores that the lull in the siege is not a sign of hope. The Babylonian army will return

not attack you or this land'? ²⁰Please hear me, my lord king! Grant my petition: do not send me back into the house of Jonathan the scribe, or I shall die there."

²¹So King Zedekiah ordered that Jeremiah be confined in the court of the guard and given a ration of bread every day from the bakers' street until all the bread in the city was eaten up. Thus Jeremiah remained in the court of the guard.

38 Jeremiah in the Muddy Cistern.
¹Shephatiah, son of Mattan, Gedaliah, son of Pashhur, Jucal, son of Shelemiah, and Pashhur, son of Malchiah, heard the words Jeremiah was speaking to all the people: ²Thus says the LORD: Those who remain in this city shall die by means of the sword, starvation, and disease; but those who go out to the Chaldeans shall live. Their lives shall be spared them as spoils of war that they may live. ³Thus says the LORD: This city shall certainly be handed over to the army of the king of Babylon; he shall capture it.

⁴Then the princes said to the king, "This man ought to be put to death. He is weakening the resolve of the soldiers left in this city and of all the people, by saying such things to them; he is not seeking the welfare of our people, but their ruin." ⁵King Zedekiah answered: "He is in your hands," for the king could do nothing with them. ⁶And so they took Jeremiah and threw him into the cistern of Prince Malchiah, in the court of the guard, letting him down by rope. There was no water in the cistern, only mud, and Jeremiah sank down into the mud.

⁷Now Ebed-melech, an Ethiopian, a court official in the king's house, heard that they had put Jeremiah in the cistern. The king happened to be sitting at the Gate of Benjamin, ⁸and Ebed-melech went there from the house of the king and said to him, ⁹"My lord king, these men have done wrong in all their treatment of Jeremiah the prophet, throwing him into the cistern. He will starve to death on the spot, for there is no more bread in the city." ¹⁰Then the king ordered

and destroy the city, even if only wounded soldiers are all that remain of their army. During the lull in fighting Jeremiah leaves the city to deal with family property in Benjamin and is arrested for treason, beaten, and imprisoned. King Zedekiah secretly sent for Jeremiah, requesting a word from the Lord. The king may have been hoping for a positive message, but Jeremiah reiterates the Lord's earlier judgment against the city. Jeremiah asks the king not to be sent back to where he was held in custody and the king grants his request. Jeremiah will remain in the court of the guard until the Babylonians take the city.

38:1-28 Jeremiah in the muddy cistern
Even though confined, Jeremiah finds an audience for his announcement of judgment against the city of Jerusalem. He insists that only those who leave the city and surrender to the Babylonians will be spared; those who remain in the city will die. Because Jeremiah's message of doom is undermining the

Ebed-melech the Ethiopian: "Take three men with you, and get Jeremiah the prophet out of the cistern before he dies." ¹¹Ebed-melech took the men with him, and went first to the linen closet in the house of the king. He took some old, tattered rags and lowered them by rope to Jeremiah in the cistern. ¹²Then he said to Jeremiah, "Put these old, tattered rags between your armpits and the ropes." Jeremiah did so, ¹³and they pulled him up by rope out of the cistern. But Jeremiah remained in the court of the guard.

¹⁴King Zedekiah summoned Jeremiah the prophet to meet him at the third entrance of the house of the LORD. "I have a question to ask you," the king said to Jeremiah. "Do not hide anything from me." ¹⁵Jeremiah answered Zedekiah: "If I tell you anything, will you not have me put to death? If I counsel you, you will not listen to me!" ¹⁶But King Zedekiah swore to Jeremiah secretly: "As the LORD lives who gave us our lives, I will not kill you, nor will I hand you over to those men who seek your life."

¹⁷Jeremiah then said to Zedekiah: "Thus says the LORD God of hosts, the God of Israel: If you will only surrender to the princes of Babylon's king, you shall save your life; this city shall not be destroyed by fire, and you and your household shall live. ¹⁸But if you do not surrender to the princes of Babylon's king, this city shall fall into the hand of the Chaldeans, who shall destroy it by fire, and you shall not escape their hand."

¹⁹King Zedekiah said to Jeremiah, "I am afraid of the Judahites who have deserted to the Chaldeans; I could be handed over to them, and they will mistreat me." ²⁰"You will not be handed over to them," Jeremiah answered. "I beg you! Please listen to the voice of the LORD regarding what I tell you so that it may go well with you and your life be spared. ²¹But if you refuse to surrender, this is what the LORD has shown: ²²I see all the women who remain in the house of Judah's king being brought out to the princes of Babylon's king, and they are crying:

'They betrayed you, outdid you,
   your good friends!
Now that your feet are sunk in
   mud,
   they slink away.'

²³All your wives and children shall be brought out to the Chaldeans, and you shall not escape their hands; you shall be handed over to the king of Babylon, and this city shall be destroyed by fire."

²⁴Then Zedekiah said to Jeremiah, "Let no one know about this conversation, or you shall die. ²⁵If the princes should hear I spoke with you and if they should come and ask you, 'Tell us what you said to the king; do not hide it from us, or we will kill you,' or, 'What did the

---

resolve of Judah's army, the princes of Judah demand Jeremiah's execution. King Zedekiah hands Jeremiah over to them and they throw Jeremiah into an empty cistern, presumably to starve him to death. The indecisiveness of King Zedekiah is underscored by his capitulation to their demand only to be persuaded by Ebed-melech, an Ethiopian who was a royal official or servant

king say to you?' ²⁶then give them this answer: 'I petitioned the king not to send me back to Jonathan's house lest I die there.'" ²⁷When all the princes came to Jeremiah and questioned him, he answered them with the very words the king had commanded. They said no more to him, for nothing had been overheard of the conversation. ²⁸Thus Jeremiah stayed in the court of the guard until the day Jerusalem was taken.

39 **The Capture of Jerusalem.** When Jerusalem was taken, ¹in the ninth year of Zedekiah, king of Judah, in the tenth month, Nebuchadnezzar, king of Babylon, and all his army marched against Jerusalem and placed it under siege. ²In the eleventh year of Zedekiah, on the ninth day of the fourth month, the city wall was breached. ³All the princes of the king of Babylon came and took their seats at the middle gate: Nergal-sharezer of Simmagir, a chief officer; Nebushazban, a high dignitary; and all the rest of the princes of the king of Babylon. ⁴When Zedekiah, king of Judah, and all his warriors saw this, they fled, leaving the city at night by way of the king's garden, through a gate between the two walls. He went in the direction of the Arabah, ⁵but the Chaldean army pursued them; they caught up with Zedekiah in the wilderness near Jericho and took him prisoner. They brought him to Nebuchadnezzar, king of Babylon, in Riblah, in the land of

to the king, to have Jeremiah rescued and returned to the court of the guard. King Zedekiah again meets Jeremiah secretly, and again Jeremiah reiterates his message that the only way the city and its people will be spared is if they surrender to the Babylonians. This message applies to the king and his family as well. The weakness of King Zedekiah is apparent in his fear of what will happen to him if he surrenders and in his fear of what the princes of Judah will do if they find out about his meeting with Jeremiah. The princes do find out, but Jeremiah lies to them as he had been advised by the king. It cannot be denied that Jeremiah lies, but given the situation in which he found himself, it is understandable. He opted to protect both the king and himself.

39:1-10 The capture of Jerusalem

The harsh judgment repeatedly announced by Jeremiah comes to pass with the capture and destruction of the city of Jerusalem, the arrest of King Zedekiah, the execution of his sons and other Judean nobles, and the blinding and exile of King Zedekiah. That verses 4-13 of this chapter are not found in the LXX suggests that this brief history of the last days of Jerusalem was incorporated into the book of Jeremiah. It has been drawn from 52:4-16 and its purpose seems to be not only to confirm the validity of Jeremiah's prophetic word but also to provide the context for the stories that follow.

Hamath, and he pronounced sentence upon him. ⁶The king of Babylon executed the sons of Zedekiah at Riblah before his very eyes; the king of Babylon also executed all the nobles of Judah. ⁷He then blinded Zedekiah and bound him in chains to bring him to Babylon.

⁸The Chaldeans set fire to the king's house and the houses of the people and tore down the walls of Jerusalem. ⁹Nebuzaradan, captain of the bodyguard, deported to Babylon the rest of the people left in the city, those who had deserted to him, and the rest of the workers. ¹⁰But Nebuzaradan, captain of the bodyguard, left in the land of Judah some of the poor who had nothing and at the same time gave them vineyards and farms.

Jeremiah Released to Gedaliah's Custody. ¹¹Concerning Jeremiah, Nebuchadnezzar, king of Babylon, gave these orders through Nebuzaradan, captain of the bodyguard: ¹²"Take him and look after him; do not let anything happen to him. Whatever he may ask, you must do for him." ¹³Thereupon Nebuzaradan, captain of the bodyguard, and Nebushazban, a high dignitary, and Nergalsharezer, a chief officer, and all the nobles of the king of Babylon, ¹⁴had Jeremiah taken out of the courtyard of the guard and entrusted to Gedaliah, son of Ahikam, son of Shaphan, to bring him home. And so he remained among the people.

A Word of Comfort for Ebed-melech. ¹⁵While Jeremiah was still imprisoned in the court of the guard, the word of the LORD came to him: ¹⁶Go, tell this to Ebed-melech the Ethiopian: Thus says the LORD of hosts, the God of Israel: See, I am now carrying out my words against this city, for evil and not for good; this will happen in your presence on that day. ¹⁷But on that day I will deliver you—oracle of the LORD; you shall not be handed over to the men you dread. ¹⁸I will make certain that you escape and

39:11-14 Jeremiah released to Gedaliah's custody

Jeremiah is released from prison by the captain of the bodyguard at the orders of Nebuchadnezzar, king of Babylon, and entrusted into the hands of Gedaliah. A different version of the release of Jeremiah is found in 40:1-6, but that is probably a variant of this tradition rather than a reference to a later imprisonment and release. There is no explicit reason given for the kindness shown to Jeremiah, but it is likely that Babylonian officials were aware of Jeremiah's pro-Babylonian stance.

39:15-18 A word of comfort for Ebed-melech

Jeremiah announces a word of salvation to Ebed-melech. Though he will see the destruction of Jerusalem, his life will be spared because he trusted in the Lord. No mention is made of Ebed-melech's rescue of Jeremiah (38:7-13). It is not clear why this word of comfort is not attached to the story of chapter 38; it may be here because its fulfillment is at hand.

do not fall by the sword. Your life will be your spoils of war because you trusted in me—oracle of the LORD.

40 **Jeremiah Still in Judah.** ¹The word which came to Jeremiah from the LORD, after Nebuzaradan, captain of the bodyguard, had released him in Ramah, where he found him a prisoner in chains among the captives of Jerusalem and Judah being exiled to Babylon. ²The captain of the bodyguard took charge of Jeremiah and said to him, "The LORD, your God, decreed ruin for this place. ³Now he has made it happen, accomplishing what he decreed; because you sinned against the LORD and did not listen to his voice, this decree has been realized against you. ⁴Now, I release you today from the chains upon your hands; if you want to come with me to Babylon, then come: I will look out for you. But if you do not want to come to Babylon, very well. See, the whole land lies before you; go wherever you think good and proper. ⁵Or go to Gedaliah, son of Ahikam, son of Shaphan, whom the king of Babylon has set over the cities of Judah. Stay with him among the people. Or go wherever you want!" The captain of the bodyguard gave him food and gifts and let him go. ⁶So Jeremiah went to Gedaliah, son of Ahikam, in Mizpah, and dwelt with him among the people left in the land.

⁷When the military leaders still in the field with their soldiers heard that the king of Babylon had set Gedaliah, son of Ahikam, over the land and had put him in charge of men, women, and children, from the poor of the land who had not been deported to Babylon, ⁸they and their soldiers came to Gedaliah in Mizpah: Ishmael, son of Nethaniah; Johanan, son of Kareah; Seraiah, son of Tanhumeth; the sons of Ephai of Netophah; and Jezaniah of Beth-maacah. ⁹Gedaliah, son of Ahikam, son of Shaphan, swore an oath to them and their men: "Do not be afraid to serve the Chaldeans. Stay in the land and serve the king of Babylon, so that everything may go well with you. ¹⁰As for me, I will remain in Mizpah, as your representative before the Chaldeans when they

40:1-12 Jeremiah still in Judah

In this alternate version (cf. 38:11-14) of the fate of Jeremiah after Jerusalem was destroyed, he was taken in chains to Ramah with other exiles, but then was given the choice to go to Babylon, to go wherever he wanted, or to go to Gedaliah, son of Ahikam, who had been appointed governor by the Babylonian king. That Jeremiah chooses to go to Gedaliah in Mizpah, and so remain in Judah, is surprising, for he had prophesied that the future of Israel rests with the remnant that has gone into exile (24:4-7; 29:5-7).

The early days of Gedaliah's governorship appear to go well. When he is met by the military leaders of Judah and their troops, he advises them to return to their lands and harvest their crops, which they do. In the days that follow, peace and abundance seem to have returned to the land of Judah.

come to us. You, for your part, harvest the wine, the fruit, and the oil, store them in jars, and remain in the cities you occupied." ¹¹Then all the Judahites in Moab, in Ammon, in Edom, and those in all other lands heard that the king of Babylon had left a remnant in Judah and had set over them Gedaliah, son of Ahikam, son of Shaphan. ¹²They all returned to the land of Judah from the places to which they had scattered. They went to Gedaliah at Mizpah and had a rich harvest of wine and fruit.

Assassination of Gedaliah. ¹³Now Johanan, son of Kareah, and all the military leaders in the field came to Gedaliah in Mizpah ¹⁴and said to him, "Surely you are aware that Baalis, the Ammonite king, has sent Ishmael, son of Nethaniah, to assassinate you?" But Gedaliah, son of Ahikam, would not believe them. ¹⁵Then Johanan, son of Kareah, said secretly to Gedaliah in Mizpah: "Please let me go and kill Ishmael, son of Netha-

niah; no one will know it. What if he assassinates you? All the Judahites who have now rallied behind you would scatter and the remnant of Judah would perish." ¹⁶Gedaliah, son of Ahikam, answered Johanan, son of Kareah, "You must not do that. What you are saying about Ishmael is a lie!"

41 ¹In the seventh month, Ishmael, son of Nethaniah, son of Elishama, of royal descent, one of the king's nobles, came with ten men to Gedaliah, son of Ahikam, at Mizpah. While they were together at table in Mizpah, ²Ishmael, son of Nethaniah, and the ten with him, stood up and struck down Gedaliah, son of Ahikam, son of Shaphan, with swords. They killed him, since the king of Babylon had set him over the land; ³Ishmael also killed all the Judahites of military age who were with Gedaliah and the Chaldean soldiers stationed there.

⁴The day after the murder of Gedaliah, before anyone learned about it,

40:13–41:10 Assassination of Gedaliah

The rival pro- and anti-Babylonian factions that dominated Judean politics before the fall of Jerusalem did not disappear after the Babylonians destroyed the city. Many accepted Gedaliah's policy of accommodation to Babylonian rule, but others refused to submit. Johanan made Gedaliah aware of a plot against his life that was instigated by the Ammonite king, Baalis, but was to be carried out by Ishmael, a member of the royal line of David (41:1). Gedaliah refuses to take action against Ishmael, and when Ishmael and ten of his men come to him, Gedaliah takes no precautions to protect his life. Ishmael and his forces assassinate Gedaliah, but they also kill Judahites of military age and the Babylonian soldiers at the outpost. The killing spree continues the next day as Ishmael and his men slaughter men from the north who were coming to Mizpah to offer grain offerings and incense. Only men who have hidden provisions to offer as barter for their lives are spared. Ishmael then captures the rest of the people at Mizpah and brings them to Ammon, whose king had supported his rebellion.

⁵eighty men, in ragged clothes, with beards shaved off and gashes on their bodies, came from Shechem, Shiloh, and Samaria, bringing grain offerings and incense for the house of the LORD. ⁶Weeping as he went, Ishmael son of Nethaniah, set out from Mizpah to meet them. "Come to Gedaliah, son of Ahikam," he said as he met them. ⁷Once they were inside the city, Ishmael, son of Nethaniah, and his men slaughtered them and threw them into the cistern. ⁸Ten of them said to Ishmael: "Do not kill us! We have stores of wheat and barley, oil and honey hidden in the field." So he spared them and did not kill them as he had killed their companions. ⁹The cistern into which Ishmael threw all the bodies of the men he had killed was the large one King Asa made to defend himself against Baasha, king of Israel; Ishmael, son of Nethaniah, filled this cistern with the slain.

¹⁰Ishmael led away the rest of the people left in Mizpah, including the princesses, whom Nebuzaradan, captain of the bodyguard, had consigned to Gedaliah, son of Ahikam. With these captives, Ishmael, son of Nethaniah, set out to cross over to the Ammonites.

Flight to Egypt. ¹¹But when Johanan, son of Kareah, and the other army leaders with him heard about the crimes Ishmael, son of Nethaniah, had committed, ¹²they took all their men and set out to attack Ishmael, son of Nethaniah. They overtook him at the great pool in Gibeon. ¹³At the sight of Johanan, son of Kareah, and the other army leaders, the people with Ishmael rejoiced; ¹⁴all of those whom Ishmael had taken captive from Mizpah went back to Johanan, son of Kareah. ¹⁵But Ishmael, son of Nethaniah, escaped from Johanan with eight men and fled to the Ammonites. ¹⁶Then Johanan, son of Kareah, and all the military leaders took charge of all the rest of the people whom Ishmael, son of Nethaniah, had taken away from Mizpah after he killed Gedaliah, son of Ahikam—the soldiers, the women with children, and court officials, whom he brought back from Gibeon. ¹⁷They set out and stopped at Geruth Chimham near Bethlehem, intending to go into Egypt. ¹⁸They were afraid of the Chaldeans, because Ishmael, son of Nethaniah, had slain Gedaliah, son of Ahikam, whom the king of Babylon had set over the land.

42 ¹Then all the military leaders, including Johanan, son of Kareah, Azariah, son of Hoshaiah, and all the people, from the least to the greatest, ²approached Jeremiah the prophet and said, "Please grant our petition; pray for us to the LORD, your God, for all this remnant. As you see, only a few of us remain, but once we were many. ³May the LORD, your God, show us the way we should take and what we should do." ⁴"Very well!" Jeremiah the prophet answered them: "I will pray to the LORD, your God, as you desire; whatever the

41:11–43:7 Flight to Egypt

When Johanan, who had warned Gedaliah of the assassination plot, hears of Ishmael's insurrection, he and those with him confront Ishmael. The captives that had been taken by Ishmael welcome Johanan and join with him. Ishmael and eight of his men escape, never to be heard from

LORD answers, I will tell you; I will withhold nothing from you." [5]And they said to Jeremiah, "May the LORD be a true and faithful witness against us if we do not follow all the instructions the LORD, your God, sends us through you. [6]Whether we like it or not, we will obey the command of the LORD, our God, to whom we are sending you, so that it may go well with us for obeying the command of the LORD, our God."

[7]Ten days passed before the word of the LORD came to Jeremiah. [8]Then he called Johanan, son of Kareah, his army leaders, and all the people, from the least to the greatest, [9]and said to them: Thus says the LORD, the God of Israel, to whom you sent me to offer your petition: [10]If indeed you will remain in this land, I will build you up, and not tear you down; I will plant you, not uproot you; for I repent of the evil I have done you. [11]Do not fear the king of Babylon, as you do now. Do not fear him—oracle of the LORD—for I am with you to save you, to rescue you from his power. [12]I will take pity on you, so that he will have pity on you and let you return to your land. [13]But if you keep saying, "We will not stay in this land," thus disobeying the voice of the LORD, your God, [14]and saying, "No, we will go to the land of Egypt, where we will not see war, nor hear the trumpet alarm, nor hunger for bread. There we will live!" [15]then listen to the word of the LORD, remnant of Judah: Thus says the LORD of hosts, the God of Israel: If you are set on going to Egypt and settling down there once you arrive, [16]the sword you fear shall overtake you in the land of Egypt; the hunger you dread shall pursue you to Egypt and there you shall die. [17]All those determined to go to Egypt to live shall die by the sword, famine, and disease: not one shall survive or escape the evil that I am bringing upon them. [18]For thus says the LORD of hosts, the God of Israel: Just as my furious wrath was poured out upon the inhabitants of Jerusalem, so shall my anger be poured out on you when you reach Egypt. You shall become a malediction and a horror, a curse and a reproach, and you shall never see this place again.

[19]The LORD has spoken to you, remnant of Judah. Do not go to Egypt! Mark well that I am warning you this day. [20]At the cost of your lives you have been deceitful, for you yourselves sent me to the LORD, your God, saying, "Pray for us to the LORD, our God; whatever the LORD, our God, shall say, tell us and we will do it." [21]Today I have told you, but you have not listened to the voice of the LORD your God, in anything that he has sent me to tell you. [22]Have no doubt about this: you shall die by the sword, famine, and disease in the place where you want to go and live.

43 [1]When Jeremiah finished telling the people all the words the LORD, their God, sent to them, [2]Azariah, son of Hoshaiah, Johanan, son of Kareah, and

---

again. Johanan and the people with him are afraid of Babylonian reprisals, so they do not return to Mizpah but head for Egypt. Only at this time does Jeremiah return to center stage. The people seek a word of the Lord from Jeremiah regarding the direction the community should take and they vow

all the others had the insolence to say to Jeremiah: "You lie; the LORD, our God, did not send you to tell us, 'Do not go to Egypt to live there.' ³Baruch, son of Neriah, is inciting you against us, to hand us over to the Chaldeans to be killed or exiled to Babylon."

⁴So Johanan, son of Kareah, and the rest of the leaders and the people did not listen to the voice of the LORD to stay in the land of Judah. ⁵Instead, Johanan, son of Kareah, and the military leaders took along all the remnant of Judah who had been dispersed among the nations and then had returned to dwell in the land of Judah: ⁶men, women, and children, the princesses and everyone whom Nebuzaradan, captain of the bodyguard, had consigned to Gedaliah, son of Ahikam, son of Shaphan; also Jeremiah, the prophet, and Baruch, son of Neriah. ⁷They went to Egypt—they did not listen to the voice of the LORD—and came to Tahpanhes.

Jeremiah in Egypt. ⁸The word of the LORD came to Jeremiah in Tahpanhes: ⁹Take some large stones in your hand and set them in mortar in the terrace at the entrance to the house of Pharaoh in Tahpanhes, while the Judahites watch. ¹⁰Then say to them: Thus says the LORD of hosts, the God of Israel: I will send for my servant Nebuchadnezzar, king of Babylon. He will place his throne upon these stones which I, Jeremiah, have set up, and stretch his canopy above them. ¹¹He shall come and strike the land of Egypt: with death, those marked for

to follow that word. The first part of the word from the Lord (42:9-12) is consistent with the message that Jeremiah has repeatedly given: if they settle down and submit to Babylon, all will go well for them in the land. The second part of the Lord's word (42:13-17) is an emphatic warning not to go to Egypt, for "sword, famine, and disease" will follow them and they shall die in a foreign land. The Lord's word is reiterated by Jeremiah in 42:19-22. Underlying the harsh punishment upon those who would go to Egypt is a theological perspective that sees their journey to Egypt as a reversal of the exodus and thus a rejection of the Lord's greatest salvific act on their behalf. Their rejection of Jeremiah's word is surprising in light of their vow to obey whether they agree with the word or not (43:5-6), but it is not surprising in light of the many affirmations throughout the book of Jeremiah that the people time and again refuse to listen to and obey the Lord. It is not clear why Baruch is blamed for inciting Jeremiah against the people, for Jeremiah's position is consistent with his prophetic message. Jeremiah and Baruch will go to Egypt, but it is assumed that they were taken against their will, even though this is not explicitly stated.

43:8–44:30 Jeremiah in Egypt

Even in Egypt Jeremiah continues to function as prophet. He is commanded to perform a final symbolic act; he is to place stones in mortar at

death; with exile, those marked for exile; with the sword, those marked for the sword. ¹²He shall set fire to the temples of Egypt's gods, burn the gods and carry them off. He shall pick the land of Egypt clean, as a shepherd picks lice off his cloak, and then depart victorious. ¹³He shall smash the obelisks at the Temple of the Sun in the land of Egypt and destroy with fire the temples of the Egyptian gods.

44 ¹The word that came to Jeremiah for all the Judahites who were living in Egypt, those living in Migdol, Tahpanhes, and Memphis, and in Upper Egypt: ²Thus says the LORD of hosts, the God of Israel: You yourselves have seen all the evil I brought upon Jerusalem and the other cities of Judah. Today they lie in ruins uninhabited, ³because of the evil they did to provoke me, going after other gods, offering incense and serving other gods they did not know, neither they, nor you, nor your ancestors. ⁴Though I repeatedly sent you all my servants the prophets, saying: "You must not commit this abominable deed I hate," ⁵they did not listen or incline their ears in order to turn from their evil, no longer offering incense to other gods. ⁶Therefore the fury of my anger poured forth and kindled fire in the cities of Judah and the streets of Jerusalem, to turn them into the ruined wasteland they are today.

⁷Now thus says the LORD God of hosts, the God of Israel: Why inflict so great an evil upon yourselves, cutting off from Judah man and woman, child and infant, not leaving yourselves even a remnant? ⁸Why do you provoke me with the works of your hands, offering sacrifice to other gods here in the land of Egypt where you have come to live? Will you cut yourselves off and become a curse, a reproach among all the nations of the earth? ⁹Have you forgotten the evil of your ancestors, the evil of the kings of Judah, the evil of their wives, and your own evil and the evil of your wives—all that they did in the land of Judah and in the streets of Jerusalem? ¹⁰To this day they have not been crushed down, nor have they shown fear. They have not followed my law and my statutes that I set before you and your ancestors.

¹¹Therefore, thus says the LORD of hosts, the God of Israel: I have set my face against you for evil, to cut off all Judah. ¹²I will take away the remnant of Judah who insisted on going to the land of Egypt to live there; in the land of Egypt they shall meet their end. They shall fall by the sword or be consumed by hunger. From the least to the greatest, they shall die by sword or hunger; they shall become a malediction, a horror, a curse, a reproach. ¹³Thus I will punish those who live in Egypt, just as I punished Jerusalem, with sword, hunger, and disease, ¹⁴so that none of the remnant of Judah who came to live in the land of Egypt shall escape or survive. No one shall return to the land of Judah. Even though they long to return and live

the entrance of Pharaoh's house in Tahpanhes. This action is done to affirm the dominance of Babylon, for upon the stones Nebuchadnezzar will place his throne, symbolizing that the Babylonian Empire will rule over Egypt.

there, they shall not return except as refugees.

¹⁵They answered Jeremiah—all the men who knew that their wives were offering sacrifices to other gods, all the women standing there in the immense crowd, and all the people who lived in Lower and Upper Egypt: ¹⁶"Regarding the word you have spoken to us in the name of the LORD, we are not listening to you. ¹⁷Rather we will go on doing what we proposed; we will offer incense to the Queen of Heaven and pour out libations to her, just as we have done, along with our ancestors, our kings and princes, in the cities of Judah and in the streets of Jerusalem. Then we had plenty to eat, we prospered, and we suffered no misfortune. ¹⁸But ever since we stopped offering sacrifices to the Queen of Heaven and pouring out libations to her, we lack everything and are being destroyed by sword and hunger." ¹⁹And the women said, "When we offered sacrifices to the Queen of Heaven and poured out libations to her, did we bake cakes in her image and pour out libations to her without our husbands' consent?"

²⁰To all the people, men and women, who gave him this answer, Jeremiah said: ²¹As for the sacrifices you offered in the cities of Judah and in the streets of Jerusalem—you, your ancestors, your kings and princes, and the people of the land—did not the LORD remember them? Did it not enter his mind? ²²The LORD could no longer bear the evil of your deeds, the abominations you were doing; then your land became a waste, a horror, a curse, without even one inhabitant, as it is today. ²³Because you offered sacrifice and sinned against the LORD, not listening to the voice of the LORD, not following his law, his statutes, and his decrees, therefore this evil has overtaken you, as it is today.

²⁴Jeremiah said to all the people and to all the women: Hear the word of the LORD, all you Judahites in the land of Egypt: ²⁵Thus says the LORD of hosts, the God of Israel: You and your wives have carried out with your hands what your mouths have spoken: "We will go on fulfilling the vows we have made to offer sacrifice to the Queen of Heaven and to pour out libations to her." Very well! keep your vows, fulfill your vows! ²⁶And then listen to the word of the LORD, all you Judahites living in Egypt; I swear by my own great name, says the

---

The last public words of Jeremiah delivered to the Judeans in Egypt are consistent with the prophetic message that he has proclaimed throughout his life. After rehearsing the history of Israel's persistence in the worship of other gods and the judgment visited upon them on that account, Jeremiah raises a series of questions that underscore that even now as refugees in a foreign land the people provoke the Lord's anger by continuing to worship other gods. They have learned nothing from the destruction of Jerusalem and their temple. As before, their sin calls forth punishment, but there will be no remnant left and thus no future for this community of Judeans in Egypt. The Judeans reject Jeremiah's word and insist that they will return to the worship of the Queen of Heaven. They believe their present suffering

LORD: in the whole land of Egypt, my name shall no longer be pronounced by the lips of any Judahite, saying, "As the Lord GOD lives." ²⁷I am watching over them for evil, not for good. All the Judahites in Egypt shall come to an end by sword or famine until they are completely destroyed. ²⁸Those who escape the sword to return from the land of Egypt to the land of Judah shall be few in number. The whole remnant of Judah who came to Egypt to live shall know whose word stands, mine or theirs.

²⁹And this shall be a sign to you— oracle of the LORD—I will punish you in this place so that you will know that my words stand solidly against you for evil. ³⁰Thus says the LORD: See! I will hand over Pharaoh Hophra, king of Egypt, to his enemies, to those seeking his life, just as I handed over Zedekiah, king of Judah, to his enemy Nebuchadrezzar, king of Babylon, to the one seeking his life.

45 **A Message to Baruch.** ¹The word that Jeremiah the prophet spoke to Baruch, son of Neriah, when he wrote on a scroll words from Jeremiah's own mouth in the fourth year of Jehoiakim, son of Josiah, king of Judah: ²Thus says the LORD, God of Israel, to you, Baruch. ³You said, "Woe is me! the LORD has added grief to my pain. I have worn myself out with groaning; rest eludes me." ⁴You must say this to him. Thus says the LORD: What I have built, I am tearing down; what I have planted, I am uprooting: all this land. ⁵And you, do you seek great things for yourself? Do not seek them! I am bringing evil on all flesh— oracle of the LORD—but I will grant you your life as spoils of war, wherever you may go.

---

is the result of abandoning the worship of this goddess, but Jeremiah disagrees. Jeremiah's response is to reiterate the Lord's judgment against them. That all the Judahites in Egypt will be destroyed (44:27) may be hyperbole, for it is countered in the very next verse by a reference to a few who will escape (44:28).

45:1-5 A message to Baruch

The delivery of a message of hope to Baruch is set in the fourth year of the reign of Jehoiakim (605 B.C.), but the basis for Baruch's grief at that time is not clear. Baruch will see the destruction of Jerusalem in 587 B.C. and a few months later he was uprooted from his homeland (43:6); both experiences may provide the basis for his cry of lament in verses 3-4. It is not clear what "great things" Baruch was seeking (45:5). It is unlikely that the Lord is referring to self-serving ambition on Baruch's part; it is more likely that Baruch harbored the hope that through Jeremiah's prophecy and his service to Jeremiah Jerusalem will not be destroyed. The Lord affirms in language drawn from the call of Jeremiah (1:10) that the time of "tearing down" and "uprooting" has come (45:4), but guarantees that Baruch's life will be spared. A similar promise was made to Ebed-melech in 39:18.

VIII. Oracles Against the Nations

46 ¹The word of the LORD that came to Jeremiah the prophet concerning the nations.

Against Egypt. ²Concerning Egypt. Against the army of Pharaoh Neco, king of Egypt, defeated at Carchemish on the Euphrates by Nebuchadrezzar, king of Babylon, in the fourth year of Jehoiakim, son of Josiah, king of Judah: .

> ³Prepare buckler and shield!
>   move forward to battle!
> ⁴Harness the horses,
>   charioteers, mount up!
> Fall in, with helmets on;
>   polish your spears, put on your
>   armor.

> ⁵What do I see?
>   Are they panicking, falling
>   apart?
> Their warriors are hammered
>   back,
> They flee headlong
>   never making a stand.
> Terror on every side—
>   oracle of the LORD!
> ⁶The swift cannot flee,
>   nor the warrior escape:
> There up north, on the banks of the
>   Euphrates
>   they stumble and fall.
> ⁷Who is this? Like the Nile, it rears
>   up;
>   like rivers, its waters surge.
> ⁸Egypt rears up like the Nile,
>   like rivers, its waters surge.

ORACLES AGAINST THE NATIONS

Jeremiah 46:1–51:64

The oracles in this section are traditionally called "oracles against the nations" and we find similar oracles in other prophetic books, for example, Isaiah 13–23; Ezekiel 25–32; Amos 1:1–2:3; Nahum; and Obadiah. The origin of oracles against the nations is unknown, but they are linked to the holy war tradition by language and themes. It is doubtful that Jeremiah is the author of these oracles against the nations. The heading (45:1) sets them apart as a separate collection, as does the fact that they have a different placement in the Hebrew text of Jeremiah (chs. 46–51) than in the LXX (after 25:13a). Also it is difficult to reconcile the harsh tone of the oracles against Babylon (chs. 50–51) with Jeremiah's pro-Babylonian stance. These oracles link Jeremiah, who is not presented in the book as prophesying to the nations, to his call to be a "prophet to the nations" (1:5, 10).

The oracles against the nations of chapters 46–49 are distinct from those of chapters 50–51. In the first set of oracles divine judgment is mediated through Babylon against various nations, but in chapters 50–51 Babylon is judged by the other nations. The oracles against Babylon are considerably longer than the oracles of chapters 46–49. The dating of the oracles from the fourth year of Jehoiakim (605 B.C.; 46:2) to the fourth year of Zedekiah (593 B.C.) provides a suitable context for these oracles, but a preexilic date

"I will rear up," it says, "and cover
the earth,
destroying the city and its people.
⁹Forward, horses!
charge, chariots!
March forth, warriors,
Cush and Put, bearing shields,
Archers of Lud, stretching bows!"
¹⁰Today belongs to the Lord GOD of
hosts,
a day of vengeance, vengeance
on his foes!
The sword devours and is sated,
drunk with their blood:
for the Lord GOD of hosts holds
a sacrifice
in the land of the north, on the
River Euphrates.
¹¹Go up to Gilead, procure balm,
Virgin daughter Egypt!
No use to multiply remedies;
for you there is no healing.
¹²The nations hear your cries,
your screaming fills the earth.
Warrior stumbles against warrior,
both collapse together.

¹³The word that the LORD spoke to Jeremiah the prophet when Nebuchadrezzar, king of Babylon, came to attack the land of Egypt:

¹⁴Proclaim in Egypt, announce in
Migdol,

announce in Memphis and
Tahpanhes!
Say: Fall in, get ready,
the sword has devoured your
neighbors.
¹⁵Why has Apis fled?
Your champion did not stand,
Because the LORD thrust him down;
¹⁶he stumbled repeatedly then
collapsed.
They said to each other,
"Get up! We must return to our
own people,
To the land of our birth,
away from the destroying
sword."
¹⁷Give Pharaoh, king of Egypt, the
name
"Braggart-missed-his-chance."
¹⁸As I live, says the King
whose name is LORD of hosts,
Like Tabor above mountains,
like Carmel above the sea, he
comes.
¹⁹Pack your bags for exile,
enthroned daughter Egypt;
Memphis shall become a wasteland,
an empty ruin.
²⁰Egypt is a beautiful heifer,
a horsefly from the north keeps
coming.
²¹Even the mercenaries in her ranks
are like fattened calves;

---

for the oracles against Babylon (chs. 50–51) is unlikely in view of the pro-Babylonian stance taken by Jeremiah. The judgment against the nations is not because of idolatry; rather it is because of their crimes against other nations and their arrogance. These oracles against the nations do not just announce judgment against the nations but also allow for the restoration of fortunes of these nations after the time of judgment.

46:2-28 Against Egypt

Two oracles against Egypt dominate this section, verses 2-12 and 13-26, though verses 24-26 may constitute a separate oracle. A short final oracle,

They too turn and flee together—
 they do not stand their ground,
For their day of ruin comes upon
  them,
 their time of punishment.
²²Her voice is like a snake!
 Yes, they come in force;
They attack her with axes,
 like those who fell trees.
²³They cut down her forest—oracle
  of the LORD—
 impenetrable though it be;
More numerous than locusts,
 they cannot be counted.
²⁴Shamed is daughter Egypt,
 handed over to a people from
  the north.

²⁵The LORD of hosts, the God of Israel, has said: See! I will punish Amon of Thebes and Egypt, gods, kings, Pharaoh, and those who trust in him. ²⁶I will hand them over to those who seek their lives, to Nebuchadrezzar, king of Babylon, and to his officers. But later, Egypt shall be inhabited again, as in days of old—oracle of the LORD.

²⁷But you, my servant Jacob, do not
  fear;
 do not be dismayed, Israel!
Listen! I will deliver you from
  far-off lands;
 your offspring, from the land of
  their exile.
Jacob shall again find rest,
 secure, with none to frighten
  him.
²⁸You, Jacob my servant, must not
  fear—oracle of the LORD—
 for I am with you;
I will make an end of all the nations
 to which I have driven you,
But of you I will not make an end:
 I will chastise you as you
  deserve,
 I cannot let you go unpunished.

47 Against the Philistines. ¹The word of the LORD that came to Jere-

directly addressed to Israel (46:27-28), concludes the chapter. The first oracle against Egypt is put in the context of the defeat of Egyptian forces at Carchemish in 605 B.C.; the second envisions a later invasion of Egypt that is about to begin or has already begun. In both oracles vivid metaphors concretize the preparation for war and the horror of the experience of war. The war itself is seen as the Lord's judgment upon Egypt, which stands as helpless as Judah in the face of the Lord's vengeance. The final oracle (46:27-28) is virtually identical to 30:10-11 and intrudes into the oracles against the nations with a message of hope for Israel. Israel itself has been judged and exiled, but the judgment against Egypt will open the way for the future restoration of Israel. Israel should not fear, for the Lord is at work in the affairs of the nations to effect what is desired for the people. It was never the Lord's purpose to bring the people to an end but only to punish them for a time, as justice demanded.

47:1-7 Against the Philistines
The opening statement sets this oracle against the Philistines before an attack upon Gaza by a pharaoh, but this verse is missing from the LXX.

121

miah the prophet concerning the Philistines, before Pharaoh attacked Gaza:

²Thus says the LORD:
See: waters are rising from the
     north,
   to become a torrent in flood;
They shall flood the land and all it
     contains,
   the cities and their inhabitants.
People will howl and wail,
   every inhabitant of the land.
³At the noise of the pounding
     hooves of his steeds,
   the clanking chariots, the
        rumbling wheels,
Parents do not turn back for their
     children;
   their hands hang helpless,
⁴Because of the day that is coming
   to destroy all the Philistines
And cut off from Tyre and Sidon
   the last of their allies.
Yes, the LORD is destroying the
     Philistines,
   the remnant from the coasts of
        Caphtor.
⁵Baldness is visited upon Gaza,

Ashkelon is reduced to silence;
Ashdod, remnant of their strength,
   how long will you gash
        yourself?
⁶Ah! Sword of the LORD!
   When will you find rest?
Return to your scabbard;
   stop, be still!
⁷How can it find rest
   when the LORD has commanded
        it?
Against Ashkelon and the seacoast,
   there he has appointed it.

48 **Against Moab.** ¹Concerning Moab.
   Thus says the LORD of hosts, the
God of Israel:

Ah, Nebo! it is ravaged;
   Kiriathaim is disgraced,
        captured;
Disgraced and overthrown is the
     stronghold:
²Moab's glory is no more.
In Heshbon they plot evil against
     her:
   "Come! We will put an end to
        her as a nation."

Pharaoh Neco II led a series of campaigns into the region in 609 B.C., but
references to waters "rising from the north" (47:2) and the destruction of
Ashkelon (47:5, 7) suggest Babylonian rather than Egyptian involvement.
The Babylonian army under Nebuchadnezzar destroyed Ashkelon in 604
B.C. There is no indictment against Philistia in this oracle; there is only a
description of the people's reaction to the horrors wrought by an invading
army. The Lord is behind this invasion (47:4, 7). There is a certain poignancy
that finds expression in questions such as, "[H]ow long?" and "When will
you [the sword] find rest?" (47:5, 6). It may be the prophet's voice that
comes to the fore asking the sword of the Lord to cease (47:6), even while
recognizing that it cannot rest until the Lord commands it (47:7).

48:1-47 Against Moab

There is no superscription that sets these oracles against Moab within
a historical context, but the advance of the Babylonian army into the region
in the late seventh and early sixth centuries B.C. may be in the background.

You, too, Madmen, shall be
  silenced;
  you the sword stalks!
³Listen! an outcry from Horonaim,
  "Ruin and great destruction!"
⁴"Moab is crushed!"
  their outcry is heard in Zoar.
⁵Up the ascent of Luhith
  they go weeping;
At the descent to Horonaim
  they hear cries of anguish:
⁶"Flee, save your lives!
  Be like a wild donkey in the
    wilderness!"
⁷Because you trusted in your works
  and your treasures,
  you also shall be captured.
Chemosh shall go into exile,
  his priests and princes with him.
⁸The destroyer comes upon every
    city,
  not a city escapes;
Ruined is the valley,
  wasted the plateau—oracle of
    the Lord.
⁹Set up a tombstone for Moab;
  it will soon become a complete
    wasteland,
Its cities turned into ruins
  where no one dwells.
¹⁰Cursed are they who do the
    Lord's work carelessly,
  cursed those who keep their
    sword from shedding
    blood.
¹¹"Moab has been resting from its
    youth,
  suspended above its dregs,
Never poured from flask to flask,
  never driven into exile.

Thus it retained its flavor,
  its bouquet is not lost.

¹²Be assured! The days are coming—
oracle of the Lord—when I will send
him wine-makers to decant the wine;
they shall empty its flasks and smash its
jars. ¹³Chemosh shall disappoint Moab,
just as the house of Israel was disap-
pointed by Bethel, in which they trusted.

¹⁴How can you say, "We are heroes,
  mighty warriors"?
¹⁵The one who ravages Moab and
    its cities comes up,
  the best of its youth go down to
    slaughter—
  oracle of the King, whose name
    is Lord of hosts.
¹⁶Moab's ruin is near at hand,
  its disaster approaches swiftly.
¹⁷Mourn, all you neighbors,
  all you who know its name!
Say: How the mighty scepter is
    broken,
  the glorious staff!
¹⁸Come down from glory, sit on the
    parched ground,
  enthroned daughter Dibon;
Moab's destroyer has fallen upon
    you,
  has shattered your strongholds.
¹⁹Stand along the road, keep watch,
  enthroned Aroer;
Ask the fleeing man, the escaping
    woman:
  ask them what has happened.
²⁰"Moab is put to shame, destroyed."
  Wail and cry out,
Proclaim it at the Arnon:
  "Moab is destroyed!"

Moab shared kinship with Israel (Gen 19:37-38), but little is made of that
relationship. The focus of these oracles is on the suffering experienced by
the Moabites because armies have ravaged its land. The chapter is remark-
able in its length and in the language of mourning that is interspersed

²¹Judgment has come upon the plateau: on Holon, Jahzah, and Mephaath, ²²on Dibon, Nebo, and Beth-diblathaim, ²³on Kiriathaim, Beth-gamul, and Beth-meon, ²⁴on Kerioth and on Bozrah: on all the cities of the land of Moab, far and near.

²⁵The horn of Moab is cut off,
 its arm is broken—oracle of the
  LORD.

²⁶Make him drunk because he set himself over against the LORD; let Moab swim in his vomit and become a laughingstock. ²⁷Has Israel not been a laughingstock to you? Was he caught among thieves that you wag your heads whenever you speak of him?

²⁸Abandon the cities, take shelter in
 the crags,
  inhabitants of Moab.
Be like the dove that nests
 in the walls of a gorge.
²⁹We have heard of the pride of
 Moab,
  pride beyond bounds:
His loftiness, his pride, his scorn,
 his insolent heart.
³⁰I myself know his arrogance—
  oracle of the LORD—
 liar in word, liar in deed.
³¹And so I wail over Moab,
 over all Moab I cry,
  over the people of Kir-heres I
   moan.
³²More than for Jazer I weep for you,
 vine of Sibmah.

Your tendrils trailed down to the
 sea,
  as far as Jazer they stretched.
Upon your summer harvest and
 your vintage,
  the destroyer has fallen.
³³Joy and gladness are taken away
 from the garden land, the land
  of Moab.
I dry up the wine from the wine
 vats,
  the treader treads no more,
  the vintage shout is stilled.

³⁴The cry of Heshbon and Elealeh is heard as far as Jahaz; they call from Zoar to Horonaim and to Eglath-shelishiyah; even the waters of Nimrim turn into a wasteland. ³⁵I will leave no one in Moab—oracle of the LORD—to offer burnt offerings on the high place or to make sacrifices to their gods. ³⁶Hence my heart wails like a flute for Moab; my heart wails like a flute for the people of Kir-heres: the wealth they accumulated has perished. ³⁷Every head has been shaved bald, every beard cut off; every hand gashed, and all their loins are draped in sackcloth. ³⁸On all the rooftops of Moab and in all its squares there is mourning. I have shattered Moab like a pot that no one wants—oracle of the LORD. ³⁹How terrified they are, how they wail! How Moab turns its back in shame! Moab has become a laughingstock and a horror to all its neighbors!

---

throughout the oracles. Moab's failings, especially its pride and arrogance (48:7, 14, 26, 29-30, 42), receive some attention, but it is the vivid portrayal of devastation and desolation accompanied by weeping and wailing that pervades the chapter. It is not only Moab that mourns but also its neighbors and even the Lord (48:31-32, 36). The description of Moab's suffering and the mournful tone of the chapter evoke sympathy for its people rather than

⁴⁰For thus says the Lᴏʀᴅ:
Look there! Like an eagle he
    swoops,
        spreading his wings over Moab.
⁴¹Cities are captured,
    strongholds seized:
On that day the hearts of Moab's
    warriors
        become like the heart of a
            woman in labor.
⁴²Moab shall be wiped out, a people
    no more,
        because it set itself over against
            the Lᴏʀᴅ.
⁴³Terror, pit, and trap be upon you,
    enthroned Moab—oracle of the
        Lᴏʀᴅ.
⁴⁴Those fleeing the terror
    fall into the pit;
Those climbing out of the pit
    are caught in the trap;
Ah, yes! I will bring these things
    upon Moab
        in the year of their punishment—
            oracle of the Lᴏʀᴅ.
⁴⁵In Heshbon's shadow the fugitives
    stop short, exhausted;
For fire blazes up from Heshbon,
    and flames up from the house of
        Sihon:
It consumes the forehead of Moab,
    the scalp of the noisemakers.

⁴⁶Woe to you, Moab!
    You are finished, people of
        Chemosh!
Your sons are taken into exile,
    your daughters into captivity.
⁴⁷Yet I will restore the fortunes of
    Moab
        in the days to come—oracle of
            the Lᴏʀᴅ.

Thus far the judgment on Moab.

49 **Against the Ammonites.** ¹Concerning the Ammonites. Thus says the Lᴏʀᴅ:

Has Israel no sons?
    none to inherit?
Why has Milcom disinherited Gad,
    why are his people living in its
        cities?
²Therefore the days are coming—
    oracle of the Lᴏʀᴅ—
        when I will sound the battle
            alarm
        against Rabbah of the
            Ammonites;
It shall become a mound of ruins,
    and its villages destroyed by
        fire.
Israel shall then inherit those who
    disinherited it—
        oracle of the Lᴏʀᴅ.

---

a vindictive satisfaction in the judgment meted out to them. The oracle ends with the announcement of the restoration of Moab's fortunes.

49:1-6 Against the Ammonites

The Ammonites also shared kinship with the Israelites (Gen 19:38), but there was an ongoing antagonism between these two groups that is evidenced frequently in the Old Testament (e.g., Judg 10–11; 2 Sam 10). The opening verses of this passage allude to a territorial dispute between Israel's tribe of Gad and Ammon as the basis for judgment against Ammon. The Ammonites' reliance on their strength and wealth (49:4) will not prevent their destruction when the Lord's judgment comes upon them (49:5). The destruction of Ammon will be followed by exile; even Ammon's god, Milcom,

³Wail, Heshbon, "The ruin is
    destroyed!"
  shriek, villages of Rabbah!
Put on sackcloth and lament!
  Run back and forth in the sheep-
    folds.
For Milcom is going into exile,
  taking priest and prince with
    him.
⁴Why boast in your strength,
  your ebbing strength, rebellious
    daughter?
Why trust in your treasures, saying,
  "Who would dare attack me?"
⁵See, I am bringing terror upon
    you—
  oracle of the Lord GOD of hosts—
from all around you;
You shall be scattered, each in
    headlong flight,
  with no one to gather the
    fugitives.
⁶But afterward I will restore the
    fortunes
  of the Ammonites—oracle of the
    LORD.

Against Edom. ⁷Concerning Edom. Thus says the LORD of hosts:

  Is there no more wisdom in Teman,
    has counsel perished from the
      prudent,
    is their wisdom gone?

⁸Flee, retreat, hide deep for lodging,
  inhabitants of Dedan:
For I bring disaster upon Esau
  when I come to punish them.
⁹If vintagers came upon you,
  they would leave no gleanings;
If thieves by night,
  they would destroy as they
    pleased.
¹⁰So I myself will strip Esau;
  I will uncover his lairs so he
    cannot hide.
Offspring and family are destroyed,
  neighbors, too; he is no more.
¹¹Leave your orphans behind, I will
  keep them alive;
  your widows, let them trust in
    me.

¹²For thus says the LORD: Look, even those not sentenced to drink the cup must drink it! Shall you then go unpunished? You shall not! You shall drink every bit of it! ¹³By myself I have sworn—oracle of the LORD—Bozrah shall become an object of horror, a disgrace, a desolation, and a curse. Bozrah and all its cities shall become ruins forever.

¹⁴I have heard a report from the
    LORD,
  a herald has been sent among
    the nations:

---

will go into exile, taking Ammon's leaders with him. This oracle also ends on a positive note with the restoration of the fortunes of Ammon (49:6).

49:7-22 Against Edom

The absence of a tone of lament from this oracle against Edom may be explained as the result of the frequent and often bitter antagonism between Israel and Edom. Edom is often the object of prophetic denunciations (Isa 34:1-17; 63:1-6; Lam 4:21-22; Ezek 25:12-14; 35:1-15; Amos 1:11-12; Obad; Mal 1:2-5). There are similarities between this oracle and the book of Obadiah (49:9-10a with Obad 5-6; and 49:14-16 with Obad 1-4), but this may be due to the reliance upon a common source rather than direct borrowing of one

"Gather together, move against it,
    get ready for battle!"
[15]I will make you the least among
        the nations,
    despised by all people!
[16]The terror you spread,
    the pride of your heart, beguiled
        you.
You denizens of rocks and crevices,
    occupying towering peaks:
Though you build your nest high as
        the eagle,
    from there I will bring you
            down—oracle of the
            LORD.

[17]Edom shall become an object of horror. Passersby recoil in terror, hissing at all its wounds. [18]As when Sodom, Gomorrah, and their neighbors were overthrown—oracle of the LORD—no one shall live in it, nor anyone settle there.

[19]As when a lion comes up from a
        thicket of the Jordan
    to a permanent pasture,
So in an instant, I will chase them
        off;
    I will establish there whomever
        I choose.
For who is like me? Who holds me
        accountable?
    What shepherd can stand
        against me?

[20]Therefore, listen to the strategy
    the LORD devised for Edom;
The plans he has drawn up
    against the inhabitants of
        Teman:
They shall be dragged away, even
        the smallest of the flock;
    their pasture shall be aghast
        because of them.
[21]With the din of their collapse the
        earth quakes,
    to the Red Sea the outcry is
        heard!
[22]Look! like an eagle he soars aloft,
    and spreads his wings over
        Bozrah;
On that day the hearts of Edom's
        warriors become
    like the heart of a woman in
        labor.

Against Damascus

[23]Concerning Damascus.

Hamath and Arpad are shamed,
    for they have heard bad news;
Anxious, they surge like the sea
    which cannot calm down.
[24]Damascus loses heart, turns to
        flee;
    panic has seized it.
Distress and pangs take hold,
    like the pain of a woman in
        labor.

upon the other. Verses 18-21 are virtually identical to 50:40, 44-46 of the oracle against Babylon and there are marked similarities between what is said of Moab in 48:41-44 and of Edom in 49:22. These parallels suggest that there were stock phrases used in oracles against the nations. There are no historical references in the oracle; rather there is a collage of images assembled to vividly display the destruction of Edom without this destruction being anchored in time. Edom was noted for its wisdom (49:7), but that is now gone as it is judged for its pride. A reference to the incomparability of the Lord stands out in the midst of this judgment against Edom, but it is typical of Israel's prophets to present the Lord as in control of history.

25How can the glorious city be
abandoned,
the town of joy!
26But now its young men shall fall
in its squares,
all the warriors destroyed on
that day—
oracle of the LORD of hosts.
27I will set fire to the wall of
Damascus;
it shall devour the palaces of
Ben-hadad.

Against Arabia. 28About Kedar and
the kingdoms of Hazor, which Nebuchadnezzar, king of Babylon, defeated.

Thus says the LORD:
Rise up, attack Kedar,
destroy the people from the east.
29Their tents and flocks shall be
taken away,
their tent curtains and all their
goods;
Their camels they carry off,
they shout over them, "Terror
on every side!"
30Flee! wander about, hide deep for
lodging,
inhabitants of Hazor—oracle of
the LORD;
For Nebuchadnezzar, king of Babylon, has devised a strategy
against you,
drawn up a plan against you,
31Get up! set out against a tranquil
nation,
living in security—oracle of the
LORD—
Without gates or bars,
dwelling alone.
32Their camels shall become spoils,
their hordes of cattle, plunder;

49:23-27 Against Damascus

Damascus, as the capital of Syria, stands in for the nation itself. Syria
and Israel were often at war prior to 721 B.C., but their enmity receded into
the background after the northern kingdom was destroyed. The inclusion
of Syria among these oracles may be due to the help given to Nebuchadnezzar by the Syrian armies when he invaded Jerusalem and Judah in 597 B.C.
(35:11), but there is no information in the oracle to locate it as a response
to a particular historical situation. The oracle focuses on Syria's fear and
distress at the abandonment of its once glorious city and the destruction of
its warriors, but no reason is given for the judgment against Syria.

49:28-33 Against Arabia

Little is known of the Arabian tribes located south and east of Canaan.
Kedar was noted for its commerce and its people were desert-dwellers, but
Hazor, not to be confused with the city in Palestine, is unknown. There is
no antipathy against these people expressed here or in the rest of the Old
Testament. The reason for judgment against them is perhaps alluded to in
verse 31, but it is not clear that there is anything wrong with being a "tranquil nation, living in security," being "[w]ithout gates or bars" and "dwelling alone." It may be that such a description suggests complacency and
arrogance. Nebuchadnezzar is explicitly mentioned and it is known that

I will scatter to the winds those
  who shave their temples;
  from every side I will bring their
    ruin—
  oracle of the LORD.
³³Hazor shall become a haunt for
    jackals,
  a wasteland forever,
Where no one lives,
  no mortal stays.

Against Elam. ³⁴The word of the LORD that came to Jeremiah the prophet concerning Elam at the beginning of the reign of Zedekiah, king of Judah:

³⁵Thus says the LORD of hosts:
Look! I will break the bow of Elam,
  the mainstay of their might.
³⁶I will bring upon Elam the four
    winds
  from the four ends of the heavens:

I will scatter them to all these
  winds, until there is no
    nation
  to which the outcasts of Elam
    have not gone.
³⁷I will terrify Elam before their foes,
  those seeking their life;
I will bring evil upon them,
  my burning wrath—oracle of
    the LORD.
I will send sword after them
  until I have finished them off;
³⁸I will set up my throne in Elam
  and destroy from there king and
    princes—
  oracle of the LORD.
³⁹But at the end of days I will restore
  the fortunes of Elam—oracle of
    the LORD.

50 **The First Oracle Against Babylon.**
¹The word the LORD spoke against

he subjugated the Arabian tribes. The Lord addresses both the Babylonian armies and the people whom they will attack. The Babylonians are commanded to attack and plunder Kedar and Hazor; the people of these tribes are warned to flee. The severity of this judgment is indicated by Hazor becoming "a haunt for jackals" and "a wasteland forever" (49:33).

49:34-39 Against Elam

Unlike the other oracles against the nations, the oracle against Elam is dated; it is set at the beginning of the reign of Zedekiah (49:34). It differs from the other oracles against the nations in other ways as well. There are no direct addresses either to enemies or to the Elamites. Other than Elam there are no place names and there are no references to life in Elam. No one laments; indeed, nothing is said of the actions of anyone other than the Lord. There is no reason given for the announcement of judgment against Elam; the judgment alone dominates the oracle. The subject of each verb is the Lord, as a series of calamities against Elam is announced in terms that echo similar judgments in the book of Jeremiah. The conclusion rather surprisingly makes a brief announcement that the fortunes of Elam will be restored at the end of time.

Babylon, against the land of the Chaldeans, through Jeremiah the prophet:

²Proclaim this among the nations,
   announce it!
      Announce it, do not hide it, but
         say:
Babylon is captured, Bel put to
   shame, Marduk terrified;
      its images are put to shame, its
         idols shattered.
³A nation from the north advances
   against it,
      making the land desolate
So that no one can live there;
   human beings and animals have
      fled.
⁴In those days and at that time—
   oracle of the LORD—
      Israelite and Judahite shall come
         together,
Weeping as they come, to seek the
   LORD, their God;
⁵They shall ask for Zion,
   seeking out the way.
"Come, let us join ourselves to the
   LORD
      in an everlasting covenant,
         never to be forgotten."

⁶Lost sheep were my people,
   their shepherds misled them,
      leading them astray on the
         mountains;
From mountain to hill they
   wandered,
      forgetting their fold.
⁷Whoever happened upon them
   devoured them;
      their enemies said, "We are not
         guilty,
Because they sinned against the
   LORD,
      the abode of justice, the hope of
         their ancestors."
⁸Flee from the midst of Babylon,
   leave the land of the Chaldeans,
      be like rams at the head of the
         flock.
⁹See, I am stirring up against
   Babylon
      a band of great nations from the
         land of the north;
They are arrayed against her,
   from there she shall be taken.
Their arrows are like the arrows of
   a skilled warrior
      who never returns empty-
         handed.

50:1-46 The first oracle against Babylon

Oracles against Babylon bring the section on the oracles against the nations to a close. These oracles are considerably longer than the others, suggesting the dominance of Babylon in Judah's last days and the importance of the defeat of Babylon for the restoration of the exiles to their land. This first oracle gives a vivid description of the destruction of Babylon, drawing much of its language and imagery from other oracles against the nations. The overriding reason given for Babylon's demise is its arrogance in challenging the Lord (50:24, 31-32). Babylon was the mediator of the Lord's judgment, but it went beyond what the Lord required of it by its brutality against the land of Judah and its people. The destruction of Babylon is linked to a proclamation of hope for the exiles. With the land of their oppressor in ruins the exiles are free to return home.

¹⁰Chaldea shall become plunder;
 all its plunderers shall be
  enriched—
 oracle of the LORD.
¹¹Yes, rejoice and exult,
 you that plunder my heritage;
Frisk like calves on the grass,
 neigh like stallions!
¹²Your mother will indeed be put to
 shame,
 she that bore you shall be
  abashed;
See, the last of the nations,
 a wilderness, a dry wasteland.
¹³Because of the LORD's wrath it
 shall be uninhabited,
 become an utter wasteland;
Everyone who passes by Babylon
 will be appalled
 and hiss at all its wounds.
¹⁴Take your posts encircling Babylon,
 you who bend the bow;
Shoot at it, do not spare your arrows,
 ¹⁵raise the war cry against it on
  every side.
It surrenders, its bastions fall,
 its walls are torn down:
This is retribution from the LORD!
 Take retribution on her,
 as she has done, do to her;
 for she sinned against the LORD.
¹⁶Cut off the sower from Babylon
 and those who wield sickles at
  harvest time!
Before the destroying sword,
 all of them turn back to their
  own people,
 all flee to their own land.
¹⁷Israel was a stray sheep
 that lions pursued;
The king of Assyria once devoured
 him;
 now Nebuchadnezzar of Babylon gnaws his bones.
¹⁸Therefore, thus says the LORD of
 hosts, the God of Israel:
I will punish the king of Babylon
 and his land,

as I once punished the king of
 Assyria;
¹⁹But I will bring Israel back to its
 pasture,
 to feed on Carmel and Bashan,
And on Mount Ephraim and Gilead,
 until they have their fill.

²⁰In those days, at that time—oracle of
the LORD:

 The guilt of Israel may be sought,
  but it no longer exists,
  the sin of Judah, but it can no
   longer be found;
  for I will forgive the remnant I
   preserve.
²¹Attack the land of Merathaim,
 and those who live in Pekod;
Slaughter and put them under the
 ban—oracle of the LORD—
 do all I have commanded you.
²²Battle alarm in the land,
 great destruction!
²³How the hammer of the whole
 earth
 has been cut off and broken!
What an object of horror
 Babylon has become among the
  nations!
²⁴You ensnared yourself and were
 caught,
 Babylon, before you knew it!
You were discovered and seized,
 because you challenged the
  LORD.
²⁵The LORD opens his armory,
 brings out the weapons of his
  wrath;
The Lord GOD of hosts has work to
 do
 in the land of the Chaldeans.
²⁶Come upon them from every side,
 open their granaries,
Pile them up in heaps and put them
 under the ban;
 do not leave a remnant.
²⁷Slay all the oxen,
 take them down to slaughter;

Woe to them! their day has come,
the time of their punishment.
²⁸Listen! the fugitives, the refugees
from the land of Babylon:
They announce in Zion
the retribution of the Lord, our
God.
²⁹Call archers out against Babylon,
all who bend the bow;
Encamp around them;
let no one escape.
Repay them for their deeds;
what they have done, do to
them,
For they insulted the Lord,
the Holy One of Israel.
³⁰Therefore their young men shall
fall in the squares,
all their warriors shall be stilled
on that day—
oracle of the Lord.
³¹I am against you, O Insolence—
oracle of the Lord God of hosts;
For your day has come,
the time for me to punish you.
³²Insolence stumbles and falls;
there is no one to raise him up.
I will kindle a fire in his cities
to devour everything around
him.
³³Thus says the Lord of hosts:
Oppressed are the people of Israel,
together with the people of
Judah;
All their captors hold them fast
and refuse to let them go.
³⁴Strong is their Redeemer,
whose name is Lord of hosts,
The sure defender of their cause,
who gives rest to their land,
but unrest to those who live in
Babylon.
³⁵A sword upon the Chaldeans—
oracle of the Lord—
upon the inhabitants of Babylon,
her princes and sages!
³⁶A sword upon the soothsayers,

and they become fools!
A sword upon the warriors,
and they tremble;
³⁷A sword upon their motley
throng,
and they become women!
A sword upon their treasures,
and they are plundered;
³⁸A drought upon the waters,
and they dry up!
For it is a land of idols,
soon made frantic by phantoms.
³⁹Hence, wildcats shall dwell there
with hyenas,
and ostriches occupy it;
Never again shall it be inhabited or
settled,
from age to age.
⁴⁰As happened when God over-
turned Sodom
and Gomorrah and their
neighbors—oracle of the
Lord—
No one shall dwell there,
no mortal shall settle there.
⁴¹See, a people comes from the north,
a great nation, and mighty kings
rising from the ends of the earth.
⁴²Bow and javelin they wield,
cruel and pitiless are they;
They sound like the roaring sea,
as they ride forth on horses,
Each in place for battle
against you, daughter Babylon.
⁴³The king of Babylon hears news of
them,
and his hands hang helpless;
Anguish takes hold of him,
like the pangs of a woman giving
birth.
⁴⁴As happens when a lion comes up
from a thicket of the Jordan
to permanent pasture,
So I, in an instant, will chase them
off,
and establish there whomever I
choose!

For who is like me? Who can call
  me to account?
What shepherd can stand
  against me?
⁴⁵Therefore, hear the strategy of the
  Lord,
which he has devised against
  Babylon;
Hear the plans drawn up
against the land of the
  Chaldeans:
They shall be dragged away, even
  the smallest sheep;
their own pasture aghast because
  of them.
⁴⁶At the cry "Babylon is captured!"
  the earth quakes;
the outcry is heard among the
  nations.

The Second Oracle Against Babylon

51 ¹Thus says the Lord:

See! I rouse against Babylon,
and the inhabitants of Chaldea,
a destroyer wind.
²To Babylon I will send winnowers
to winnow and lay waste the
  land;
They shall besiege it on every side
on the day of affliction.
³How can the archers draw back
  their bows,
lift their armor?

Do not spare her young men,
put the entire army under the
  ban.
⁴The slain shall fall in the land of
  Chaldea,
the wounded, in its streets;
⁵For Israel and Judah are not left
  widowed
by their God, the Lord of hosts,
Even though the land is full of guilt
against the Holy One of Israel.
⁶Flee from Babylon;
each of you save your own life,
do not perish because of her
  guilt;
This is a time of retribution from
  the Lord,
⁷who pays out her due.
Babylon was a golden cup in the
  hand of the Lord
making the whole earth drunk;
The nations drank its wine,
thus they have gone mad.
⁸Babylon suddenly falls and is
  broken:
wail over her!
Bring balm for her wounds,
in case she can be healed.
⁹"We have tried to heal Babylon,
but she cannot be healed.
Leave her, each of us must go to
  our own land."
The judgment against her reaches
  the heavens,
it touches the clouds.

51:1-58 The second oracle against Babylon

The forcefulness of this second oracle is found in its lengthy description of the total devastation that will be visited upon Babylon. Images of destruction wrought by war dominate, but the unrelenting announcement of judgment is punctuated by a concern for the exiles. Assurance is given that the Lord's people will be vindicated (51:5-6, 10, 11b, 24, 36) because Israel is the Lord's own "portion"/"tribe" (51:18-19). The power of the Lord to carry out the punishment of Babylon is affirmed, for it is God who rules over all of creation (51:14-16, 19).

¹⁰The LORD has brought forth our
  vindication;
  come, let us tell in Zion
  what the LORD, our God, has
    done.
¹¹Sharpen the arrows,
  fill the quivers;
The LORD has stirred up the spirit
  of the kings of the Medes,
  for his resolve is Babylon's
    destruction.
Yes, it is retribution from the LORD,
  retribution for his temple.
¹²Over the walls of Babylon raise a
    signal,
  reinforce the watch;
Post sentries,
  arrange ambushes!
For the LORD has both planned and
    carried out
  what he spoke against the
    inhabitants of Babylon.
¹³You who dwell by mighty waters,
  rich in treasure,
Your end has come,
  the time at which you shall be
    cut off!
¹⁴The LORD of hosts has sworn by
    himself:
  I will fill you with people as
    numerous as locusts,
  who shall raise over you a joyous
    shout!
¹⁵He made the earth by his power,
  established the world by
    wisdom,
  and by his skill stretched out the
    heavens.
¹⁶When he thunders, the waters in
    the heavens roar,
  he summons clouds from the
    ends of the earth,
Makes lightning flash in the rain,
  and brings out winds from their
    storehouses.
¹⁷Every man is stupid, ignorant;

every artisan is put to shame by
    his idol:
He molds a fraud,
  without life-breath.
¹⁸They are nothing, a ridiculous
    work,
  that will perish at the time of
    punishment.
¹⁹Jacob's portion is nothing like
    them:
  he is the creator of all things.
Israel is his very own tribe;
  LORD of hosts is his name.
²⁰You are my hammer,
  a weapon for war;
With you I shatter nations,
  with you I destroy kingdoms.
²¹With you I shatter horse and rider,
  with you I shatter chariot and
    driver.
²²With you I shatter man and
    woman,
  with you I shatter old and
    young,
  with you I shatter the young
    man and young woman.
²³With you I shatter shepherd and
    flock,
  with you I shatter farmer and
    team,
  with you I shatter governors
    and officers.
²⁴Thus I will repay Babylon,
  all the inhabitants of Chaldea,
For all the evil they committed
    against Zion,
  before your very eyes—oracle of
    the LORD.
²⁵Beware! I am against you,
  destroying mountain—oracle of
    the LORD—
  destroyer of the entire earth,
I will stretch forth my hand against
    you,
  roll you down over the cliffs,
  and make you a burnt mountain:

²⁶They will not take from you a
cornerstone,
or a foundation stone;
You shall remain ruins forever—
oracle of the Lord.
²⁷Raise a signal in the land,
sound the trumpet among the
nations;
Dedicate nations for war against
her,
summon against her the
kingdoms:
Ararat, Minni, and Ashkenaz;
Appoint a recruiting officer against
her,
dispatch horses like bristling
locusts.
²⁸Dedicate nations for war against
her:
the king of the Medes,
Its governors and all its officers,
every land in its domain.
²⁹The earth quakes and writhes,
the Lord's plan against Babylon
is carried out,
Turning the land of Babylon
into a wasteland without inhabitants.
³⁰Babylon's warriors have ceased to
fight,
they remain in their strongholds;
Dried up is their strength,
they have become women.
Burned down are their homes,
broken their gates.
³¹One runner meets another,
herald meets herald,
Telling the king of Babylon
that his entire city has been
taken.
³²The fords have been seized,
marshes set on fire,
warriors panic.

³³For thus says the Lord of hosts, the
God of Israel:

Daughter Babylon is like a threshing
floor
at the time of treading;
Yet a little while,
and the harvest time will come
for her.
³⁴"He consumed me, defeated me,
Nebuchadnezzar, king of
Babylon;
he left me like an empty vessel,
Swallowed me like a sea monster,
filled his belly with my delicacies
and cast me out.
³⁵Let my torn flesh be visited upon
Babylon,"
says enthroned Zion;
"My blood upon the inhabitants of
Chaldea,"
says Jerusalem.
³⁶But now, thus says the Lord:
I will certainly defend your cause,
I will certainly avenge you;
I will dry up her sea,
and drain her fountain.
³⁷Babylon shall become a heap of
ruins,
a haunt of jackals;
A place of horror and hissing,
without inhabitants.
³⁸They roar like lions,
growl like lion cubs.
³⁹When they are parched, I will set
drink before them
to make them drunk, that they
may be overcome
with everlasting sleep, never to
awaken—
oracle of the Lord.
⁴⁰I will bring them down like lambs
to slaughter,
like rams and goats.
⁴¹How she has been seized, taken
captive,
the glory of the whole world!
What a horror Babylon has become
among the nations:

⁴²against Babylon the sea rises,
she is overwhelmed by roaring
waves!
⁴³Her cities have become wasteland,
a parched and arid land
Where no one lives,
no one passes through.
⁴⁴I will punish Bel in Babylon,
and make him vomit up what
he swallowed;
nations shall no longer stream to
him.
Even the wall of Babylon falls!
⁴⁵Leave her, my people; each of
you save your own life
from the burning wrath of the
LORD.

⁴⁶Do not be discouraged when rumors spread through the land; this year one rumor comes, next year another: "Violence in the land!" or "Ruler against ruler!" ⁴⁷Realize that the days are coming when I will punish the idols of Babylon; the whole land shall be put to shame, all her slain shall fall in her midst. ⁴⁸Then heaven and earth and everything in them shall shout over Babylon with joy, when the destroyers come against her from the north—oracle of the LORD. ⁴⁹Babylon, too, must fall, you slain of Israel, because by the hand of Babylon the slain of all the earth have fallen.

⁵⁰You who have escaped the sword,
go, do not stand idle;
Remember the LORD from far away,
let Jerusalem come to mind.
⁵¹We are ashamed because we have
heard taunts,
disgrace covers our faces;
strangers have entered sanctuaries in the LORD's house.
⁵²Therefore see, the days are coming—oracle of the LORD—
when I will punish her idols,
and throughout the land the
wounded will groan.
⁵³Though Babylon scale the heavens,
and make her strong heights
inaccessible,
my destroyers shall reach her—
oracle of the LORD.
⁵⁴A sound of crying from Babylon,
great destruction from the land
of the Chaldeans;
⁵⁵For the LORD lays Babylon waste,
silences her loud cry,
Waves roaring like mighty waters,
a clamor resounding.
⁵⁶For the destroyer comes upon her,
upon Babylon;
warriors are captured, their
bows broken;
The LORD is a God of recompense,
he will surely repay.

⁵⁷I will make her princes and sages drunk, with her governors, officers, and warriors, so that they sleep an everlasting sleep, never to awaken—oracle of the King, whose name is LORD of hosts.

⁵⁸Thus says the LORD of hosts:
The walls of spacious Babylon shall
be leveled to the ground,
its lofty gates destroyed by fire.
The toil of the peoples is for nothing;
the nations weary themselves
for what the flames
consume.

The Prophecy Sent to Babylon. ⁵⁹The mission Jeremiah the prophet gave to

51:59-64 The prophecy sent to Babylon

Jeremiah's commission to Seraiah is set in the fourth year of King Zedekiah's reign and brings the oracles against Babylon to conclusion.

Seraiah, son of Neriah, son of Mahseiah, when he went to Babylon with King Zedekiah, king of Judah, in the fourth year of his reign; Seraiah was chief quartermaster. ⁶⁰Jeremiah wrote down on one scroll the disaster that would befall Babylon; all these words were written against Babylon. ⁶¹And Jeremiah said to Seraiah: "When you reach Babylon, see that you read all these words aloud, ⁶²and then say: LORD, you yourself spoke against this place in order to cut it down so that nothing, human being or beast, could live in it, because it is to remain a wasteland forever. ⁶³When you have finished reading this scroll, tie a stone to it and throw it into the Euphrates, ⁶⁴and say: Thus Babylon shall sink. It will never rise, because of the disaster I am bringing upon it." Thus far the words of Jeremiah.

IX. Historical Appendix

52 **Capture of Jerusalem.** ¹Zedekiah was twenty-one years old when he became king; he reigned eleven years in Jerusalem. His mother's name was Hamutal, daughter of Jeremiah from Libnah. ²He did what was evil in the sight of the LORD, just as Jehoiakim had done. ³Indeed, the things done in Jerusalem and in Judah so angered the LORD that he cast them out from his presence. Thus Zedekiah rebelled against the king of Babylon. ⁴In the tenth month of the ninth year of his reign, on the tenth day of the month, Nebuchadnezzar, king of Babylon, and his entire army advanced against Jerusalem, encamped around it, and built siege walls on every side. ⁵The siege of the city continued until the eleventh year of King Zedekiah.

⁶On the ninth day of the fourth month, when famine had gripped the city and the people had no more bread, ⁷the city walls were breached. All the soldiers fled and left the city by night through the gate between the two walls which was near the king's garden. With

---

Seraiah is to read a scroll written by Jeremiah announcing judgment against Babylon and then he is to throw the scroll into the Euphrates, symbolizing that Babylon will never rise again.

HISTORICAL APPENDIX

Jeremiah 52:1-34

A shorter version of the destruction of Jerusalem and the capture of King Zedekiah is found in 39:1-10. This longer version is taken from 2 Kings 24:18–25:30 with minor changes. The chapter brings to a close the book of Jeremiah showing the fulfillment of the words of judgment from Jeremiah; Jeremiah's message of hope awaits fulfillment in the future.

52:1-11 Capture of Jerusalem

The punishment of the city of Jerusalem and its kings is the main focus of chapter 52. Typical of the theological perspective of the books of Kings

the Chaldeans surrounding the city, they went in the direction of the Arabah. ⁸But the Chaldean army pursued the king and overtook Zedekiah in the wilderness near Jericho; his whole army fled from him.

⁹The king, therefore, was arrested and brought to Riblah, in the land of Hamath, to the king of Babylon, who pronounced judgment on him. ¹⁰As Zedekiah looked on, the king of Babylon slaughtered his sons before his eyes! All the nobles of Judah were slaughtered at Riblah. ¹¹And the eyes of Zedekiah he then blinded, bound him with chains, and the king of Babylon brought him to Babylon and kept him in prison until the day he died.

Destruction of Jerusalem. ¹²On the tenth day of the fifth month, this was in the nineteenth year of Nebuchadnezzar, king of Babylon, Nebuzaradan, captain of the bodyguard, came to Jerusalem as the representative of the king of Baby-

lon. ¹³He burned the house of the Lord, the palace of the king, and all the houses of Jerusalem; every large building he destroyed with fire. ¹⁴Then the Chaldean troops with the captain of the guard tore down all the walls that surrounded Jerusalem.

¹⁵Nebuzaradan, captain of the guard, led into exile the remnant of people left in the city, those who had deserted to the king of Babylon, and the rest of the artisans. ¹⁶But Nebuzaradan, captain of the guard, left behind some of the country's poor as vinedressers and farmers.

¹⁷The bronze pillars that belonged to the house of the Lord, and the wheeled carts and the bronze sea in the house of the Lord, the Chaldeans broke into pieces; they carried away all the bronze to Babylon. ¹⁸They also took the pots, shovels, snuffers, bowls, pans, and all the bronze vessels used for service; ¹⁹the basins, fire holders, bowls, pots, lampstands, pans, the sacrificial bowls made

and also of the book of Jeremiah, the disaster is blamed on the evil actions of both king and people. The siege of the city by the Babylonians lasted eighteen months (January 588 B.C.–August 587 B.C.) and resulted in widespread starvation. King Zedekiah and his army escaped but were caught near Jericho by the Babylonian army. The army fled, but the king was forced to see his sons and officers executed. He was blinded, brought to Babylon, and imprisoned for life.

52:12-30 Destruction of Jerusalem

It is not clear why a month passed before the Babylonian army burned down Jerusalem's houses and large buildings, including the temple and palace, and tore down the city walls. Among those exiled were deserters and artisans, but some of the poor were left behind to tend the land. Temple furnishings were broken into pieces and its vessels were carried into exile. References to additional executions and the numbers of those deported bring to a close the Babylonian destruction and decimation of the kingdom of Judah.

of gold or silver. Along with these furnishings the captain of the guard carried off ²⁰the two pillars, the one sea and its base of twelve oxen cast in bronze, and the wheeled carts King Solomon had commissioned for the house of the LORD. The bronze from all these furnishings was impossible to weigh.

²¹As for the pillars, each of them was eighteen cubits high and twelve cubits in diameter; each was four fingers thick and hollow inside. ²²A bronze capital five cubits high crowned the one pillar, and a network with pomegranates encircled the capital, all of bronze; and so for the other pillar, with pomegranates. ²³There were ninety-six pomegranates on the sides, a hundred pomegranates surrounding the network.

²⁴The captain of the guard also took Seraiah the high priest, Zephaniah the second priest, and the three keepers of the entrance. ²⁵From the city he took one courtier, a commander of soldiers, and seven men in the personal service of the king still in the city, the scribe of the army commander who mustered the people of the land, and sixty of the common people remaining in the city. ²⁶The captain of the guard, Nebuzaradan, arrested them and brought them to the king of Babylon at Riblah, ²⁷who had them struck down and executed in Riblah, in the land of Hamath.

Thus Judah was exiled from the land. ²⁸This is the number of people Nebuchadnezzar led away captive: in his seventh year, three thousand twenty-three people of Judah; ²⁹in the eighteenth year of Nebuchadnezzar, eight hundred thirty-two persons from Jerusalem; ³⁰in the twenty-third year of Nebuchadnezzar, Nebuzaradan, captain of the guard, deported seven hundred forty-five Judahites: four thousand six hundred persons in all.

Favor Shown to Jehoiachin. ³¹In the thirty-seventh year of the exile of Jehoiachin, king of Judah, on the twenty-fifth day of the twelfth month, Evil-merodach, king of Babylon, in the inaugural year of his reign, raised up Jehoiachin, king of Judah, and released him from prison. ³²He spoke kindly to him and gave him a throne higher than the thrones of the other kings who were with him in Babylon. ³³Jehoiachin took off his prison garb and ate at the king's table as long as he lived. ³⁴The allowance given him by the king of Babylon was a perpetual allowance, in fixed daily amounts, all the days of his life until the day of his death.

52:31-34 Favor shown to Jehoiachin

The final verses, drawn from 2 Kings 25:27-30, take place in the year 561/560 B.C. King Jehoiachin, Zedekiah's predecessor, had been exiled and imprisoned in 597 B.C. (2 Kgs 24:15), but he is now released from prison. He is not allowed to return to Jerusalem, but he enjoys a position of privilege in relation to other exiled kings. He is given new clothes and provisions at the king's table, presumably as signs of his elevated status. Though King Jehoiachin will never return from exile and rule over his people, this final notice is often seen as a sign of hope for the future.

The Book of Baruch

The book of Baruch is found in the Catholic canon of Scripture, but it has not been accepted into either the Jewish or Protestant canons. It is sometimes called 1 Baruch to distinguish it from other works attributed to Baruch. These are 2 Baruch, a Syriac Apocalypse, and 3 Baruch, a Greek Apocalypse. "The *Paraleipomena* of Jeremiah" ("things omitted from the prophet Jeremiah") is sometimes designated 4 Baruch. These works are attributed to Baruch, but it is unlikely that he authored any of them. The Letter of Jeremiah is a separate book in the Septuagint (LXX), where it comes after the book of Lamentations, but the Catholic canon follows the order of St. Jerome's Vulgate and places the Letter of Jeremiah at the end of the book of Baruch.

We know of Baruch from the book of Jeremiah, where he is presented as a scribe and secretary to Jeremiah (Jer 32:10-16; 36:1-31). After the assassination of Gedaliah, Baruch is accused of inciting Jeremiah against military leaders from Judah, who had asked Jeremiah for a word from the Lord (Jer 43:1-3). Both Jeremiah and Baruch are taken to Egypt by these military leaders (Jer 43:5-7), presumably against their will. Baruch is a recipient of an oracle of hope from Jeremiah, assuring Baruch that he would survive the exile (Jer 45:1-5). We have no certain knowledge of what became of Baruch after he was taken to Egypt, but the book of Baruch situates him among the exiles in Babylon. It may be that Baruch played an important role in the postexilic community either among the exiles in Babylon, among the refugees in Egypt, or with those who remained in Jerusalem. He became a significant figure over the next several hundred years. Not only were several books attributed to him but he is also assigned roles beyond that of scribe: biographer, sage, prophet, and apocalyptist.

The author, date, and language

The book of Baruch is composed of four independent sections: 1:1–3:8; 3:9–4:4; 4:5–5:9; 6:1-72. Though traditionally the first three sections have been attributed to Baruch, he is explicitly mentioned only in the introduction (1:1-9) to the first section. The opening verses situate the delivery of

Baruch's message in the exilic period, specifically 582 B.C.; the Letter of Jeremiah is said to have been sent by Jeremiah to the Babylonian exiles, though it does not specify whether these are the exiles of 597 B.C. or 587 B.C. These chronological indications cannot be reconciled with the content of the book; for example, the temple cannot be in ruins (presumed in 2:26) and still intact and fully operational (1:10, 14). The identification of Belshazzar as the son of Nebuchadnezzar (1:11) is an error best explained by attributing a late date to the book of Baruch (cf. Dan 5:1-2, where the same mistake is made). The issues and themes taken up in the various sections of the book of Baruch, including the Letter of Jeremiah, reflect the concerns of the late postexilic period and even later. The content of the book betrays a heavy reliance on the Old Testament, especially Second Isaiah (Isa 40–55) and the book of Daniel, which also suggests a late date. It is unlikely that the book was composed prior to 300 B.C., but dates as late as 70 A.D. have been proposed. Our earliest copies of the book of Baruch are in Greek, but it is possible that one or more sections were originally in Hebrew.

Historical situation of the book

The last years of Judah were characterized by political turmoil. It was a vassal of the Babylonian Empire, but after repeated attempts to secure help from Egypt, presumably in a bid for independence, Judah was destroyed by Babylon. The first concerted Babylonian effort against this small kingdom was in 597 B.C. and resulted in the exile of King Jehoiachin and many of Judah's leading citizens, but it was the Babylonian attack of 587 B.C. that resulted in the destruction of the city of Jerusalem and its temple, and another exile. The exile of 587 B.C. was a turning point in the history of Israel. The nation that for centuries had struggled to survive was destroyed. Many were forced into exile to Babylon; others escaped the path of destruction and became refugees in foreign lands. The people scattered among the nations became known as the Jews of the Diaspora. Identity and faith became critically important for those separated from their homeland. Without a nation, who were they? Without a temple, where would they worship? How would they worship? Who would lead them? And, perhaps most important, where was God? Had God abandoned them or was God still with them? The book of Baruch addresses some concerns of the Jews of the Diaspora.

The book of Baruch

The first section of the book of Baruch begins with an introduction that sets the historical context (1:1-9) for the confession of guilt (1:10–2:10) and prayer for deliverance (2:11–3:8). The second section is a praise of wisdom that addresses the importance of wisdom (3:9-23), its inaccessibility (3:24-36), and the relation of wisdom and law (3:37–4:4). The third section is a poem of consolation that consists of a series of addresses: Baruch to the Diaspora (4:5-9a), Jerusalem to its neighbors (4:9b-16), Jerusalem to the Diaspora (4:17-29), and Baruch to Jerusalem (4:30–5:9). Finally, chapter 6 purports to be a letter from Jeremiah warning the exiles against idols and idolatry.

The Book of Baruch

I. Letter to Jerusalem

1 **A. Historical Setting.** ¹Now these are the words of the scroll which Baruch, son of Neriah, son of Mahseiah, son of Zedekiah, son of Hasadiah, son of Hilkiah, wrote in Babylon, ²in the fifth year, on the seventh day of the month, at the time the Chaldeans took Jerusalem and destroyed it with fire. ³Baruch read the words of this scroll in the hearing of Jeconiah, son of Jehoiakim, king of Judah, and all the people who came to the reading: ⁴the nobles, kings' sons, elders, and all the people, small and great—all who lived in Babylon by the river Sud.

LETTER TO JERUSALEM
Baruch 1:1–3:8

1:1-9 Historical setting

Baruch reads a scroll to the exiles in Babylon in 582 B.C., five years after the destruction of Jerusalem. The exiles respond with acts of contrition and they take up a collection to send to Jerusalem in support of the temple. The return of the temple vessels may be seen as a fulfillment of the prophecy in Jeremiah 28:1-6, even though that prophecy was uttered by a false prophet.

1:10–2:10 Confession of guilt

The exiles send to the "people back home" the collection with a request for sacrifices to be offered and prayers to be said on their behalf. They also ask that the scroll they are sending be read aloud. There is no clear beginning of the reading of the scroll itself, but as verse 14 mentions the scroll, presumably it begins in verse 15.

The confession of guilt draws a sharp contrast between God who acts justly (1:15; 2:6, 9) and the people and their leaders who are characterized as "shamefaced" (1:15; 2:6). As the passage develops the people acknowledge their sin and recognize that the punishment they have endured was justified. They recount their sinful actions in general terms: they "sinned"

⁵They wept, fasted, and prayed before the Lord, ⁶and collected such funds as each could afford. ⁷These they sent to Jerusalem, to Jehoiakim the priest, son of Hilkiah, son of Shallum, and to the priests and the whole people who were with him in Jerusalem. ⁸(At the same time he received the vessels of the house of the LORD that had been removed from the temple, to restore them to the land of Judah, on the tenth of Sivan. These silver vessels Zedekiah, son of Josiah, king of Judah, had had made ⁹after Nebuchadnezzar, king of Babylon, carried off as captives Jeconiah and the princes, the skilled workers, the nobles, and the people of the land from Jerusalem, and brought them to Babylon.)

B. Confession of Guilt. ¹⁰The message was: "We send you funds, with which you are to procure burnt offerings, sin offerings, and frankincense, and to prepare grain offerings; offer these on the altar of the LORD our God, ¹¹and pray for the life of Nebuchadnezzar, king of Babylon, and of Belshazzar, his son, that their lifetimes may be as the days of the heavens above the earth. ¹²Pray that the LORD may give us strength, and light to our eyes, that we may live under the protective shadow of Nebuchadnezzar, king of Babylon, and of Belshazzar, his son, to serve them many days, and find favor in their sight. ¹³Pray for us to the LORD, our God, for we have sinned against the LORD, our God. Even to this day the wrath of the LORD and his anger have not turned away from us. ¹⁴On the feast day and during the days of assembly, read aloud in the house of the LORD this scroll that we send you:

¹⁵"To the Lord our God belongs justice; to us, people of Judah and inhabitants of Jerusalem, to be shamefaced, as on this day—¹⁶to us, our kings, rulers, priests, and prophets, and our ancestors. ¹⁷We have sinned in the LORD's sight ¹⁸and disobeyed him. We have not listened to the voice of the LORD, our God, so as to follow the precepts the LORD set before us. ¹⁹From the day the LORD led our ancestors out of the land of Egypt until the present day, we have been disobedient to the LORD, our God, and neglected to listen to

---

(1:17; 2:5), "disobeyed" (1:18, 19), "have not listened" to the Lord's voice (1:18, 19, 21; 2:5, 10), did not follow the Lord's precepts (1:18; 2:10), "followed the inclinations of [their] wicked hearts" (1:22; 2:7), have "done evil" (1:22), and did not turn "from the designs of [their] evil hearts" (2:8). The only specific sin mentioned is that they "served other gods" (1:22).

The people acknowledge that their sinfulness continued in spite of the warnings they had received from the prophets (1:21). That the Lord carried through with the threats contained in these warnings (1:20; 2:1, 7) is justified, because the people refused to heed these warnings. They knew the precepts of the Lord (1:18; 2:10) but chose to disobey them, as had their ancestors (1:15, 19). Their obstinacy is set against the Lord's actions on their behalf: the exodus (1:19, 20) and the gift of the land (1:20), as well as the repeated warnings that they would be punished if they did not repent.

"Now these are the words of the scroll which Baruch . . . wrote in Babylon" (Bar 1:1).

his voice. ²⁰Even today evils cling to us, the curse the LORD pronounced to Moses, his servant, at the time he led our ancestors out of the land of Egypt to give us a land flowing with milk and honey. ²¹For we did not listen to the voice of the LORD, our God, in all the words of the prophets he sent us, ²²but each of us has followed the inclinations of our wicked hearts, served other gods, and done evil in the sight of the LORD, our God.

2 ¹"So the LORD carried out the warning he had uttered against us: against our judges, who governed Israel, against our kings and princes, and against the people of Israel and Judah. ²Nowhere under heaven has anything been done like what he did in Jerusalem, as was written in the law of Moses: ³that we would each eat the flesh of our sons, each the flesh of our daughters. ⁴He has made us subject to all the kingdoms around us, an object of reproach and horror among all the peoples around us,

where the LORD has scattered us. ⁵We are brought low, not raised high, because we sinned against the LORD, our God, not listening to his voice.

⁶"To the LORD, our God, belongs justice; to us and to our ancestors, to be shamefaced, as on this day. ⁷All the evils of which the LORD had warned us have come upon us. ⁸We did not entreat the favor of the LORD by turning, each one, from the designs of our evil hearts. ⁹The LORD kept watch over the evils, and brought them home to us; for the LORD is just in all the works he commanded us to do, ¹⁰but we did not listen to his voice, or follow the precepts of the LORD which he had set before us.

C. Prayer for Deliverance. ¹¹"And now, LORD, God of Israel, who led your people out of the land of Egypt with a strong hand, with signs and wonders and great might, and with an upraised arm, so that you have made for yourself a name to the present day: ¹²we have

---

The horror of the catastrophe is not passed over. It is given expression in a variety of ways: "evils cling to us" (1:20); "curse" (1:20); nowhere has anything like what the Lord did to Jerusalem been done (2:2); we ate the flesh of our sons and daughters (2:3); we are "subject to all the kingdoms around us" (2:4); we are the "object of reproach and horror" (2:4); we have been "brought low" (2:5); "[a]ll the evils . . . have come upon us" (2:7). In spite of the extent of their destruction, it is asserted repeatedly that the Lord is just and the people received the punishment that they deserved. This recounting of sin with references to the warnings of the prophet and to the Lord's past actions on Israel's behalf echoes the language and theology of the Deuteronomic school. It is thought that the prayer of Daniel (Dan 9:4-19) provided a model for this confessional prayer.

2:11–3:8 Prayer for deliverance

The confession of guilt is followed by a prayer for deliverance, which both repeats the confession of guilt and moves beyond it. Once again there are general statements acknowledging the failure of the people: "we have sinned, we have committed sacrilege, we have violated all your statutes, Lord, our God. [13]Withdraw your anger from us, for we are left few in number among the nations where you have scattered us. [14]Hear, Lord, our prayer of supplication, and deliver us for your own sake: grant us favor in the sight of those who brought us into exile, [15]that the whole earth may know that you are the Lord, our God, and that Israel and his descendants bear your name. [16]Lord, look down from your holy dwelling and take thought of us; Lord, incline your ear to hear us. [17]Open your eyes and see: it is not the dead in Hades, whose breath has been taken from within them, who will declare the glory and vindication to the Lord. [18]The person who is deeply grieved, who walks bowed and feeble, with failing eyes and famished soul, will declare your glory and justice, Lord! [19]"Not on the just deeds of our ancestors and our kings do we base our plea for mercy in your sight, Lord, our God. [20]You have sent your wrath and anger upon us, as you had warned us through your servants the prophets: [21]Thus says the Lord: Bend your necks and serve the king of Babylon, that you may continue in the land I gave your ancestors;[22] for if you do not listen to the Lord's voice so as to serve the king of Babylon, [23]I will silence from the cities of Judah and from the streets of Jerusalem the cry of joy and the cry of gladness, the voice of the bridegroom and the voice of the bride; and all the land shall be deserted, without inhabitants. [24]But we did not listen to your voice, or serve the king of Babylon, and you carried out the threats you had made through your servants the prophets, that the bones of our kings and the bones of our ancestors would be brought out from their burial places. [25]And indeed, they lie exposed to the heat of day and the frost of night. They died in great suffering, by famine and sword and plague. [26]And you reduced the house which

---

sinned" (2:12; 3:2, 4); "we did not listen" (2:24; cf. 3:4). But additional ways of speaking of the people's sin are now included: "we have committed sacrilege, we have violated all your statutes" (2:12); we did not "serve the king of Babylon" (2:24) as commanded (2:21). It is Jeremiah who insisted that it was the Lord's will that Judah submit to Babylon (Jer 27:1-22).

Also in this section there is another reference to the Lord's actions on Israel's behalf in the exodus (2:11) and against Israel in punishment for the sin of the people (2:20, 23-26). Most dominant in this section, however, is the prayer to the Lord in which the people ask the Lord to pay attention to them and reverse their present situation of exile: "Withdraw your anger" (2:13), hear our prayer (2:14, 16; 3:2), "hear the prayer of the dead" (3:4), "deliver us" (2:14), "look . . . take thought of us" (2:16), "incline your ear" (2:16), "[o]pen your eyes" (2:17), remember not "the wicked deeds of our ancestors" but rather "your power and your name" (3:5). The people plead for mercy (2:19; 3:2) and cry out to the Lord (3:1).

bears your name to what it is today, because of the wickedness of the house of Israel and the house of Judah.

God's Promises Recalled. ²⁷"But with us, Lord, our God, you have dealt in all your clemency and in all your great mercy.²⁸ Thus you spoke through your servant Moses, the day you ordered him to write down your law in the presence of the Israelites: ²⁹'If you do not listen to my voice, surely this great and numerous throng will dwindle away among the nations to which I will scatter them. ³⁰For I know they will not listen to me, because they are a stiff-necked people. But in the land of their exile they shall have a change of heart; ³¹they shall know that I, the LORD, am their God. I will give them a heart and ears that listen; ³²and they shall praise me in the land of their exile, and shall remember my name. ³³Then they shall turn back from their stiff-necked stubbornness, and from their evil deeds, because they shall remember the ways of their ancestors, who sinned against the LORD. ³⁴And I will bring them back to the land I promised on oath to their ancestors, to Abraham, Isaac, and Jacob; and they shall rule it. I will make them increase; they shall not be few. ³⁵And I will establish for them an eternal covenant: I will be their God, and they shall be my people; and I will never again remove my people Israel from the land I gave them.'

3 ¹"LORD Almighty, God of Israel, the anguished soul, the dismayed spirit cries out to you. ²Hear, LORD, and have mercy, for you are a merciful God; have mercy on us, who have sinned against

---

Throughout the prayer the people's requests are expanded by motivation clauses in an attempt to move the Lord to respond to their prayer. A variety of motivations are drawn upon to persuade the Lord to a change of heart: "for we are left few in number" (2:13), "for your own sake" (2:14), so "that the whole earth may know" that the Lord is our God and that Israel "bear[s] your name" (2:15), "for you are . . . merciful" (3:2), "for you are enthroned forever" (3:3), for "we are perishing" (3:3), for our God is the Lord and we will praise the Lord (3:6).

As the prayer draws to a conclusion there is a shift from the people's confession of their sin to blaming their suffering in exile on the sins of their ancestors (3:8). This shift may represent the position of subsequent generations that remained in exile even though they were not responsible for the exile itself.

PRAISE OF WISDOM

Baruch 3:9–4:4

The "Praise of Wisdom" is a poem that speaks of wisdom but also encourages the pursuit of wisdom. The poem begins and ends with exhortations. The first half of the poem is dominated by questions that are answered

you: ³for you are enthroned forever, while we are perishing forever. ⁴LORD Almighty, God of Israel, hear the prayer of the dead of Israel, children who sinned against you; they did not listen to the voice of the LORD, their God, and their evils cling to us. ⁵Do not remember the wicked deeds of our ancestors, but remember at this time your power and your name, ⁶for you are the LORD our God; and you, LORD, we will praise! ⁷This is why you put into our hearts the fear of you: that we may call upon your name, and praise you in our exile, when we have removed from our hearts all the wickedness of our ancestors who sinned against you. ⁸See, today we are in exile, where you have scattered us, an object of reproach and cursing and punishment for all the wicked deeds of our ancestors, who withdrew from the LORD, our God."

II. Praise of Wisdom

A. Importance of Wisdom

⁹Hear, Israel, the commandments of life:
listen, and know prudence!
¹⁰How is it, Israel,
that you are in the land of your foes,
grown old in a foreign land,
¹¹Defiled with the dead,
counted among those destined for Hades?
¹²You have forsaken the fountain of wisdom!
¹³Had you walked in the way of God,
you would have dwelt in enduring peace.
¹⁴Learn where prudence is,
where strength, where understanding;
That you may know also

---

in the second half of the poem. This intermixing of exhortations with questions and answers prevents the poem from being merely a set of commands. Through the rhetorical device of "question and answer," readers engage dialogically with the poem and become more receptive to its exhortations. The poem draws on themes found elsewhere in the Bible, but it develops these themes with great eloquence.

3:9-23 Importance of wisdom

After exhorting Israel to be attentive to the "commandments of life," the poem turns to the question of the cause of the exile (3:9-11). The prophets attributed the exile to the sinfulness of the people in worshiping other gods and/or in Israel's failure to live in justice, but the author of this poem blames the exile on Israel's abandonment of the fountain of wisdom (3:12). The theory of retribution is underscored in the assertion that if Israel had "walked in the way of God" (3:12) and learned wisdom (3:13), it would have found peace and long life (3:13, 14), but its failure in obedience resulted in its destruction and exile. In a series of rhetorical questions the author implies that rulers and the wealthy have not found wisdom (3:16-19), nor has wisdom been passed onto later generations, even among those whose

where are length of days, and
life,
where light of the eyes, and
peace.
¹⁵Who has found the place of
wisdom?
Who has entered into her
treasuries?
¹⁶Where are the rulers of the
nations,
who lorded it over the wild
beasts of the earth,
¹⁷made sport of the birds in the
heavens,
Who heaped up the silver,
the gold in which people trust,
whose possessions were
unlimited,
¹⁸Who schemed anxiously for
money,
their doings beyond discovery?
¹⁹They have vanished, gone down
to Hades,
and others have risen up in their
stead.
²⁰Later generations have seen the
light of day,
have dwelt on the earth,
But the way to understanding they
have not known,
²¹they have not perceived her
paths or reached her;
their children remain far from
the way to her.

²²She has not been heard of in
Canaan,
nor seen in Teman.
²³The descendants of Hagar who
seek knowledge on earth,
the merchants of Medan and
Tema,
the storytellers and those seeking knowledge—
These have not known the way to
wisdom,
nor have they kept her paths in
mind.

B. Inaccessibility of Wisdom
²⁴O Israel, how vast is the dwelling
of God,
how broad the scope of his
dominion:
²⁵Vast and endless,
high and immeasurable!
²⁶In it were born the giants,
renowned at the first,
huge in stature, skilled in war.
²⁷These God did not choose,
nor did he give them the way of
understanding;
²⁸They perished for lack of prudence,
perished through their own folly.
²⁹Who has gone up to the heavens
and taken her,
bringing her down from the
clouds?

---

nations were renowned for their wisdom (3:20-23). Both this section and the next draw upon Job 28 and Isaiah 40:12-31 in speaking of the inaccessibility of wisdom and the incomparability of Israel's God.

3:24-36 Inaccessibility of wisdom

God's dwelling place is not identified as the temple but as the "vast" and "immeasurable" universe (3:24-25). This notion betrays the influence of Greek thought and that of Philo of Alexandria. The poem continues to stress that wisdom has not been found, even by the heroes, the "giants," of the past (3:26-28). Again in a series of rhetorical questions the author

³⁰Who has crossed the sea and
found her,
bearing her away rather than
choice gold?
³¹None knows the way to her,
nor has at heart her path.
³²But the one who knows all things
knows her;
he has probed her by his knowledge—
The one who established the earth
for all time,
and filled it with four-footed
animals,
³³Who sends out the lightning, and
it goes,
calls it, and trembling it obeys
him;

³⁴Before whom the stars at their
posts
shine and rejoice.
³⁵When he calls them, they answer,
"Here we are!"
shining with joy for their Maker.
³⁶Such is our God;
no other is to be compared to
him:

C. Wisdom Contained in the Law

³⁷He has uncovered the whole way
of understanding,
and has given her to Jacob, his
servant,
to Israel, his beloved.
³⁸Thus she has appeared on earth,
is at home with mortals.

---

highlights the inability of anyone to find wisdom (3:29-31). Only the in-comparable, all-knowing creator God knows wisdom (3:32-36).

3:37–4:4 Wisdom contained in the law

The final section of the poem resolves the dilemma raised by exhorting Israel to pursue wisdom and at the same time insisting that wisdom cannot be found: wisdom has appeared on earth in Israel as the torah (3:37–4:1). In the Old Testament the identification of wisdom with the torah is found only here and in Sirach 24:23-29. Wisdom, embodied in the torah, is God's gift to Israel. The final exhortation to Israel is to recognize that it is privi-leged and blessed, because it knows the will of God (4:3-4).

BARUCH'S POEM OF CONSOLATION

Baruch 4:5–5:9

Often drawing upon the language and imagery of Second Isaiah, this poignant dialogue gives expression to the people's sorrow at the destruc-tion of Jerusalem and their longing for restoration and salvation.

4:5-9a Baruch addresses Diaspora

The speaker is assumed to be Baruch, even though that is never made explicit in this poem. An opening exhortation to "[t]ake courage" is fol-lowed by yet another statement that punishment has come upon the people because they angered God by their actions (4:5-6). It is unusual that the

4 ¹She is the book of the precepts of
God, the law that endures forever;
All who cling to her will live,
but those will die who forsake
her.
²Turn, O Jacob, and receive her:
walk by her light toward
splendor.
³Do not give your glory to another,
your privileges to an alien
nation.
⁴Blessed are we, O Israel;
for what pleases God is known
to us!

III. Baruch's Poem of Consolation

A. Baruch Addresses Diaspora

⁵Take courage, my people!
Remember, O Israel,
⁶You were sold to the nations
not for destruction;
It was because you angered God
that you were handed over to
your foes.
⁷For you provoked your Maker
with sacrifices to demons and
not to God;
⁸You forgot the eternal God who
nourished you,
and you grieved Jerusalem who
nurtured you.

⁹She indeed saw coming upon you
the wrath of God; and she said:

B. Jerusalem Addresses Neighbors

"Hear, you neighbors of Zion!
God has brought great
mourning upon me,
¹⁰For I have seen the captivity
that the Eternal One has brought
upon my sons and daughters.
¹¹With joy I nurtured them;
but with mourning and lament I
sent them away.
¹²Let no one gloat over me,
a widow, bereft of many;
For the sins of my children I am left
desolate,
because they turned from the
law of God,
¹³and did not acknowledge his
statutes;
In the ways of God's commandments they did not walk,
nor did they tread the disciplined
paths of his justice.

¹⁴"Let Zion's neighbors come—
Remember the captivity of my
sons and daughters,
brought upon them by the
Eternal One.

---

people are accused of sacrificing to demons (4:7), but this probably represents an intensification of the polemic against other gods by equating them
with demons. The personification of Jerusalem as a woman begins here
and is continued throughout this poem.

4:9b-16 Jerusalem addresses neighbors

Jerusalem expresses her grief over the exile of her citizens. It is the grief
of a widow who has lost her children (4:4b-12a, 16). The people have refused
to acknowledge and obey the law of God (4:12b-13) and therefore God has
made them captives of another nation. Jerusalem calls upon the neighboring countries to remember the destruction and desolation that Israel's God
brought upon her (4:14-16).

¹⁵He has brought against them a
    nation from afar,
  a nation ruthless and of alien
    speech,
That has neither reverence for old
    age
  nor pity for the child;
¹⁶They have led away this widow's
    beloved sons,
  have left me solitary, without
    daughters.

C. Jerusalem Addresses Diaspora

¹⁷What can I do to help you?
  ¹⁸The one who has brought this
    evil upon you
  must himself deliver you from
    your enemies' hands.
¹⁹Farewell, my children, farewell;
  I am left desolate.
²⁰I have taken off the garment of
    peace,
  have put on sackcloth for my
    prayer of supplication;
  while I live I will cry out to the
    Eternal One.
²¹"Take courage, my children; call
    upon God;
  he will deliver you from oppres-
    sion, from enemy hands.

²²I have put my hope for your
    deliverance in the Eternal
    One,
  and joy has come to me from the
    Holy One
Because of the mercy that will
    swiftly reach you
  from your eternal Savior.
²³With mourning and lament I sent
    you away,
  but God will give you back to me
  with gladness and joy forever.
²⁴As Zion's neighbors lately saw
    you taken captive,
  so shall they soon see God's
    salvation come to you,
  with great glory and the
    splendor of the Eternal
    One.

²⁵"My children, bear patiently the
    wrath
  that has come upon you from
    God;
Your enemies have persecuted you,
  but you will soon see their
    destruction
  and trample upon their necks.
²⁶My pampered children have
    trodden rough roads,

4:17-29 Jerusalem addresses Diaspora

Jerusalem raises the question as to what she can do, for it is God who must deliver the people and she mourns for her loss by putting on sackcloth and making supplication (4:17-20). With confidence in the mercy of God, Jerusalem encourages the people to call upon God to deliver them (4:21-22). When God's salvation comes, there will be reversals: Jerusalem's mourning will be turned to joy; those who saw the people led away as captives will now see them return (4:23-24). Jerusalem seeks to motivate the people to be patient in their suffering by continuing the contrast between the present and the future: their persecutors will be destroyed; though they were carried off, God will remember them; those who strayed away will turn back to God; the God who brought disaster will bring deliverance (4:25-29).

carried off by their enemies like
sheep in a raid.
[27]Take courage, my children; call
out to God!
The one who brought this upon
you will remember you.
[28]As your hearts have been
disposed to stray from God,
so turn now ten times the more
to seek him;
[29]For the one who has brought disaster upon you
will, in saving you, bring you
eternal joy."

D. Baruch Addresses Jerusalem

[30]Take courage, Jerusalem!
The one who gave you your
name will console you.
[31]Wretched shall be those who
harmed you,
who rejoiced at your downfall;
[32]Wretched shall be the cities where
your children were enslaved,
wretched the city that received
your children.
[33]As that city rejoiced at your
collapse,
and made merry at your downfall,
so shall she grieve over her own
desolation.
[34]I will take from her the rejoicing
crowds,
and her exultation shall be
turned to mourning:
[35]For fire shall come upon her

from the Eternal One, for many a
day,
to be inhabited by demons for a
long time.
[36]Look to the east, Jerusalem;
see the joy that comes to you
from God!
[37]Here come your children whom
you sent away,
gathered in from east to west
By the word of the Holy One,
rejoicing in the glory of God.
[1]Jerusalem, take off your
robe of mourning and misery;
put on forever the splendor
of glory from God:
[2]Wrapped in the mantle of justice
from God,
place on your head the diadem
of the glory of the Eternal One.
[3]For God will show your splendor
to all
under the heavens;
[4]you will be named by God
forever:
the peace of justice, the glory of
God's worship.
[5]Rise up, Jerusalem! stand upon the
heights;
look to the east and see your
children
Gathered from east to west
at the word of the Holy One,
rejoicing that they are
remembered by God.
[6]Led away on foot by their enemies
they left you:

4:30–5:9 Baruch addresses Jerusalem

Jerusalem is addressed in this final section with a series of exhortations:
"Take courage" (4:30); "[l]ook to the east" (4:36); "take off your robe of
mourning and misery" (5:1); "[r]ise up . . . stand upon the heights; / look
. . . and see" (5:4). All these actions are in response to the salvation that is
at hand. As before, a contrast is drawn between the time of mourning and
the triumph of Jerusalem's enemies, and the time of rejoicing and the defeat

but God will bring them back to
   you
carried high in glory as on royal
   thrones.
⁷For God has commanded
   that every lofty mountain
   and the age-old hills be made
      low,
That the valleys be filled to make
      level ground,
   that Israel may advance securely
      in the glory of God.
⁸The forests and every kind of
      fragrant tree
   have overshadowed Israel at
      God's command;
⁹For God is leading Israel in joy
   by the light of his glory,
   with the mercy and justice that
      are his.

IV. Letter of Jeremiah

6 ¹A copy of the letter which Jeremiah
sent to those led captive to Babylon

by the king of the Babylonians, to tell
them what God had commanded him:
   For the sins you committed before
God, you are being led captive to Babylon by Nebuchadnezzar, king of the
Babylonians. ²When you reach Babylon
you will be there many years, a long
time—seven generations; after that I will
bring you back from there in peace. ³And
now in Babylon you will see gods of silver and gold and wood, carried shoulder high, to cast fear upon the nations.
⁴Take care that you yourselves do not
become like these foreigners and let not
such fear possess you. ⁵When you see
the crowd before them and behind worshiping them, say in your hearts, "You,
Lord, are the one to be worshiped!" ⁶For
my angel is with you, and he will keep
watch on you.
   ⁷Their tongues are smoothed by
woodworkers; they are covered with
gold and silver—but they are frauds,

of those who led the Jerusalem's citizens into exile (4:31-34). The splendor
of the time of salvation is highlighted by terms such as joy, rejoice, glory,
peace, mercy, and justice, which dominate the last verses of this passage.

THE LETTER OF JEREMIAH

Baruch 6:1-72

   This final chapter is said to be a letter from Jeremiah sent, at God's command, to the people who had been carried into exile, either the exile of 597
B.C. or 587 B.C. The letter begins by stating the reason for the exile (sinfulness, 6:1) and the duration of the exile (up to seven generations, 6:2), but
the rest of the poem is a warning against idolatry. The pomp and circum-
stance associated with the worship of idols made the worship of other gods
attractive to those exiled to Babylon (6:3), especially if the exiles felt abandoned by God or thought that their God was powerless before the gods of
their conquerors. Jeremiah's letter is a sustained warning against the worship of idols, but it reads more like a caustic sermon than a letter. It is similar

and cannot speak. [8]People bring gold, as though for a girl fond of dressing up, [9]and prepare crowns for the heads of their gods. Then sometimes the priests filch the gold and silver from their gods and spend it on themselves, [10]or give part of it to harlots in the brothel. They dress them up in clothes like human beings, these gods of silver and gold and wood. [11]Though they are wrapped in purple clothing, they are not safe from rust and corrosion. [12]Their faces are wiped clean of the cloud of dust which is thick upon them. [13]Each has a scepter, like the human ruler of a district, but none can do away with those that offend against it. [14]Each has in its right hand an ax or dagger, but it cannot save itself from war or pillage. Thus it is known they are not gods; do not fear them.

[15]As useless as a broken pot [16]are their gods, set up in their temples, their eyes full of dust from the feet of those who enter. [17]Their courtyards are walled in like those of someone brought to execution for a crime against the king; the priests reinforce their temples with gates and bars and bolts, so they will not be carried off by robbers. [18]They light more lamps for them than for themselves, yet not one of these can they see. [19]They are like any timber in the temple; their hearts, it is said, are eaten away. Though crawling creatures from the ground consume them and their garments, they do not feel it. [20]Their faces become sooty from the smoke in the temple. [21]Bats and swallows alight on their bodies and heads—any bird, and cats as well. [22]Know, therefore, that they are not gods; do not fear them.

[23]Gold adorns them, but unless someone wipes away the corrosion, they do not shine; they felt nothing when they were molded. [24]They are bought at whatever price, but there is no spirit in them. [25]Since they have no feet, they are carried shoulder high, displaying to all how worthless they are; even those who worship them are put to shame [26]because, if they fall to the ground, the worshipers must pick them up. They neither move of themselves if one sets them upright, nor come upright if they are tipped over; offerings are set out for them as for the dead. [27]Their priests sell their sacrifices

in tone to the mockery of idols, such as we find in Second Isaiah (40:18-20; 41:6-7; 44:9-20; 46:5-7), but its mockery is carried to a greater extreme.

There is a great deal of repetition that serves to underscore the futility of worshiping idols: "they are not gods" (6:14, 22, 28, 49, 50, 51, 64, 71); they cannot be "thought," "called," or "claimed" as gods (6:29, 39, 44, 47, 56, 63, 68); they are "false gods" (vv. 58 [3x], 62); because idols are not gods, they are not to be feared (6:14, 22, 28, 64, 68). Interspersed between these assertions are descriptions of the idols that show why it is ridiculous to worship these false gods. As with the mockery of the idols in Second Isaiah, the author points out that the idols are made by artisans (6:7, 45, 50); they cannot speak (6:7), cannot see (6:18), and cannot move on their own (6:25, 26). Those who worship idols do not have sense (6:35-37).

"As useless as a broken pot are their gods, . . . their eyes full of dust from the feet of those who enter" (Bar 6:15).

for their own advantage. Likewise their wives cure some of the meat, but they do not share it with the poor and the weak; ²⁸women ritually unclean or at childbirth handle their sacrifices. From such things, know that they are not gods; do not fear them.

²⁹How can they be called gods? Women set out the offerings for these gods of silver and gold and wood, ³⁰and in their temples the priests squat with torn tunic and with shaven hair and beard, and with their heads uncovered. ³¹They shout and wail before their gods as others do at a funeral banquet. ³²The priests take some of the clothing from their gods and put it on their wives and children. ³³Whether these gods are treated well or badly by anyone, they cannot repay it. They can neither set up nor remove a king. ³⁴They cannot give anyone riches or pennies; if one fails to fulfill a vow to them, they will not exact

it. ³⁵They neither save anyone from death, nor deliver the weak from the strong, ³⁶nor do they restore sight to the blind, or rescue anyone in distress. ³⁷The widow they do not pity, the orphan they do not help. ³⁸These gilded and silvered wooden statues are no better than stones from the mountains; their worshipers will be put to shame. ³⁹How then can it be thought or claimed that they are gods?

⁴⁰Even the Chaldeans themselves have no respect for them; for when they see a deaf mute, unable to speak, they bring forward Bel and expect him to make a sound, as though he could hear. ⁴¹They themselves are unable to reflect and abandon these gods, for they have no sense. ⁴²And the women, with cords around them, sit by the roads, burning chaff for incense; ⁴³and whenever one of them is taken aside by some passerby who lies with her, she mocks her neighbor who

---

To this modest list from Second Isaiah the author expands considerably. To the inactivity of idols the author adds that they cannot dress (6:8-10) or clean themselves (6:12, 23). Idols are totally passive; they are subject to rust, corrosion, and fire (6:11, 23, 56-57); even their clothes rot (6:12, 23, 71). They are consumed by insects (6:19), their faces get sooty (6:20), and they become a perch for birds and bats and even for cats (6:21). They are imprisoned like criminals (6:17), bought (6:24), handled by the unclean (6:28), stolen (6:56), stripped (6:57), and thrown away like a corpse (6:70-71). They cannot feel (6:23) and they have "no spirit" (6:24). Indeed they are "no better than stones" (6:38) or scarecrows in a field (6:69). Idols cannot take action; they cannot do justice (6:13, 33, 63), protect (6:69), heal (6:36, 41), vindicate or rescue (6:36-37, 53), save or deliver (6:35) even themselves (6:14, 33), bless with wealth (6:34), bring rain (6:52), and bestow kingship (6:52). They are powerless (6:53) and useless (6:6); they are frauds (6:7, 47, 50). Beasts are better, for they can help themselves (6:67). Idols do not equal the forces of nature (the sun, moon, wind, lightning), which are commanded by God (6:59-62); they cannot even shine like the sun and moon (6:66).

has not been thought thus worthy, and has not had her cord broken. ⁴⁴All that is done for these gods is a fraud; how then can it be thought or claimed that they are gods?

⁴⁵They are produced by woodworkers and goldsmiths; they are nothing other than what these artisans wish them to be. ⁴⁶Even those who produce them are not long-lived; ⁴⁷how then can the things they have produced be gods? They have left frauds and disgrace to their successors. ⁴⁸For when war or disaster comes upon them, the priests deliberate among themselves where they can hide with them. ⁴⁹How then can one not understand that these are not gods, who save themselves neither from war nor from disaster? ⁵⁰Beings that are wooden, gilded and silvered, they will later be known for frauds. To all nations and kings it will be clear that they are not gods, but human handiwork; and that God's work is not in them. ⁵¹Is it not obvious that they are not gods?

⁵²They set no king over the land, nor do they give rain. ⁵³They neither vindicate their own rights, nor do they rescue anyone wronged, for they are powerless. ⁵⁴They are like crows in midair. For when fire breaks out in the temple of these wooden or gilded or silvered gods, though the priests flee and are safe, they themselves are burned up in the fire like timbers. ⁵⁵They cannot resist a king or enemy forces. ⁵⁶How then can it be admitted or thought that they are gods?

They are safe from neither thieves nor bandits, these wooden and silvered and gilded gods. ⁵⁷Anyone who can will strip off the gold and the silver, and go away with the clothing that was on them; they cannot help themselves. ⁵⁸How much better to be a king displaying his valor, or a handy tool in a house, the joy of its owner, than these false gods; better the door of a house, protecting whatever is within, than these false gods; better a wooden post in a palace, than these false gods! ⁵⁹The sun and moon and stars are bright, obedient in the task for which they are sent. ⁶⁰Likewise the lightning, when it flashes, is a great sight; and the one wind blows over every land. ⁶¹The clouds, too, when commanded by God to proceed across the whole world, fulfill the command; ⁶²and fire, sent from on high to burn up the mountains and the forests, carries out its command. But these false gods are not their equal, whether in appearance or in power. ⁶³So it is unthinkable, and cannot be claimed that they are gods. They can neither execute judgment, nor benefit anyone. ⁶⁴Know, therefore, that they are not gods; do not fear them.

The priests who serve these idols are not left unscathed by the author of this letter. He accuses them of stealing gold and silver offered to the idols and giving it to harlots (6:9-10). They even steal the clothing of the idols and give it to their wives (6:32). They sell sacrifices for their own gain; their wives do not share cured meat with the poor and weak (6:27). The devotion of the priests is called into question, for they abandon their idols when war or fire threatens (6:49, 54).

⁶⁵Kings they can neither curse nor bless. ⁶⁶They show the nations no signs in the heavens, nor do they shine like the sun, nor give light like the moon. ⁶⁷The beasts are better than they—beasts can help themselves by fleeing to shelter. ⁶⁸Thus is it in no way apparent to us that they are gods; so do not fear them.

⁶⁹For like a scarecrow in a cucumber patch, providing no protection, are their wooden, gilded, silvered gods. ⁷⁰Just like a thornbush in a garden on which perches every kind of bird, or like a corpse hurled into darkness, are their wooden, gilded, silvered gods. ⁷¹From the rotting of the purple and the linen upon them, you can know that they are not gods; they themselves will in the end be consumed, and be a disgrace in the land. ⁷²Better the just who has no idols; such shall be far from disgrace!

This rather scathing treatment of idols is meant to deter the exiles from the worship of other gods; the Lord alone is to be worshiped (6:5). Only the God who commands the forces of nature and brings justice and salvation is worthy of worship.

REVIEW AIDS AND DISCUSSION TOPICS

The Book of Jeremiah

Introduction *(pages 5–7)*

1. What is the historical background of the book of Jeremiah (pp. 5–6)?

2. How does the prophet Jeremiah's persona come through in his poetry (p. 7)?

1:1–6:30 Oracles in the Days of Josiah *(pages 9–28)*

1. What is significant about the use of the words "knew" and "dedicated" in 1:5?

2. What two images are used to describe the relationship between the Lord and Israel in 2:1-3?

3. How can we interpret the sexual imagery that is present in chapter 2?

4. Describe how the Lord's tone changes in 3:11-18 and 3:19–4:4.

5. What is the purpose of the war imagery in 4:5-31?

6. In 5:1-31, how does the Lord justify his judgment of the people?

7. Discuss Jeremiah's role in 6:27-30.

7:1–20:18 Oracles Primarily from the Days of Jehoiakim *(pages 28–64)*

1. Summarize the temple sermon in 7:1–8:3.

2. How does the Lord view the people's sacrifices, and what does he prefer instead (7:21-23)?

3. What purpose do the rhetorical questions serve in 8:4-9?

4. Describe the different voices/speakers in 8:18-23.

5. The Lord gives the people a reason to boast—what is it (9:22-23)?

6. Examine the similarities between 10:1-16 and Isaiah 44:9-20.

7. How does the tone shift in 11:1-14?

8. Why is the first part of chapter 11 often considered to be Deuteronomic?

9. The six passages in 11:18–12:6 are identified as the "Confessions of Jeremiah." What are some of the interpretations of these "confessions"?

10. What does the loincloth symbolize in 13:1-11?

11. Describe the different points of view/voices expressed in the laments of 14:1–15:4.

12. What does Jeremiah "complain" about in 15:10-21?

13. What three commands does the Lord give Jeremiah in 16:1-9?

14. Discuss how 17:5-11 is part of the wisdom tradition.

15. How can we reconcile with the fact that Jeremiah prays for vengeance (17:14-18; 18:18-23)?

16. What is the symbolism of the potter and the clay in 18:1-12?

17. What is the purpose of the potter's flask in 19:1-13?

18. Describe Jeremiah's range of emotions expressed in 20:7-18.

21:1–25:38 Oracles in the Last Years of Jerusalem *(pages 64–78)*

1. In 22:9 Jeremiah gives a different reason, rather than idolatry, for the destruction of Jerusalem. What is it?

2. Compare 23:1-8 to Genesis 1:28; 17:1-8, 20; 28:3-4; 48:4. What themes do these passages share?

3. Does 23:9-40 indicate how the people can determine which prophets are false? Look at how this issue is addressed in Deuteronomy 13:1-6; 18:9-22.

4. What do the two baskets of figs represent in 24:1-10?

5. Read through 25:15-38. Do you think this passage is "a report of a symbolic act, the expansion of a vivid metaphor, or the explanation of a vision" (pp. 76–78)? What is your interpretation of the passage?

27:1–29:32 Controversies with the False Prophets *(pages 80–85)*

1. How do Jeremiah's teachings conflict with those of the false prophets in 27:1-22?

2. In what ways is chapter 28 similar to chapter 27?

3. Why does the Lord tell the exiles to "[b]uild houses," "plant gardens," "find wives," and so forth in 29:4-7?

30:1–35:19 Oracles of the Restoration of Israel and Judah
(pages 86–102)

1. 30:23-24 is almost exactly the same as 23:19-20, but the context is different—explain how this is so.

2. In chapter 31 the Lord is no longer portrayed as a judge. What images are used here instead?

3. What do Rachel and Ephraim represent (31:15-20)?

4. How do you interpret 31:22 (p. 91)?

5. Describe the meaning of the new covenant in 31:31-34.

6. What is significant about Jeremiah's purchase of a field in chapter 32?

7. Chapters 30–33 are often called "the book of consolation." Explain how this is an appropriate title for this section of Jeremiah.

8. Discuss the subject of slavery after reading "the pact broken" (34:8-22).

9. Why does chapter 35 take us back to a story that occurred ten years earlier than previous chapters?

36:1–45:5 Jeremiah and the Fall of Jerusalem *(pages 103–18)*

1. Read about the scroll in chapter 36 and then reflect on how communication was accomplished in ancient times.

2. Jeremiah lies to the princes in 38:27. Considering his situation, does this fact change your opinion of his character?

3. 39:4-13 is taken from 52:4-16. What is a possible reason for this?

4. What does Jeremiah warn the people of if they choose to go to Egypt (42:15-22)?

5. Discuss this statement: there "is a theological perspective that sees their [the people's] journey to Egypt as a reversal of the exodus and thus a rejection of the Lord's greatest salvific act on their behalf" (p. 115).

6. Why do the Judeans insist on worshiping the Queen of Heaven (44:17-19)?

7. Summarize the message to Baruch in 45:1-5.

46:1–51:64 Oracles against the Nations (*pages 119–37*)

1. The oracles against the nations (46:1–51:64) were likely authored by someone other than Jeremiah. What are the reasons for assuming this fact (p. 119)?

2. Compare the oracles against the nations in Jeremiah (46:1–51:64) to those found in other prophetic books (Isa 13–23; Ezek 25–32; Amos 1:1–2:3; Nahum; and Obadiah).

3. While reading through chapter 46, how does the tone change drastically in verses 27-28?

4. Why does the oracle against Edom (49:7-22) lack a tone of lament?

5. How does the oracle against Elam (49:34-39) differ from the other oracles against the nations?

6. Why are the oracles against Babylon (50:1-46; 51:1-58) much longer than the others?

52:1-34 Historical Appendix (*pages 137–39*)

1. 52:1-34 is taken from 2 Kings 24:18–25:30. Discuss the theological similarities between Jeremiah and the books of Kings.

The Book of Baruch

Introduction (*pages 140–42*)

1. Who was Baruch (p. 140), and what is the historical background of this book (p. 141)?

1:1–3:8 Letter to Jerusalem (*pages 143–48*)

1. How could 1:1-9 be related to Jeremiah 28:1-6?

2. Identify the Deuteronomic qualities of 1:10–2:10.

3. Daniel 9:4-19 may have been a model for Baruch 1:10–2:10. Compare the two passages.

4. What is the tone of the people's prayer for deliverance (2:11–3:8)?

3:9–4:4 Praise of Wisdom *(pages 148–51)*

1. The "Praise of Wisdom" poem (3:9–4:4) urges the people to pursue wisdom. According to this passage, is wisdom considered to be accessible?

2. Do you think that the "theory of retribution" is an adequate explanation of disasters and war (p. 149; 3:12-13)?

3. Compare 3:9-36 to Job 28 and Isaiah 40:12-31 (see p. 151).

4:5–5:9 Baruch's Poem of Consolation *(pages 151–55)*

1. Do you see any similarities in the language and images used between Baruch 4:5–5:9 and Second Isaiah?

2. What do you think about the personification of Jerusalem as a woman in 4:9–5:9?

3. What does Baruch exhort Jerusalem to do in response to salvation (4:30–5:9)?

6:1-72 The Letter of Jeremiah *(pages 155–60)*

1. Why was idolatry appealing to those who were exiled to Babylon (p. 155)?

2. The Letter of Jeremiah (Bar 6:1-72) goes further than Second Isaiah (40:18-20; 41:6-7; 44:9-20; 46:5-7) in its treatment of idolatry. Give examples of how this is so.

3. Why does the Letter of Jeremiah condemn idolatry so strongly (p. 157)? Identify some modern-day "idols" that influence our day-to-day lives.

INDEX OF CITATIONS FROM THE
CATECHISM OF THE CATHOLIC CHURCH

The arabic number(s) following the citation refer(s) to the paragraph number(s) in the *Catechism of the Catholic Church*. The asterisk following a paragraph number indicates that the citation has been paraphrased.

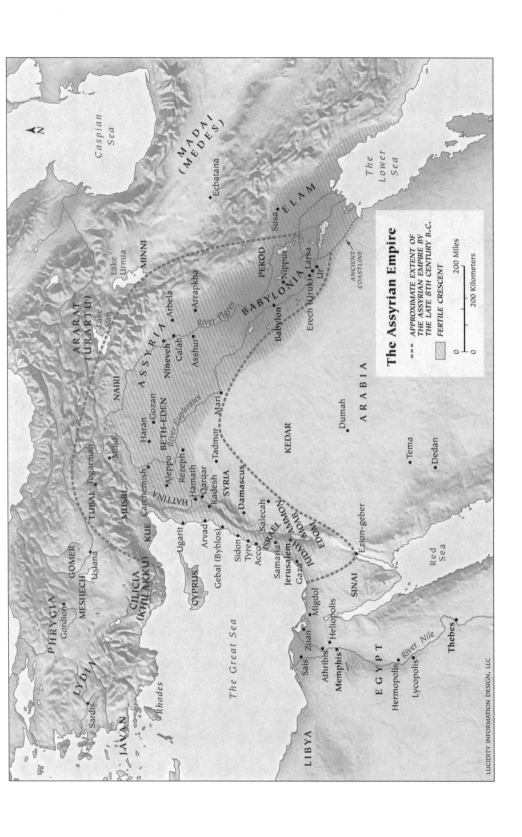

The Assyrian Empire

- - - - APPROXIMATE EXTENT OF
THE ASSYRIAN EMPIRE BY
THE LATE 8TH CENTURY B.C.

░░░ FERTILE CRESCENT

0   200 Miles

0   200 Kilometers

LUCIDITY INFORMATION DESIGN, LLC

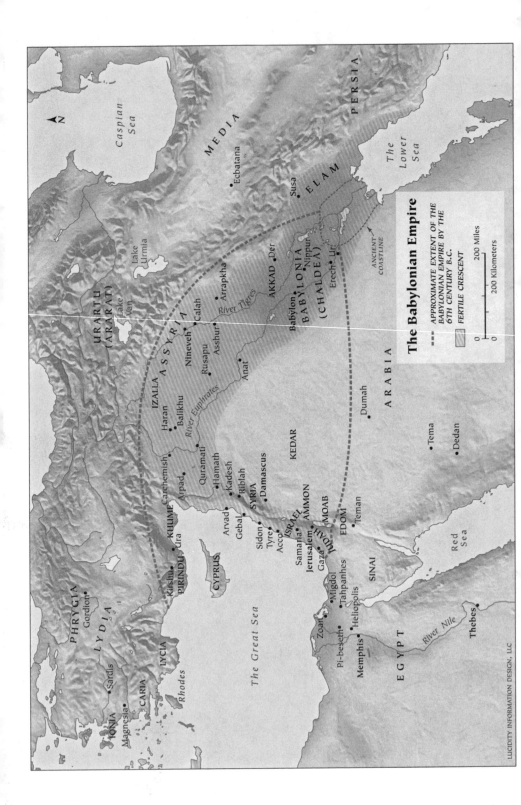

The Babylonian Empire